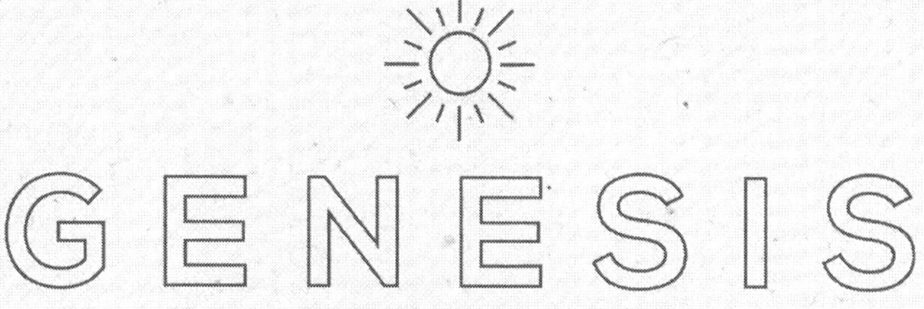

IN THE BEGINNING

by Dr. Randy T. Johnson
with contributions by:

ROGER ALLEN
NOBLE BAIRD
PAT BEDELL
HOLLY BOSTON
JOHN CARTER
JAMES CLOUSE
CALEB COMBS
CAROLE COMBS
ISAIAH COMBS
JEN COMBS
JOSHUA COMBS
SIERRA COMBS
MATT DARDEN
BRETT EBERLE
DONNA FOX
MICHAEL FOX
DEBBIE GABBARA
LARRY GABBARA
SUE HARRINGTON
RICHIE HENSON
KENNY HOVIS
JOHN HUBBARD
MARY JANE JOHNS
DEBBIE KERR
BEN KIRKMAN
JOSH LAHRING
CHUCK LINDSEY
PAT MACDERMAID
WES MCCULLOUGH
MARK O'CONNOR
JILL OSMON
PHILIP PIASECKI
DANI REYNOLDS
RYAN STORY
GARETH VOLZ

DESIGNED BY: CASEY MAXWELL
FORMATTED BY: SHAWNA JOHNSON

First Edition, March 2019

Published by:
The River Church
8393 E. Holly Rd.
Holly, MI 48442

Scriptures are taken from the Bible, English Standard Version (ESV)

Printed in the United States of America

CONTENTS

LESSON 1 • CREATION

LESSON 2 • THE FALL

LESSON 3 • ADAM & EVE

LESSON 4 • CAIN & ABEL

LESSON 5 • THE FLOOD

LESSON 6 • TOWER OF BABEL

LESSON 7 • ABRAHAM'S CALL

LESSON 8 • LOT'S LIFE

LESSON 9 • ABRAHAM, HAGAR, & ISHMAEL

LESSON 10 • ABRAHAM, SARAH, & ISAAC

LESSON 11 • ABRAHAM "SACRIFICES" ISAAC

LESSON 12 • ISAAC & REBEKAH

LESSON 13 • JACOB & ESAU

LESSON 14 • LEAH & RACHEL

LESSON 15 • JOSEPH & BROTHERS

LESSON 16 • JOSEPH & POTIPHAR'S WIFE

LESSON 17 • PRISON TO PALACE

LESSON 18 • JOSEPH FORGIVES HIS BROTHERS

PREFACE

"In the beginning, God created the heavens and the earth."
Genesis 1:1

Four words into the Bible, we find the principal character. It is God. All of the world and our very lives should be focused around Him.

GENESIS: In the beginning covers the first book of the Bible (Genesis) and about twenty-five hundred years. It is a study on the holiness of God, man's sinfulness, and God's way of redemption. God offers a new beginning for all of us.

We are introduced to many characters in the book of Genesis: Adam, Eve, Cain, Abel, Noah, Abraham, Sarah, Lot, Isaac, Rebekah, Jacob, Esau, Leah, Rachel, and Joseph. Also included are creation, forbidden fruit, murder, the flood, many languages, Sodom and Gomorrah, a pillar of salt, a birthright, romance, a coat of many colors, prison, and even the Palace.

GENESIS: In the beginning consists of eighteen study guides on the people and events in Genesis. These are written for personal or group discussion. There are also over one hundred devotions covering character qualities found in their interactions that we should emulate in our daily lives.

01

CREATION

DR. RANDY T. JOHNSON,
GROWTH PASTOR

I enjoy the story of the scientist who went to God and said, "I do not need you anymore. I can clone animals and people, transplant organs, create artificial organs, and do all kinds of things people used to consider miraculous."

God sighed, "You do not need me? Are you as powerful as Me? Have you replaced Me? Then why don't we see if this is true? Let's have a competition to see who can make a male human being, just like I did before." The scientist agreed.

God reached down and scooped up some dirt. At the same time, the scientist reached for the dirt, too. God said, "Get your own dirt."

That may be a silly story, but it reminds us that no matter how far science advances, God created everything out of nothing.

Genesis 1:1-2:3 records the creation account. After reading just four words, we find out who the main character is.

"In the beginning, God created the heavens and the earth. The earth was without form and void, and darkness was over the face of the deep. And the Spirit of God was hovering over the face of the waters." Genesis 1:1-2

When did God become more than just a name to you?

____

____

____

Realize, God did not begin when the beginning began; He began the beginning. He did not start when start got started; He started start. He is eternal. Yet, He was not alone.

Who else is listed in these verses (1:1-2) of the creation account?

John 1:1-3 says, ***"In the beginning was the Word, and the Word was with God, and the Word was God. He was in the beginning with God. All things were made through him, and without him was not any thing made that was made."***

Colossians 1:16 adds, ***"For by him all things were created, in heaven and on earth, visible and invisible, whether thrones or dominions or rulers or authorities—all things were created through him and for him."***

Who are these verses addressing and what do they add to this topic?

Genesis 1:3-5 continue, ***"And God said, 'Let there be light,' and there was light. And God saw that the light was good. And God separated the light from the darkness. God called the light Day, and the darkness he called Night. And there was evening and there was morning, the first day."***

What was created on day one and how does this relate to time?

God created everything in six literal days. He created time for our sake. It would not be easier or harder for Him to create everything in 6 days, 600 days, or 6,000,000 days. He is God. He spoke, and it happened.

Verses 6-8 cover day two, ***"And God said, 'Let there be an expanse in the midst of the waters, and let it separate the waters from the waters.' And God made the expanse and separated the waters that were under the expanse from the waters that were above the expanse. And it was so. And God called the expanse Heaven. And there was evening and there was morning, the second day."***

What was created on the second day?

____

____

____

Verses 9-13 address day three, ***"And God said, 'Let the waters under the heavens be gathered together into one place, and let the dry land appear.' And it was so. God called the dry land Earth, and the waters that were gathered together he called Seas. And God saw that it was good. And God said, 'Let the earth sprout vegetation, plants yielding seed, and fruit trees bearing fruit in which is their seed, each according to its kind, on the earth.' And it was so. The earth brought forth vegetation, plants yielding seed according to their own kinds, and trees bearing fruit in which is their seed, each according to its kind. And God saw that it was good. And there was evening and there was morning, the third day."***

What was created on the third day?

____

____

____

Day four is described in verses 14-19, ***"And God said, 'Let there be lights in the expanse of the heavens to separate the day from the night. And let them be for signs and for seasons, and for days and years, and let them be lights in the expanse of the heavens to give light upon the earth.' And it was so. And God made the two great lights—the greater light to rule the day and the lesser light to rule the night—and the stars. And God set them in the expanse of the heavens to give light on the earth, to rule over the day and over the night, and to separate the light from the darkness. And God saw that it was good. And there was evening and there was morning, the fourth day."***

What was created on the fourth day?

____

____

____

Verses 20-23 say, ***"And God said, 'Let the waters swarm with swarms of living creatures, and let birds fly above the earth across the expanse of the heavens.' So God created the great sea creatures and every living creature that moves, with which the waters swarm, according to their kinds, and every winged bird according to its kind. And God saw that it was good. And God blessed them, saying, 'Be fruitful and multiply and fill the waters in the seas, and let birds multiply on the earth.' And there was evening and there was morning, the fifth day."***

What was created on the fifth day?

____

____

____

How did God create things?

____

____

____

What was God's opinion of His creation each step of the way?

____

____

____

Verses 24-31 give the pinnacle of creation, ***"And God said, 'Let the earth bring forth living creatures according to their kinds—livestock and creeping things and beasts of the earth according to their kinds.' And it was so. And God made the beasts of the earth according to their kinds and the livestock according to their kinds, and everything that creeps on the ground according to its kind. And God saw that it was good. Then God said, 'Let us make man in our image, after our likeness. And let them have dominion over the fish of the sea and over the birds of the heavens and over the livestock and over all the earth and over every creeping thing that creeps on the earth.' So God created man in his own image, in the image of God he created him; male and female he created them. And God blessed them. And God said to them, 'Be fruitful and multiply and fill the earth and subdue it, and have dominion over the fish of the sea and over the birds of the heavens and over every living thing that moves on the earth.' And God said, 'Behold, I have given you every plant yielding seed that is on the face of all the earth, and***

every tree with seed in its fruit. You shall have them for food. And to every beast of the earth and to every bird of the heavens and to everything that creeps on the earth, everything that has the breath of life, I have given every green plant for food.' And it was so. And God saw everything that he had made, and behold, it was very good. And there was evening and there was morning, the sixth day."

What was created on the sixth day?

____

____

____

What makes man different from the other land creatures?

____

____

____

Finally, Genesis 2:1-3 speaks of God's response after His work is done, ***"Thus the heavens and the earth were finished, and all the host of them. And on the seventh day God finished his work that he had done, and he rested on the seventh day from all his work that he had done. So God blessed the seventh day and made it holy, because on it God rested from all his work that he had done in creation."***

What did God do on the seventh day?

____

____

____

How does this relate to us? Be specific.

____

____

____

Genesis 2:18-22 goes into a little more depth on the creation of woman, ***"Then the Lord God said, 'It is not good that the man should be alone; I will make him a helper fit for him.' Now out of the ground the Lord God had formed every beast of the field and every bird of the heavens and brought them to the man to see what he would call them. And whatever the man called every living creature, that was its name. The man gave names to all livestock and to the birds of the heavens and to every beast of the field. But for Adam there was not found a helper fit for him. So the Lord God caused a deep sleep to fall upon the man, and while he slept took one of his ribs and closed up its place with flesh. And the rib that the Lord God had taken from the man he made into a woman and brought her to the man."***

Why was woman created?

____

____

____

What is implied since nothing was needed to be created after woman?

____

____

____

Matthew Henry made an interesting observation, "Eve was not taken out of Adam's head to top him, neither out of his feet to be trampled on by him, but out of his side to be equal with him, under his arm to be protected by him, and near his heart to be loved by him."

Romans 1:20-25 ties creation to salvation, ***"For his invisible attributes, namely, his eternal power and divine nature, have been clearly perceived, ever since the creation of the world, in the things that have been made. So they are without excuse. For although they knew God, they did not honor him as God or give thanks to him, but they became futile in their thinking, and their foolish hearts were darkened. Claiming to be wise, they became fools, and exchanged the glory of the immortal God for images resembling mortal man and birds and animals and creeping things. Therefore God gave them up in the lusts of their hearts to impurity, to the dishonoring of their bodies among themselves, because they exchanged the truth about God for a lie and worshiped and served the creature rather than the Creator, who is blessed forever! Amen."***

What does Paul say about creation, God, and man's response?

____

____

____

Why would people reject a Creator?

____

____

____

"You weren't an accident. You weren't mass produced. You aren't an assembly-line product. You were deliberately planned, specifically gifted, and lovingly positioned on the Earth by the Master Craftsman." Max Lucado

GOD EXISTS

CREATION, DEVOTION 1

Donna Fox | *Assistant to the Growth Pastor*

"In the beginning, God..." Genesis 1:1a

The Bible begins with God (Genesis chapter 1) and ends with God (Revelation chapter 22). He was there at the beginning and will be there at the end. He is omnipresent (all-present), omnipotent (all-powerful), and omniscient (all-knowing). He has no timeline; He just has always been.

God exists. Period. If you profess to be a Christian, you have a relationship with the Son, you have faith, and you just know He exists. What about those who do not yet have that relationship? How can they know God exists?

Creation and nature were my first clue. Before salvation, I would look at the earth, the trees and flowers, the human body, the eyeball, and birth of a baby, and just know that there had to be a God that existed and created such intricate, beautiful things. How could the planets not crash into each other? How could a baby grow into a child, then an adult, from some "Big Bang?" I knew that could not be true. The Holy Spirit was pursuing me, it was very evident to me, and that was another clue. I resisted for a long time, but I kept feeling that tug on my heartstrings wanting to have a relationship. Of course, God existed, He wanted to have a relationship with ME!

The existence of Jesus was, of course, the most compelling! It has been proven time and time again that Jesus did, in fact, live on this Earth. As you study the Bible, learn the stories, hear of the miracles, and compare it to other historical events, it becomes more and more evident that the Bible is the truth. God did exist, does exist, and always will exist.

If you have not researched it for yourself, if you have not read the Bible, if you have not seen the proof and developed the faith, you need to start that journey NOW! Open your Bible. ***"In the beginning, God…"*** That says it all right there. Keep reading, and as the stories unfold, you cannot help but fall in love with God over and over again!

ELOHIM

CREATION, DEVOTION 2

Noble Baird | *Community Center Director*

One of my favorite movie series is *Harry Potter*. Now, I do not necessarily agree with everything that is in the movies; however, I do appreciate and enjoy the adventure which Harry, Hermione, and Ron experience. Throughout the series, Harry uses various "tools" to carry out tasks and solve his many mysteries. One of my favorite tools he uses is the cloak of invisibility. As you have probably guessed, for those of you who have not seen the movies, this cloak makes Harry and whoever wears it invisible. This allowed Harry to sneak around Hogwarts without ever being seen.

As we continue to take a deeper look into creation, it is important that we make sure to stop and establish who was there at the beginning. In Genesis 1:2 it reads, ***"The earth was without form and void, and darkness was over the face of the deep. And the Spirit of God was hovering over the face of the waters."*** So, right from the very beginning, we have established that we not only have God the Father during creation, but also the Spirit of God, or the Holy Spirit for a more familiar name. Fast forward to Colossians, Paul writes in 1:15-16, ***"He is the image of the invisible God, the firstborn of all creation. For by him all things were created, in heaven and on earth, visible and invisible, whether thrones or dominions or rulers or authorities - all things were created through him and for him."*** Here, Paul establishes that we also have Jesus' existence at the very beginning of creation. Now, we have this completed picture where we not only have God the Father at creation but also the Spirit and Christ, completing the Trinity.

Some days, I wish that I could put on the cloak of invisibility and just disappear. Maybe sneak into a Dierks Bentley concert, snag a free pizza at Little Caesars, or simply hide at home knowing no one would see me! Now, I know this cloak is not real and it is just all in fun; however, when we talk about the Spirit of God, He has the same character trait of being invisible, yet so much more powerful. When Christ ascended after His forty days here on earth, He told us how He would be sending the Helper. In Acts 1:8 Jesus says, ***"But you will receive power when the Holy Spirit has come upon you."*** You see, although we cannot physically see the Holy Spirit, we will be able to see His works through us and others, but not see Him, yet.

Personally, I have found this understanding of the Spirit so comforting. Knowing that Jesus left this earth, but made sure we were never alone, blows my mind. He knew exactly what the Disciples needed then and what we need now. So, as you continue in your week and we continue this study on Genesis, I encourage you to remember the Spirit of God. Knowing that although we may not be able to physically see Him, He is covering us and His power is at work in and through us always.

CREATED IN THE IMAGE OF GOD

CREATION, DEVOTION 3

Ryan Story | *Location Pastor - Burton*

I recently returned from a mission trip to Guatemala. It was a great week seeing God use our group in some amazing ways. We partnered with an organization called Potter's House. There are many things that I enjoy about Potter's House in how they view the people they serve. In Guatemala, Central America's largest trash dump is in Guatemala City. This landfill is the size of 23 football fields. Potter's House ministers to many of the people who live in and around the dump too. While we were there, we went from ministering to the poor to ministering to "treasures." Potter's House believes that every person we minister to is a treasure because that is how God views him or her.

Genesis 1:26 says, ***"Then God said, 'Let us make man in our image, after our likeness. And let them have dominion over the fish of the sea and over the birds of the heavens and over the livestock and over all the earth and over every creeping thing that creeps on the earth.'"*** There are many ways a person can look at what being made in God's image is. I have read it has authoritarian roots. Since God has authority over everything, God passed His authority to man to take care of His creation. I have read the being created in God's image has relational roots. Since God exists in Trinity, He is always in relationship with Himself. When God created everything, He desired us to have a relationship with each other. While God had angels and heavenly hosts, there was something special about having a relationship with something with free will. I have read that being created in God's image has emotional roots. Since we all long for love, joy, peace, and compassion, all of those are rooted in God. We resemble God because we are capable of showing those emotions, whereas, a platypus is not.

Regardless of all the studying we do, understanding exactly what being created in God's image exactly means will keep one busy for longer than the amount of time I have in this devotional. This one truth we do know, God created everything, but humans were special to Him. God made the sun and the stars. A star is a massively huge ball of energy that illuminates light bright enough to reach millions of light years (reminder: a light year is a measurement of distance not time). Because of this, sun life could not be sustained. The most powerful thing we see every morning, outside of God, is the sun. Even in every star's majestic beauty and amazement, God did not look at them as in His image. Personally, that rocked my world. I gaze at stars whenever I am in a new place. I love looking at stars. I get lost in how amazing they are. While I am doing that, God is looking at me thinking, those people on Earth are amazing.

We live in a world that does not value human life. Somehow this exists inside God's Church. We are losing the ability to look at each other with value. We look at unsaved bus kids as a nuisance because they mess up our building or cause us to teach our children that they should not swear. We view people struggling with addictions as lost causes who will never get right. We look at the elderly in the church as hindering progress, while young people as a bunch of disrespectful punks. We all have such horrid ways we look at each other. We have lost the ability to look at every person we come in contact with as a treasure that God has made. I went to a third world country and saw the most beautiful children in the world. I went to a trash dump and found treasure. It took God showing me this truth to understand just how amazing ever person is. We have two choices on how to view people. The first is if we view people as junk that means that Jesus died for junk. The second is if we view people as treasure that means that Jesus died for something special. I like the second choice.

NEED FOR COMMUNITY

CREATION, DEVOTION 4

Roger Allen | *Recovery Director*

I love people. When in a crowd, I seek out those that look out of place, the "wallflowers" you might say. I believe that all should feel welcome. Even as a child, I would search out those who did not seem to be accepted. I encouraged those that would isolate themselves from others. I sought out the introverts. I would not allow you to leave without knowing at least one person in that room. Often that person was me!

I was constantly roaming in search of new friends. I remember one afternoon when I was about seven years old, after opening our Christmas gifts that morning, we traveled to my Grandmother's apartment in Romeo, Michigan. A short time after arriving the search for me began. It finally ended at the end of the hall where I had introduced myself to my Grandmother's neighbor. Excited, with a full plate of cookies and a huge smile, I proceeded to tell my story of how I introduced myself at every apartment on that floor. Did I tell you, "I love people?"

Ecclesiastes 4:9-10 reminds us, ***"Two are better than one, because they have a good reward for their toil. For if they fall, one will lift up his fellow. But woe to him who is alone when he falls and has not another to lift him up!"***

As I have grown older, my desire to meet new people has not diminished. While I do seek alone time, I am quite content being surrounded by a roomful of people. Even in the most trying times, I prefer the company of others. As Ecclesiastes says, ***"Two are better than one."*** I realize that not everyone shares my enthusiasm about making friends, but there are wisdom and benefits in sharing experiences. Words of encouragement, compassion, and a helping hand make a difference. Friends, family, and most of all your spouse can comfort and console when it is needed most.

However, today we are becoming more isolated than ever. With the advent of social media, we have traded in a real and tangible relationship for a virtual one. People are never having a real commitment and end up settling for something less than intended. We are now in isolation instead of a relationship God had planned for us.

Proverbs 18:1 adds, ***"Whoever isolates himself seeks his own desire; he breaks out against all sound judgment."***

Many today have chosen a life of meaningless partnerships in place of living, breathing relationships. Devoid of any real commitment and emotional attachment, they believe there is freedom in their lifestyle. Never caring to be their brother's keeper and having the chance to leave at the first sign of trouble, they never really commit. God never intended it to be so. In Genesis, after He created the Heavens and the Earth, God looked at His creation and said, ***"It is very good"*** (Genesis 1:31). However, when it came to Adam, He said, ***"It is not good that the man should be alone."*** The whole verse in Genesis 2:18 reads, ***"Then the Lord God said, 'It is not good that the man should be alone; I will make him a helper fit for him.'"***

"Eve" as she is called, is now Adam's "help meet." Unlike the other animals of the sea, land, and air, she is part of Adam. Created from his rib, she is a suitable helper to him. She is one that will strengthen and comfort him when he is weak. She was the perfect creation for Adam just as my wife has been the perfect creation for me. After 37 years of marriage, it has become very clear what God had intended all along. We have learned to care, encourage, and lift up each other. We walk side by side as He intended.

ONE RULE

CREATION, DEVOTION 5

Brett Eberle

One of my favorite memories growing up was getting to take a spring break trip with my best friend. The day after we got out of school, both of us climbed into his truck and drove straight to Florida. Both of our parents are very involved in our lives, and my parents told me the usual things that you tell your teenage kid (use your head, make good decisions, and other bits of wisdom), but what my friend's dad said to us has echoed through my whole life since that day. His dad's only rule was "don't cause me no grief." That rule encompassed every other rule within itself; there were no loopholes or ways around it, the only way for us to not cause his dad any grief was to act the same way we would if he were on the trip with us.

At the very beginning of the Bible, after God had finished creating everything, we see Him give one single rule to Adam and Eve. The rule was that they were not to eat from the Tree of the Knowledge of Good and Evil. What Adam and Eve did not realize was that the rule encompassed so much more than just eating something that they were told to dismiss. Other than the immediate consequences that are listed in Genesis, the result of the single rule being broken ended in the people of God having six-hundred thirteen commandments. One simple overarching rule turned into six-hundred thirteen complicated rules all apart of what is known as the old covenant or the law.

If you skip forward in the Bible to when Jesus was on the Earth, one of the stories recorded that you will come across is the Pharisees attempting to trick Jesus by asking Him what the greatest commandment was. The confrontation is recorded in Matthew 22:34-40:

"But when the Pharisees heard that he had silenced the Sadducees, they gathered together. And one of them, a lawyer, asked him a question to test him. 'Teacher, which is the great commandment in the Law?' And he said to him, 'You shall love the Lord your God with all your heart and with all your soul and with all your mind. This is the great and first commandment. And a second is like it: You shall love your neighbor as yourself. On these two commandments depend all the Law and the Prophets.'"

Just as my friend's dad encompassed every rule that we had grown up with into one very simple rule, Jesus took six-hundred thirteen rules and simplified them down to two simple yet challenging rules. Jesus not only made a way for us to get to Heaven, but He gave us rules that feel more possible to achieve.

SEVENTH DAY

CREATION, DEVOTION 6

Jill Osmon | *Assistant to the Lead Team*

"And on the seventh day God finished his work that he had done, and he rested on the seventh day from all his work that he had done. So God blessed the seventh day and made it holy, because on it God rested from all his work that he had done in creation." Genesis 2:2-3

I have the privilege of coordinating most of our large events at The River Church, and I love it, I mean super nerd love it, it is what God made me to do. But, it is an intense job, very detailed, and very much requires me to expend a lot of mind muscle energy and just plain physical energy. So after a large event, I completely lose the ability to make decisions, I have been making decisions for the last few months about everything, and now all I want to do is sit and not think. After a few days, I feel refreshed, maybe, but I do not always truly feel rested, and I have struggled with why, after relaxing, getting away, why can I not find true rest?

We have all been there, right? We have been through seasons of life that are just exhausting, a new baby, a new job, teenagers, tough financial times, or health issues for yourself or a loved one; and all you want to do is rest. But what is true rest? God rested on the seventh day during Creation, making a command that we rest. Unfortunately, we have a culture that does not truly know rest, even with vacations and days off, rest alludes most of us. Exodus 20:8-11 says, ***"Remember the Sabbath day, to keep it holy. Six days you shall labor, and do all your work, but the seventh day is a Sabbath to the Lord your God. On it you shall not do any work, you, or your son, or your daughter, your male servant, or your***

female servant, or your livestock, or the sojourner who is within your gates. For in six days the Lord made heaven and earth, the sea, and all that is in them, and rested on the seventh day. Therefore the Lord blessed the Sabbath day and made it holy."

We often equate rest with time off, doing nothing, or vacation, but what is God saying here? If you look closely, verse 10 says, ***"but the seventh day is a Sabbath TO the Lord your God"*** (emphasis is mine). While we may come back from a vacation or a day off refreshed, we will not know true rest unless we rest in God.

Psalm 91:1 (NIV) says, ***"Whoever dwells in the shelter of the Most High will rest in the shadow of the Almighty."*** I know that my soul craves for true rest, and that desire, that need, can only be satisfied by resting in the shadow of the Almighty. So how do we do that? Well, I think we look at how God rested on the seventh day. Verse 31 of Genesis chapter 1 says, ***"And God saw everything that he had made, and behold, it was very good."*** We look back on all that God has done, even when we are in the deepest valleys, and we see His goodness, kindness, and love, and we rejoice in gratitude. Matthew Henry Commentary puts it this way, "The Christian Sabbath, which we observe, is a seventh day, and in it we celebrate the rest of God the Son, and the finishing the work of our redemption." Then, and only then, will we find true rest.

02

THE FALL

DR. RANDY T. JOHNSON,
GROWTH PASTOR

For years the top four sins for men centered around women, money, alcohol, and pride. It is not to say that men have learned to control themselves in these areas, but CNN has posted updated results of their survey. They found that worry, procrastination, overeating, spending too much time on media, and sloth or laziness were the favorite sins. Lust, lying, cheating, and anger finished off the list.

No matter what makes your Achilles Heel vulnerable, temptation and sin center around selfishness. John MacArthur said, "God made all of His creation to give. He made the sun, the moon, the stars, the clouds, the earth, the plants to give. He also designed His supreme creation, man, to give. But fallen man is the most reluctant giver in all of God's creation."

Do you agree sin is centered around selfishness?

____

____

____

What other sins and temptations would you list?

____

____

____

Before examining the Original Sin in the Garden of Eden, it is helpful to understand 1 John 2:16, ***"For all that is in the world, the lust of the flesh, and the lust of the eyes, and the pride of life, is not of the Father, but is of the world."***

What three areas of temptation are listed in this passage?

____

____

____

What do they mean?

Genesis 3:1-6 contains the story of the first sin, ***"Now the serpent was more crafty than any other beast of the field that the Lord God had made. He said to the woman, 'Did God actually say, 'You shall not eat of any tree in the garden?' And the woman said to the serpent, 'We may eat of the fruit of the trees in the garden, but God said, 'You shall not eat of the fruit of the tree that is in the midst of the garden, neither shall you touch it, lest you die.'' But the serpent said to the woman, 'You will not surely die. For God knows that when you eat of it your eyes will be opened, and you will be like God, knowing good and evil.' So when the woman saw that the tree was good for food, and that it was a delight to the eyes, and that the tree was to be desired to make one wise, she took of its fruit and ate, and she also gave some to her husband who was with her, and he ate."***

Who is the serpent?

What portions of the serpent's statements are true and which are false?

How consistent are Eve's statements (3:2-3) with what God said (2:9, 16-17)?

____

____

____

Matchup Eve's battle with the phrases from 1 John 2:16.

Lust of the eyes:

____

Lust of the flesh:

____

Pride of life:

____

As Jerry Falwell said, "Temptation has been here ever since the Garden of Eden." It is true, and it normally centers around ***"the lust of the flesh, and the lust of the eyes, and the pride of life."*** The problem with sin is that it is fun for awhile. However, it is not worth the consequences. It is a fool's gold.

John Piper said, "Sin gets its power by persuading me to believe that I will be happier if I follow it. The power of all temptation is the prospect that it will make me happier."

Second Samuel 11:1-5 records how David fell to the lies and promises of temptation, ***"In the spring of the year, the time when kings go out to battle, David sent Joab, and his servants with him, and all Israel. And they ravaged the Ammonites and besieged Rabbah. But David remained at Jerusalem. It happened, late one afternoon, when David arose from his couch and was walking on***

the roof of the king's house, that he saw from the roof a woman bathing; and the woman was very beautiful. And David sent and inquired about the woman. And one said, 'Is not this Bathsheba, the daughter of Eliam, the wife of Uriah the Hittite?' So David sent messengers and took her, and she came to him, and he lay with her. (Now she had been purifying herself from her uncleanness.) Then she returned to her house. And the woman conceived, and she sent and told David, 'I am pregnant.'"

Matchup David's battle with the phrases from 1 John 2:16.

Lust of the eyes:

___

Lust of the flesh:

___

Pride of life:

___

What should have David done and when?

___

___

___

How does David's struggle relate to us?

___

___

___

Temptation is not sin. Yielding to temptation is a sin. The evangelist Billy Sunday said, "Temptation is the devil looking through the keyhole. Yielding is opening the door and inviting him in."

Satan beat Eve, Adam, David, and more, but he is not undefeated. Matthew 4:1-11 describes his embarrassing losses to Jesus, ***"Then Jesus was led up by the Spirit into the wilderness to be tempted by the devil. And after fasting forty days and forty nights, he was hungry. And the tempter came and said to him, 'If you are the Son of God, command these stones to become loaves of bread.' But he answered, 'It is written, 'Man shall not live by bread alone, but by every word that comes from the mouth of God." Then the devil took him to the holy city and set him on the pinnacle of the temple and said to him, 'If you are the Son of God, throw yourself down, for it is written, 'He will command his angels concerning you,' and 'On their hands they will bear you up, lest you strike your foot against a stone." Jesus said to him, 'Again it is written, 'You shall not put the Lord your God to the test." Again, the devil took him to a very high mountain and showed him all the kingdoms of the world and their glory. And he said to him, 'All these I will give you, if you will fall down and worship me.' Then Jesus said to him, 'Be gone, Satan! For it is written, 'You shall worship the Lord your God and him only shall you serve." Then the devil left him, and behold, angels came and were ministering to him."***

Matchup Satan's tactics with the phrases from 1 John 2:16.

Lust of the flesh:

____

Lust of the eyes:

____

Pride of life:

____

How did Jesus refute Satan?

___

___

___

What verses most relate to your situation?

___

___

___

There are four things we can learn from these passages and others about temptation.

1. Jesus quoted Scripture and Satan did not have a response.

In Ephesians chapter 6, Paul writes about putting on the armor of God. In verse 17, he says, ***"And take the helmet of salvation, and the sword of the Spirit, which is the word of God."*** The armor of God is basically designed to protect us. It focuses on defense and how to be safe. However, the sword is the Word of God and is used to be on the offense. Study God's Word. Learn it. Use it against Satan.

2. We need to be prepared by praying and being watchful.

Matthew 26:41 says, ***"Watch and pray that you may not enter into temptation. The spirit indeed is willing, but the flesh is weak."*** We are not told to pray to overcome temptation; we are directed to be alert and avoid it. Chuck Swindoll said, "I'm here today to warn you: I want you to watch out for the adversary. Guard yourself from any spirit of entitlement. Restrain any and all subtle temptation to gain attention or to find ways to promote yourself." It is easier and less painful to avoid a trap then to figure out on how to get out of it.

3. You have a choice.

Temptation is normal, natural, and daily. It comes in all flavors, but we have a choice on what we will do with it. Charles Spurgeon said, "All the goodness I have within me is totally from the Lord alone. When I sin, it is from me and is done on my own, but when I act righteously, it is wholly and completely of God." He agreed that we have a choice.

I enjoy Rick Warren's advice, "Ignoring a temptation is far more effective than fighting it. Once your mind is on something else, the temptation loses its power. So when temptation calls you on the phone, don't argue with it -- just hang up!"

4. You can be victorious.

Finally, we are called to be winners. 1 Corinthians 10:13 says, ***"No temptation has overtaken you that is not common to man. God is faithful, and he will not let you be tempted beyond your ability, but with the temptation he will also provide the way of escape, that you may be able to endure it."*** Paul says temptation is a common occurrence, but we can escape it. God will not allow more than we can handle with Him. As a team, we win. ***"God is faithful."***

"Every time you defeat a temptation, you become more like Jesus!"
Rick Warren

SIN AND THE CURE

THE FALL, DEVOTION 1

Holly Boston | *Women's Ministry Director*

Whenever someone says to me, "I have good news, and I have bad news," I always ask for the bad news first. I want to get it out of the way. So, here is the bad news: ***"Therefore, just as sin came into the world through one man, and death through sin, and so death spread to all men because all sinned"*** (Romans 5:12). Sin entered the world through one man (with the help of one misguided wife). Adam enjoyed perfect fellowship with God, had a perfect job, worked for the perfect Boss, and was married to the perfect (only) woman. The one thing God denied him was fruit from the Tree of Knowledge of Good and Evil (Genesis 2:17). In one weak moment, Adam succumbed to temptation and "he ate of it" (Genesis 3:6). One man, one temptation, and one choice led to one sentence for all mankind, ***"For all have sinned and fall short of the glory of God"*** (Romans 3:23). Romans 6:23 adds, ***"For the wages of sin is death."***

However, there is Good News. Romans 5:15 says, ***"But the free gift is not like the trespass. For if many died through one man's trespass, much more have the grace of God and the free gift by the grace of that one man Jesus Christ abounded for many."*** The Sovereign God of the universe loved us so much He devised one plan, one way to save the world from eternal damnation. In 1 John 4:9 we read, ***"In this the love of God was made manifest among us, that God sent his Only Son into the world, so that we might live through him."***

Jesus said, ***"I am the way, and the truth, and the life. No one comes to the Father except through me"*** (John 14:6). Jesus laid

His life down on the cross so we can live forever in Heaven with our gracious Father. He paid our penalty so that we can live. The most amazing part is that He accepts us just the way we are, ***"while we were still sinners, Christ died for us"*** (Romans 5:8). I thank God always that my salvation has nothing to do with my ability. Ephesians 2:8-9 says, ***"For by grace you have been saved through faith. And this is not your own doing; it is the gift of God, not a result of works, so that no one may boast."***

One God, one Son, one way leads each of us to one decision, ***"For everyone who calls on the name of the Lord will be saved"*** (Romans 10:13). One decision leads to one prayer, ***"Because if you confess with your mouth that Jesus is Lord and believe in your heart that God raised him from the dead, you will be saved"*** (Romans 10:9). The one who believes and prays with a sincere heart will ultimately make one commitment, ***"By the mercies of God, to present your bodies as a living sacrifice, holy and acceptable to God, which is your spiritual worship"*** (Romans 12:1).

Incredible: One fall, one gracious God, one perfect plan, one obedient Son, and one changed heart equals one new life! That is Agape (perfect love)!

WHO WAS THE SERPENT?

THE FALL, DEVOTION 2

Michael Fox | *Creative Director*

"And the woman said to the serpent, 'We may eat of the fruit of the trees in the garden, but God said, 'You shall not eat of the fruit of the tree that is in the midst of the garden, neither shall you touch it, lest you die." But the serpent said to the woman, 'You will not surely die. For God knows that when you eat of it your eyes will be opened, and you will be like God, knowing good and evil.' So when the woman saw that the tree was good for food, and that it was a delight to the eyes, and that the tree was to be desired to make one wise, she took of its fruit and ate, and she also gave some to her husband who was with her, and he ate. Then the eyes of both were opened." Genesis 3:2-7

"Then the Lord God said to the woman, 'What is this that you have done?' The woman said, 'The serpent deceived me, and I ate.'" Genesis 3:13

The serpent is a deceiver. As I have studied this passage of Scripture, this truth jumped out at me. I have heard the story of Adam and Eve many times. I always knew the serpent tempted them to eat of the Tree of Knowledge of Good and Evil. I always knew that they were previously told by God not to eat from that tree.

For me, many times going through life, I think that there is good and evil, and in spite of the many disguises, I recognize evil. While I do not actually believe I know all evil, that is a general truth that I choose to live my life. We make daily choices to avoid evil, and seek out good. We often fail, and God provides grace and mercy.

This passage, however, has reminded me and opened my eyes. Evil can be presented as good, as it was here with Adam and Eve. It is our job to seek out the scriptures, to know what God says. Psalm 119:11 says, ***"I have stored up your word in my heart, that I might not sin against you."*** The serpent convinced Eve that if she ate of that tree, that she ***"will be like God, knowing good and evil."*** She was deceived. This is a tool I believe the devil will use against us, pretending to be good, trying to convince us that we do not know what we talk about, and allowing us to believe evil is good.

Remembering this, and seeking God through the Scripture will help us combat the serpent, a deceiver.

EVE'S ROLE IN SIN

THE FALL, DEVOTION 3

Sierra Combs | *Women's Ministry Director*

It is good to go back to the beginning, the very beginning when God created the Heavens and the Earth. He did that on the first day and then spent the next several days creating more. He made water and land, trees and flowers, the sun and the moon, and every kind of animal. On the sixth day, He made a man and named him Adam. The Bible says that He made Adam in His image, and since sin had not yet made its way onto the newly formed land, Adam was a perfect man living in a perfect garden on a perfect Earth. Despite the perfection of it all, God saw that it was not good for Adam to be alone, so He created for him a helper, a woman named Eve. I am sure Adam was thrilled to have this perfectly designed woman as his helper. What a good life that must have been! It was just the two of them hanging out with God and a whole bunch of animals in the most beautiful garden ever created! The Bible says that they were both naked and unashamed. They did not know sin and were able to walk in blissful freedom, void of any shame and guilt.

They were only given one rule. In Genesis 2:16-17, God said to them, ***"You may surely eat of every tree of the garden, but of the tree of the knowledge of good and evil you shall not eat, for in the day that you eat of it you shall surely die."*** That sounds pretty serious! We do not know how long it took until they disregarded what God had told them, but we do know that the enemy, the crafty serpent, saw a perfect opportunity to mess up the good and perfect thing that Adam and Eve were enjoying. He went to the woman and asked if God had forbidden them from eating of that one tree, and Eve confirmed what God had said, that if they ate of the tree, there would be some serious repercussions. In Genesis

3:4-7 we see the serpent's response, ***"But the serpent said to the woman, 'You will not surely die. For God knows that when you eat of it your eyes will be opened, and you will be like God, knowing good and evil.' So when the woman saw that the tree was good for food, and that it was a delight to the eyes, and that the tree was to be desired to make one wise, she took of its fruit and ate, and she also gave some to her husband who was with her, and he ate. Then the eyes of both were opened, and they knew that they were naked. And they sewed fig leaves together and made themselves loincloths."***

Just like that, sin entered the world. The serpent, the enemy, known as Satan, crept his way into Eve's world, tricked her and tempted her to disregard God's command. Not only did she sin, but she also drug her husband down with her. The fruit itself was not the issue; the sin was that she chose to disobey. Eve already knew good, but by eating the fruit and disobeying God, she gained the personal knowledge of evil. She also gained the guilt and shame that came with it. Her sin had left her exposed, she instantly knew she was naked, and the perfect relationship she had with God was broken. She could not hide from Him, and neither can we. No fig tree outfit in the world can cover our sin and shame. God sees it. The Bible says that because of the original sin back in the garden, we are all born sinners. Romans 3:23 says, ***"All have sinned and fall short of the glory of God."*** Every single one of us falls short and are separated from God because of sin. Interestingly, though Eve was the first person to sin, God would provide the solution to that sin through "her seed." That Seed is Jesus Christ, and He alone brings the atonement for our sin. Through His perfect blood that was shed on a cross, my debt was paid, and my relationship with God has been restored. Just like Adam and Eve before their sin, I am in perfect standing with the Father. The same solution is offered to you. I pray you will accept it!

ADAM'S ROLE IN SIN

THE FALL, DEVOTION 4

Caleb Combs | *Gathering Pastor*

A few days ago my 9-year-old-son and I had a disagreement. Every morning I wake both of my kids up in the kindest most wonderful way I can imagine. It is with harp music and a nice, smooth, gentle voice. Okay, that is not realistic. I wake them up by turning their light on and ripping their covers off of them, and then I tell them its time to wake up and get ready for school. Just about every morning I remind them that if they want breakfast, they need to get ready and get themselves breakfast. Usually a bowl of cereal or waffles, but something to eat is encouraged because it is the most important meal of the day. Just about every morning, my daughter jumps out of bed, gets dressed, and heads down the stairs because she loves to eat breakfast. On the other hand, my son is the exact opposite. He hates to get up and so he uses the extra ten minutes or so, when he would be eating, to get some extra sleep.

Well, this morning was very similar to most, and Colbie jumped out of bed and headed downstairs for breakfast. Carter stayed in bed and complained about having to get out of bed. I kindly reminded Carter that if he did not get up, he would not have time for breakfast. He said he was not hungry and would skip breakfast, and so I reminded him again that he would not eat until lunchtime at school. If you know my son, he does not have many fat reserves to pull from and so that would be a while before he was able to nourish his tall and skinny frame. Both of my kids finished preparing for school and grabbed their backpacks and headed for the car. As you can imagine, as soon as we pulled out of the driveway to head to school, Carter exclaimed, "I am hungry, can we stop for something on the way?" This may make me a bad parent for sending my kid to school hungry, but I told him no. I explained to him that his decision to not get up affected his ability to be able to eat something before school. He complained about being hungry but knew that I meant it when I said we were not going to stop. We made it to school and I pulled through the parent drop off area, the kids hopped out, and I told them I love them and to have a great day. As the doors shut and the kids began to walk away, I remembered that I forgot to tell Carter that I was picking him up in the afternoon to play golf. So I rolled down my window (okay really just pressed the button because we do not roll windows down anymore) and yelled for Carter to come back to the car. As he walked up to the car I noticed something, Carter had chocolate all over his lips and even on his face. I asked Carter what was on his face and he told me he was hungry, and so he grabbed a candy bar (nice and nutritional) before we left the house. I asked him why he did not ask if he could eat it in the car and he said he knew I would say no. He got caught trying to be sneaky as he disobeyed his father. I told him I would pick him up after school and we would talk about it more then.

As I pulled away, I began to think of this thing called sin. I heard my mother's voice in my head, "Be sure, your sins will find you out," a concept taken from the book of Numbers. Sin is an awful thing and has plagued our world ever since the first man, Adam, sinned.

Adam was created and put into this perfect world by God the Father. God placed him in the Garden of Eden to rule the land and animals and even gave him a wife, named Eve. Adam was put in a perfect situation with all that he would ever want and need at his fingertips. He was given only one rule, do not eat from one specific tree. He was tempted and gave in and ate from the tree. He was just like us in the process of sin, and when he got caught he quickly tried to hide. He thought that he could hide from God. Seems silly, but how often do we do things we think we can hide from God?

When God "caught" up to him, Adam tried to blame others by blaming the woman, the serpent, and even God Himself. Ultimately, God had to kick Adam out of the Garden because of this sin, and by Adam's decision death entered into the world. Romans 5:19 (NKJV) tells us, ***"For as by one man's disobedience many were made sinners, so also by one man's obedience many will be made righteous."*** We see Adam's role in sin entering this world. As a kid, I used to ask the question, "What if Adam would have never sinned, would I be perfect today?"

Well realistically, understanding that Satan is a great deceiver, sin probably would have made its way into the earth. I wish it would not have entered our world, but that is not realistic. However, the second part of that verse is what makes this conversation so exciting. Through one Man's obedience, we now have hope. Jesus went to the cross to pay for my sins, Adam's sins, and your sins. Sin is simply disobeying the Father. We fail and mess up every day. It is just like what Carter did on that morning drive to school. However, I am thankful for a God that made way for my sin.

Romans 6:23 says, ***"For the wages of sin is death, but the free gift of God is eternal life in Christ Jesus our Lord."***

BLAME GAME

THE FALL, DEVOTION 5

Isaiah Combs | *Worship Leader*

I had a problem when I was younger. I did not like to take responsibility for my actions. I was always trying to find an angle or an excuse to get me out of trouble that I had caused. My parents always said I would make a great lawyer. If I got bad grades at school, I would blame it on distractions or the teachers teaching style. Whatever I could find, I would use to try and get out of trouble. I did this with most everything. Mom would ask, "Why didn't you clean your room?" I would quickly respond, "I couldn't clean it because my bothers were still playing." It did not matter what it was, it was never my fault, and I blamed it on someone else.

My Dad would wisely counsel me every time. He would challenge me that I needed to learn to take responsibility for my actions and the things around me. He would then say that this is how leaders were made.

The very first story of a man in the Bible is a story of a blame game. Adam and Eve had just eaten from the "Tree of Knowledge of Good and Evil" and were hiding in the garden when Jesus found them. Adam immediately blamed his sin on Eve. He not only blames Eve but blames God for giving him Eve. The blame game has been a problem from the beginning.

Genesis 3:12 says, ***"The man said, 'The woman whom you gave to be with me, she gave me fruit of the tree, and I ate.'"***

Eventually, it clicked in my brain, and I stopped blaming others and began to take responsibility for my actions. It is amazing how things around you begin to change once you take an active leadership roll in your life. It was now my responsibility to make things happen, and when things go wrong, taking full responsibility.

"But let each one test his own work, and then his reason to boast will be in himself alone and not in his neighbor. For each will have to bear his own load." Galatians 6:4-5

THE GOSPEL

THE FALL, DEVOTION 6

Chuck Lindsey | *Reach Pastor*

"And I will put enmity between you and the woman, and between your seed and her Seed; He shall bruise your head, and you shall bruise His heel." Genesis 3:15 (NKJV)

Though it was 20 years ago, I remember the day like it was yesterday. That day I purchased my wife's engagement ring. It was the largest sum of money, until that point, that I had ever spent on anything in my life. As I type this, I can see it. I was up early that morning with excitement. Six months work was coming to its culmination with this purchase. I could not wait! I was at the bank when it opened that morning withdrawing the cash needed for my purchase. I carefully chose the jewelry store where I was certain I would find "the one." As I walked into the store, I was met by a salesperson who directed me to the engagement rings. I scanned the rows and surveyed the options, scrutinized each piece until I found what I knew was the right one for my bride-to-be. Then the salesperson did something that I will never forget. He did not just pull that ring out and set it on the glass for me to see. He did not just pull it out and hand it to me. No, he first reached into the drawer below him and took out a deep black suede pad that he set in front of me. He carefully took the ring from the case, turned to a machine that quickly cleaned the ring, dried it, polished it, and turned back to me. He did all of this until, at last, he set that sparkling ring onto that dark black suede pad. He knew what he was doing. Here was this beautiful, shining, sparkling heirloom set against the deepest black, void of the suede pad in front of me. The contrast was stark. It was as though I was looking at a star in the night sky.

This has always been a picture, for me, of the Gospel.

The word Gospel in the Greek language means "good news." In Jewish culture, if you had good news to share with someone you would say, "I have 'Gospel' to share with you, we have become engaged!" Or someone might say, "Gospel! You do not owe any taxes this year!" But for good news to appear to be as good of news as it is, it must be accompanied by the bad news. So, for instance, if someone just comes up to you and says, "I am not sick!" you might think, "Well, ok, thank you for that information (I did not ask for it!)." But then you learn that they had gone to the doctor a year prior, and a blood test determined that there was cancer. Now, when they say, "I am not sick!" it means something does it not?

The same is true with the Gospel of Jesus Christ. It is truly Good News. It is the best news. But it is only good news for a person who understands the bad news. It is not enough to say, "God loves you" if the person does not know why God should not love them. It is not enough to tell a person that they should "trust Jesus, follow Him, and give their lives to Him" if they do not know what will happen if they do not. If they do not know the bad news, the good news does not seem like good news. It just seems like one option among many.

So the Gospel is what that salesperson did that day. It is a presentation of the good against the bad. It is the dark black backdrop of our sinful condition before a Holy God. The bad news is that we are all sinners. The bad news is that God demands us to be sinless to enter Heaven (yes, you read that correctly), the bad news is that there is not one person who can make themselves sinless and not a sinner. The bad news gets even worse when you consider that this sin has separated us from God and it will continue to separate us from Him forever unless somehow it is removed. However, since man cannot remove his sins or to make himself sinless and not a sinner, we are stuck. We will be judged as sinners, condemned to eternity in Hell apart from God because of the wrong we have done. That is the bad news. That is the deep black cloth that shadows our lives.

But here comes "the ring" if you will. Though man could not do anything, God did. Man could do nothing to pay for sin. Man could do nothing to make himself sinless. Though man could do nothing at all, God did by coming and dying in our place. He took our sin upon Himself, as though He was the sinner. Then He was judged as a sinner in our place. Then He was condemned. He was separated from God the Father, and then He died. It was all for us. He served my sentence so that I do not have to. He paid my debt so that I now owe nothing. He was separated so that I never have to be. That is good news!

See today the black cloth of sin that shadowed our lives, and that would have separated us from Him forever in Hell. Now see the jewel of God's amazing grace. It is the sparkling ring that is His Gospel, given to us. This is the Good News of what God has done.

03

ADAM & EVE

DR. RANDY T. JOHNSON,
GROWTH PASTOR

I remember hearing an interview as a coach and his team were parting ways. The interviewer asked why he was leaving. He responded, "Fatigue and illness." The interviewer gave a sympathetic sigh, and then the former coach said, "They were sick and tired of me."

I chuckled as I heard his response. I liked his wit, but also the fact that he did not blame anyone else or make excuses. All too often, we are tempted to play the "blame game." Our pride urges us to make up an excuse or focus the failure on someone or something else.

Adam and Eve had this same problem. As we focus on their legacy, we need to remember the good, the bad, and the ugly.

How difficult are these words, "It is my fault, I am sorry," for you?

____

____

____

1. Good

The first thing we need to remember about Adam and Eve is what God initially said. Genesis 2:18-22 says, ***"Then the Lord God said, 'It is not good that the man should be alone; I will make him a helper fit for him.' Now out of the ground the Lord God had formed every beast of the field and every bird of the heavens and brought them to the man to see what he would call them. And whatever the man called every living creature, that was its name. The man gave names to all livestock and to the birds of the heavens and to every beast of the field. But for Adam there was not found a helper fit for him. So the Lord God caused a deep sleep to fall upon the man, and while he slept took one of***

his ribs and closed up its place with flesh. And the rib that the Lord God had taken from the man he made into a woman and brought her to the man."

What was the goal in creating the woman?

____

____

____

It may sound overly simplistic, but how is woman better for man than any other creation?

____

____

____

God made the woman as a perfect match for man. It was (and is) a "good" thing. Unfortunately, the story took a bad twist.

2. Bad

When it comes to sin entering the world, "bad" is quite the understatement. It was horrific, horrendous, hideous, and heinous. It was the worst day in the history of the world. It started an epidemic that has affected all of us. It brought the death sentence. Yes, it is "bad."

Genesis 3:6 records, ***"So when the woman saw that the tree was good for food, and that it was a delight to the eyes, and that the tree was to be desired to make one wise, she took of its fruit and ate, and she also gave some to her husband who was with her, and he ate."***

Where was Adam when this was happening?

___

___

___

What was the woman's goal in eating the fruit?

___

___

___

Sin entered the world. The actions and conversation that followed became ugly.

3. Ugly

We have all heard, "When you point a finger at someone, you point four (actually three) right back at yourself." Making excuses and blaming others can get very ugly. It is refreshing to hear someone admit, "It was my fault." It became historical when president Harry Truman put a sign on his desk with the inscription, "The buck stops here!" It is encouraging to know when someone is willing to take responsibility for their actions and the results that come.

Benjamin Franklin bluntly said, "He that is good for making excuses is seldom good for anything else." The life and times of Adam and Eve continue downhill after their sin as they made excuses and started blaming any and everyone else.

Genesis 3:8-13 says, ***"And they heard the sound of the Lord God walking in the garden in the cool of the day, and the man and his wife hid themselves from the presence of the Lord God among the trees of the garden. But the Lord God called to the man and said to him, 'Where are you?' And he said, 'I heard the sound of***

you in the garden, and I was afraid, because I was naked, and I hid myself.' He said, 'Who told you that you were naked? Have you eaten of the tree of which I commanded you not to eat?' The man said, 'The woman whom you gave to be with me, she gave me fruit of the tree, and I ate.' Then the Lord God said to the woman, 'What is this that you have done?' The woman said, 'The serpent deceived me, and I ate.'"

Who did the woman blame for her sin?

____

____

____

Who did Adam blame for his sin (it is not just the woman)?

____

____

____

How do we "blame God" for things in our lives?

____

____

____

What should be our response to difficulties and even failures?

____

____

____

"All blame is a waste of time. No matter how much fault you find with another, and regardless of how much you blame him, it will not change you. The only thing blame does is to keep the focus off you when you are looking for external reasons to explain your unhappiness or frustration. You may succeed in making another feel guilty of something by blaming him, but you won't succeed in changing whatever it is about you that is making you unhappy." Wayne W. Dyer

With whom do you need to get things corrected?

____

____

____

It is amazing how powerful three words can be:

"I was wrong."

"I am sorry."

"I love you."

WHO DID ADAM BLAME?

ADAM & EVE, DEVOTION 1

Larry Gabbara | *Financial Bookkeeper*

"So when the woman saw that the tree was good for food, and that it was a delight to the eyes, and that the tree was to be desired to make one wise, she took of its fruit and ate, and she also gave some to her husband who was with her, and he ate. Then the eyes of both were opened, and they knew that they were naked." Genesis 3:6-7a

I was brought up in a religious home. We knew of God but not who He really was. As I got older, I heard about being born again, but that meant nothing to me. I heard about Billy Graham Crusades, but I thought he was just a Jesus freak! Once I accepted the truth about how to receive Christ, my heart and eyes were opened. When I first thought about the chances I missed to hear and understand the Gospel, I blamed it on the fact that no one told me. But that was not true.

Adam and Eve both knew what God had told them concerning the Tree of the Knowledge of Good and Evil; they knew exactly what they were both risking. Adam was the one who should have been responsible for following God's commands. Before Eve took a bite and then offered it to Adam, Adam should have led Eve to make a better decision. Adam then blamed both Eve and God for his disobedience.

"The Lord God took the man and put him in the garden of Eden to work it and keep it. And the Lord God commanded the man, saying, 'You may surely eat of every tree of the garden, but of

the tree of the knowledge of good and evil you shall not eat, for in the day that you eat of it you shall surely die.'" Genesis 2:15-17

Now both Adam and Eve realized what sin was, and that they were naked. They knew that they needed to cover up and wear clothing. They were ashamed to be seen by God.

This sin was transmitted to all mankind through Adam's sin of disobedience. The devil tricked them, as he tries to trick us daily. We must continually fight the good fight, as to not be tricked by the devil.

"The man said, 'The woman whom you gave to be with me, she gave me fruit of the tree, and I ate.'" Genesis 3:12

We must own the blame for our actions. Like Adam, we cannot blame someone else; we know what is the right path if we follow God's instruction. Do not give into the world's temptation.

We need to ask ourselves "Is this the right decision?"

What would we do if Jesus were next to us?

WHO DID EVE BLAME?

ADAM & EVE, DEVOTION 2

Debbie Gabbara | *Assistant to the Gathering Pastor*

I do not remember exactly what happened, but I do remember my response, "Your sister did not do that. She is a baby, and she cannot walk." The blame game comes easy and starts early. My son must have been about two because my daughter was an infant when her brother blamed her for something that he did. My son loved his baby sister; he did not want to hurt her. However, he also did not want to be in trouble. Somehow, just as we see Satan do in Genesis chapter 3, my little one knew how to twist the truth.

"Now the serpent was more cunning than any beast of the field which the Lord God had made. And he said to the woman, 'Has God indeed said, 'You shall not eat of every tree of the garden'?'" Genesis 3:1 (NKJV)

I had often wondered how long Adam and Eve were in the garden before sin crept in to find them. One day the serpent came with his twisted truth and Adam and Eve did eat from the tree that God told them not to. Later when they heard God walking in the garden, the hiding and the blaming began.

"And He said, 'Who told you that you were naked? Have you eaten from the tree of which I commanded you that you should not eat?' Then the man said, 'The woman whom You gave to be with me, she gave me of the tree, and I ate.' And the Lord God said to the woman, 'What is this you have done?' The woman said, 'The serpent deceived me, and I ate.'" Genesis 3:11-13 (NKJV)

Adam blamed Eve, and Eve blamed the serpent. In the blame game, everyone is talking, but no one is taking responsibility. Eve quickly followed the example of Adam and shifted the blame to someone else. Eve disobeyed God, Adam followed along, and their days would never be the same. They now knew good and also the evil from which God had tried to protect them.

In Deuteronomy 30:16, God promises us life and blessings when we keep His commandments. Because of Adam and Eve's choice in the garden we are all born into sin. Just like them, we all play the blame game. We blame our past, our circumstances, our lack of knowledge, and others. In 2 Corinthians 11:3 we are told that our minds can be led astray by the serpent's lies. The more grounded we are in Christ, the better we will be able to withstand the deceptions of the serpent. Satan is busy; his plan is always to find ways to twist the truths and promises of God, to cause us to stumble and even fall away from the Lord.

Trust in the Lord, keep His commandments, and do not put yourself in a place where you find yourself blaming someone or something for your decisions and actions.

FROM THE DUST WE SHALL RISE

ADAM & EVE, DEVOTION 3

James Clouse | *Student Pastor*

I do not like waking up in the morning. This is strange because I also do not like going to bed. At night, I will read, watch television, play video games, and numerous other things to not have to go to sleep. My mind is too busy for sleep! But when I need to arise in the morning, there is some bellyaching happening. Most of the time, I will ask Amanda to make coffee and I know I still have a few minutes left before that sweet aroma hits my nostrils. When I awake and start my day, I feel like a brand new man. When I start waking up and walking around, I feel like the world is ready to be explored!

I can only imagine how Adam felt when God created him. When Adam stood and stretched for the first time, I wonder what was going on through his head. Was there an automatic response to God for creating him? Was he ready to start working the garden that God made right away or did God have to teach him? It is amazing to read the text and let the questions float around in your mind!

Genesis 2:7-8 records, ***"Then the Lord God formed the man of dust from the ground and breathed into his nostrils the breath of life, and the man became a living creature. And the Lord God planted a garden in Eden, in the east, and there he put the man whom he had formed."***

God formed Adam out of the dust that He just created. He took earth and literally molded Adam from His original creation. After God had His perfect model for Adam, He breathed the breath of life into him. Imagine everything that came with that breath of life. God made Adam's body work physically. Everything that was formed to make the body work was now working. God breathed Adam's heart and lungs to life. The veins that started pumping Adam's blood starting working the way God molded them.

God also breathed a mental life into Adam. Adam's mind started working as God intended. Adam started to feel the warmth of the air, to see the blueness of the sky, and to see the green of the fields. Adam could now talk with his creator and laugh with his God.

But most importantly, God now breathed a spiritual existence into Adam. It was a spirit that had a desire to love God and to have companionship with God. This spirit had the desire to love his creator.

I believe that we are all born to have this same want and desire to love our God. That is how we were formed. We were formed, just as Adam was, and grown in our mother's womb. God also breathes the breath of life into each of us as we are born and with that comes the physical, mental, and spiritual aspect of our lives. Grow a desire to want that companionship with God as Adam did when he was created.

DO THE WORK SON

ADAM & EVE, DEVOTION 4

Ryan Story | *Location Pastor - Burton*

I love reading God's Word. I have many shortcomings in certain spiritual disciplines, but reading the Bible has always been the one habit that brings me closest to God. While I am nowhere near as learned as I would like to be, and I am by no means as disciplined in my studies as I wish I could be, I have always enjoyed my time in the Word. If you struggle with reading the Bible, I want to push you into developing disciplines to read the Bible more often. The truth is reading the Bible can be hard. For me, the hardest part of reading is my mind jumps ahead. I am that guy who while reading, my mind is already on the "next part." This makes it hard to really take in what God has in one area of His Word. For this devotion, I ended up doing the same thing. When I saw that I had to write about Adam and Eve, my mind was already racing past Genesis chapters one and two and was already thinking about the work that Jesus did on the cross. I jumped past the Garden of Eden and was already studying about the fallen world we live in through sin entering the world because of Adam.

It is so easy to skip Genesis chapter two. We read the creation account in Genesis chapter one and then skip right to chapter three and the fall of the world into sin. I have to admit; I was doing the exact same thing. In one moment ordained by God, He showed me how Adam and Eve were sinless for a period of time which brings amazing truths. We can look at Genesis chapter two as a brief moment of how things were before sin entered the world.

Genesis 2:5 says, ***"When no bush of the field was yet in the land and no small plant of the field had yet sprung up—for the Lord***

God had not caused it to rain on the land, and there was no man to work the ground." God's timing is so perfect. A snowflake cannot fall outside of God's will. When God created the world, God did not fill it with flora. Not only that, God did not plant anything; He did not allow it to rain and there was no person to tend the ground. While the Earth was taking form, God waited until man was created to begin the work of tending the grounds. I look at life in the same light. It is a blank slate of infinite possibilities, God is there to sustain everything, direct everything to His purpose, but someone has to work it. Work is not a by-product of sin; work is a godly responsibility which man has been given.

I have a guy I sit with every few weeks who has been mentoring me through the last few years of my life, and he has always said, "Opportunity is often hidden in coveralls and work gloves." Let us be honest; we live in a lazy culture. We have lost the idea that work is a good thing. Sin did not create work; sin made work hard. Be honest; there is nothing better than sitting back after you build a car or you do mass amounts of yard work. The feeling that comes over you is so satisfying. Work was created and given by God; laziness is the devil's way of scaring people off from getting closer to God. Just as a note to the armchair theologian: I am not talking about salvation in any way. The work of salvation is only accomplished by what Jesus did on the cross.

Do you think the church is known for working hard? I do not want to diminish any good that churches around the world have done for the cause of Christ, for neighborhoods, and for third world countries. However, there are secular organizations that are not motivated by the love of Jesus that are working at the same pace if not more to help people. It has been said, "10 percent does 90 percent of the work." It is always the quick answer to the problem, and then we just gaze at those not serving with condescending looks.

My question for you, "When was the last time you put work into helping disciple a person?" In Genesis 2:15-16, it says, ***"The Lord God took the man and put him in the garden of Eden to work it and keep it. And the Lord God commanded the man."*** Notice how God moves in Adam's life and commands Him what to do. I struggle with the idea that Christians put so much time in working, stacking chairs, moving dirt, cutting down trees, and driving buses all in the name of Jesus. Those are good things, but the best thing is to make sure that we are teaching others to work hard for the cause of Christ. Jesus' last words to His disciples in Matthew 28:20 say, ***"Teaching them to observe all that I have commanded you. And behold, I am with you always, to the end of the age."*** We must teach people all the things about Jesus, and this includes a Christ-centered work ethic.

We work hard for our Savior. We work hard for our Father. We work hard for the One who saved us. Your work often shows where you place your faith. It is not a person or an organization. Work hard for the One who is our eternal reward.

"Whatever you do, work heartily, as for the Lord and not for men, knowing that from the Lord you will receive the inheritance as your reward. You are serving the Lord Christ."
Colossians 3:23-24

EVE'S CURSE AND POSITION

ADAM & EVE, DEVOTION 5

Jen Combs | *Women's Ministry*

"To the woman he said, 'I will surely multiply your pain in childbearing; in pain you shall bring forth children. Your desire shall be contrary to your husband, but he shall rule over you.'" Genesis 3:16

When Adam and Eve sinned, a curse from the Lord was given to them. Sometimes when I think of Eve and the curse, I wonder if she is the most unpopular person in Heaven. Like, does every lady go to her and just eye roll and sigh? Or want to punch her? Sounds harsh, but so was the curse. It is good to break it down a bit.

"I will surely multiply your pain in childbearing." I have yet to meet a woman who says, I just love to give birth. I have had five children, relatively speedy, uncomplicated deliveries and I look back thinking, birth is one of the hardest things I have been through in life. It is painful and full of anguish. But this is also what the Lord felt when sin occurred in the garden - Pain and Anguish. So, ladies, this is part of our curse passed down from Eve. Guys, sorry but you have to watch your woman being in the most miserable pain of her life, and there is nothing you can do about it.

"In pain you shall bring forth children." As I sat here rereading the curses, it hit me that this was not just talking about birth pains. This is talking about child rearing. Scripture is telling us that raising our children is going to be painful. Our children are going to make decisions that hurt us. They are going to do things that grieve our hearts as mothers. But again, these are all emotions that we make the Lord feel. We sin and grieve His heart continually.

"Your desire shall be contrary to your husband, but he shall rule over you." Just when you thought the curse was tough enough, the Lord sticks this one in there. Now guys, do not get all excited thinking this is a sexual desire that your wife will have for you. Nope, this is a desire to want to lead and tell you what to do. So we were given this curse to want to be in charge, yet the Lord says that the husband will rule the home and be in charge. That is like putting oil and water together. Talk about a recipe for some friction and repelling of each other.

You are probably wondering, well that is all a Debbie Downer. How do we fix it? First Timothy 2:15 says, ***"Yet she will be saved through childbearing- if they continue in faith and love, holiness, with self-control."*** We do not fix it. Jesus fixes it. He restores. He renews. If we have surrendered our life to Him, we will be women of faith, love, holiness, and self-control. If we are godly women, we will be raising godly children with these attributes and lessening our pain. I love how John MacArthur put it, "And in the lives of these godly children, the work of the Lord will go on, mitigating sin in their own lives, sanctifying them and therefore reducing her pain." What about the whole husband part? Ephesians 5:22 says, ***"Wives, submit to your own husbands, as to the Lord."*** I know that probably makes a lot of you bristle. But sometimes we need to push our feelings aside and just obey. If the Lord says this is how you grow a loving, God-honoring marriage, then we just need to do it. If you dig into Scripture enough, the Lord does answer so many of our questions and even gives us formulas for some situations. Sometimes the answer is to merely obey His commands regardless of how it makes us feel.

ADAM'S CURSE AND POSITION

ADAM & EVE, DEVOTION 6

Joshua Combs | *Lead Pastor*

"And to Adam he said, 'Because you have listened to the voice of your wife and have eaten of the tree of which I commanded you, 'You shall not eat of it,' cursed is the ground because of you; in pain you shall eat of it all the days of your life; thorns and thistles it shall bring forth for you; and you shall eat the plants of the field. By the sweat of your face you shall eat bread, till you return to the ground, for out of it you were taken; for you are dust, and to dust you shall return.'" Genesis 3:17-19

There is an old saying attributed to several different authors and statesmen, that the only two certainties in the world are death and taxes. I suppose we could modify this saying ever so slightly to reflect what God says in Genesis chapter 3. The curse that is spoken over Adam, summarized, is simply, "Adam, work is going to be hard and then you die." Adam was given the joyful task of maintaining the Garden of Eden and was never going to die, but sin and Adam's rebellion ruined all of that. The work that had once been so wonderful became extremely burdensome. Food that had been so readily available to provide for his family's needs would now come at an extremely high cost. Only through tireless sweat, that would simultaneously zap the life from him, would Adam be able to eat and provide for his family. Sin had undoubtedly changed everything, including work.

But Jesus came to redeem us from the curse. He died on the cross and rose from the grave to restore what was broken in Eden. This amazing redeeming work rescues more than just our souls from the powerful grip of sin but redeems work. The Scripture is filled with important passages concerning work that point us to its greater meaning, purpose, and mission.

Paul writes in Colossians 3:22-24, ***"Bondservants, obey in everything those who are your earthly masters, not by way of eye-service, as people-pleasers, but with sincerity of heart, fearing the Lord. Whatever you do, work heartily, as for the Lord and not for men, knowing that from the Lord you will receive the inheritance as your reward."***

Just as Adam in the garden was "hired" by the Lord and "paid" by the Lord (the room and board were pretty great), in Christ, we are the same. Yes, we will have human supervisors, but they are not who we ultimately answer to or pay us. The Bible is very clear, as followers of Jesus, we are to work diligently not to impress our direct supervisor, but because we know the Lord gave us our job. Not only did the Lord bless us with our job, but it is the Lord who rewards us (Colossians 2:24).

Without a doubt, we live in a fallen world that was dramatically changed that day in Eden. But Jesus the Redeemer has come to buy back what was stolen through sin. The Lord's redemptive work includes redeeming us and even our work.

Bonus Scripture: Read 2 Thessalonians 3:6-12; Ecclesiastes 9:10; 1 Peter 2:18-25

04

CAIN & ABEL

DR. RANDY T. JOHNSON,
GROWTH PASTOR

There are a number of famous brothers from history:

Wilbur and Orville Wright
The Brothers Grimm
John, Robert, and Ted Kennedy
Frank and Jesse James
The Jacksons
The Jonases
The Marx Brothers
Cain and Abel

Who are some other famous brothers?

___

___

___

I do not have a brother. I have a couple of great brothers-in-law. I would do anything for them, and I know they would do the same for me, but I am told it is still different. There is something about a biological brother. I learned at an early age not to break up a fight of brothers; they will team up against you. No one loves like brothers, and no one can fight like brothers.

Brothers do not always get along. Jealousy, envy, rage, and anger can fill the room. It is not something new as the first brothers had their problems, too. Genesis chapter 4 records the account of Cain and Abel.

Genesis 4:1-7 says, ***"Now Adam knew Eve his wife, and she conceived and bore Cain, saying, 'I have gotten a man with the help of the Lord.' And again, she bore his brother Abel. Now Abel was a keeper of sheep, and Cain a worker of the ground. In the course of time Cain brought to the Lord an offering of the fruit***

of the ground, and Abel also brought of the firstborn of his flock and of their fat portions. And the Lord had regard for Abel and his offering, but for Cain and his offering he had no regard. So Cain was very angry, and his face fell. The Lord said to Cain, 'Why are you angry, and why has your face fallen? If you do well, will you not be accepted? And if you do not do well, sin is crouching at the door. Its desire is contrary to you, but you must rule over it.'"

What was each son's occupation?

____

____

____

God accepted both animal and grain sacrifices (Leviticus 6:14-30). Why do you think God rejected Cain's offering?

____

____

____

What does the phrase, ***"sin is crouching at the door,"*** mean in your life?

____

____

____

How can anger motivate you to do good?

____

____

____

How can anger incline you to lose control or do something evil?

Anger has many faces. When left unchecked, we can let it lead us in a direction of destruction. Be it verbal or physical it can become very abusive. The more someone else is hurt, the more you hurt yourself.

Genesis 4:8-12 continue, ***"Cain spoke to Abel his brother. And when they were in the field, Cain rose up against his brother Abel and killed him. Then the Lord said to Cain, 'Where is Abel your brother?' He said, 'I do not know; am I my brother's keeper?' And the Lord said, 'What have you done? The voice of your brother's blood is crying to me from the ground. And now you are cursed from the ground, which has opened its mouth to receive your brother's blood from your hand. When you work the ground, it shall no longer yield to you its strength. You shall be a fugitive and a wanderer on the earth.'"***

Why do you think God approached Cain the way He did?

Cain responded to God with the now famous statement, ***"Am I my brother's keeper?"*** Are we to be each other's keeper? If so, how?

What all did Cain do wrong? What should he have done at each stage of this story?

___

___

___

There is righteous anger, but typically anger needs to be avoided at all costs. Scripture repeatedly voices caution.

"Refrain from anger, and forsake wrath! Fret not yourself; it tends only to evil." Psalm 37:8

"Whoever is slow to anger has great understanding, but he who has a hasty temper exalts folly." Proverbs 14:29

"A hot-tempered man stirs up strife, but he who is slow to anger quiets contention." Proverbs 15:18

"Good sense makes one slow to anger, and it is his glory to overlook an offense." Proverbs 19:11

"A man of wrath stirs up strife, and one given to anger causes much transgression." Proverbs 29:22

"For pressing milk produces curds, pressing the nose produces blood, and pressing anger produces strife." Proverbs 30:33

"Be not quick in your spirit to become angry, for anger lodges in the heart of fools." Ecclesiastes 7:9

"Know this, my beloved brothers: let every person be quick to hear, slow to speak, slow to anger; for the anger of man does not produce the righteousness of God." James 1:19-20

Which of these verses stands out most to you?

___

___

___

It has been said, "Anger is one letter short of danger." That is so true. Cain let jealousy, envy, rage, and anger get the best or worst of him.

Where might God be looking on your life with favor or disfavor?

___

___

___

"Hot heads and cold hearts never solved anything." Billy Graham

CAIN'S SACRIFICE

CAIN & ABEL, DEVOTION 1

Richie Henson | *Production Director*

I attended Bible college at Baptist Bible College in Springfield, Missouri. While there, I had numerous wonderful professors, but there were a few that became easily distracted by intriguing topics of discussion. Due to this, many students would purposefully pose questions and quandaries that required hours of discussion. One topic that came up more than once is Cain's sacrifice in Genesis chapter 4 and why God did not accept the sacrifice. There are entire books written concerning this topic, and it is quite interesting. However, based on the text, no airtight argument can be made concerning the issue with the physical sacrifice Cain brought. There are some who would claim the sacrifice was not worthy as it did not fulfill the blood requirement for forgiveness. Although this is the clear and definitive practice later in the Old Testament, there is no indication that said the practice was a requirement at the time.

That being the case, I think there is one definitive and airtight argument we can make about Cain and his sacrifice. Cain had an attitude or disposition that would have disqualified any offering he would bring. If you look at the result of Cain's interaction with God concerning his sacrifice, the murder of Abel, I think it is entirely apparent that Cain had a serious heart condition. How full of anger and spite must a heart be to act upon the desire to murder a brother? Cain struggled with an ailment of hatred and discontent. It is this wrong attitude that eventually makes all of Cain's worship null and void.

As Christians living in the time of the Church, we can struggle to understand the sacrificial system. We have never been required to live within the confines of the law and therefore struggle to gain our bearing in the system. However, we are still called upon to make sacrifices.

In Matthew 16:24-26, Jesus details the way in which the church must give sacrifice, ***"Then Jesus told his disciples, 'If anyone would come after me, let him deny himself and take up his cross and follow me. For whoever would save his life will lose it, but whoever loses his life for my sake will find it. For what will it profit a man if he gains the whole world and forfeits his soul? Or what shall a man give in return for his soul?'"***

Whether we take the time to argue the validity of Cain's fruit sacrifice or not, the principle remains that God does not ask for our offerings and sacrifices because He needs them, but rather, God asks for them that we may learn to die to ourselves and embrace the reality of Jesus as the Lord of our lives. As we "lose" our life, that is to say, lay aside our short sided misconceptions of fulfillment and happiness, we grow to understand true contentment in God.

ABEL'S SACRIFICE

CAIN & ABEL, DEVOTION 2

Debbie Kerr | *Office Administrator*

When you worship God, do you ever wonder if your offering is acceptable? I fear we often enter into worship with self-serving or impure motives. In our corporate gatherings, we worship by singing, giving our tithes and offerings, praying, and listening to the Word of God. Many people enter through the doors of a church with their agenda and ideas as to what worship looks like to them. They will only sing certain songs, or listen to the message if the pastor uses the proper translation. These ideas and motives are completely self-serving. Did you know that God has specific requirements for our offerings of sacrifice and worship? Jesus said we are to worship Him in Spirit and Truth! Worship is not about us, and if we make it about us, we run the risk of our worship being rejected.

God delivered a very serious and sobering message to the people of Israel in Amos 5:21-24 regarding acceptable worship, ***"I hate, I despise your feasts, and I take no delight in your solemn assemblies. Even though you offer me your burnt offerings and grain offerings, I will not accept them; and the peace offerings of your fattened animals, I will not look upon them. Take away from me the noise of your songs; to the melody of your harps I will not listen. But let justice roll down like waters, and righteousness like an ever-flowing stream."*** Can you say, Ouch? We do not get to define acceptable worship, God does!

It is helpful to take a look at the first account of offering sacrifices to God. In Genesis chapter 4, we learn that Adam and Eve's sons, Cain and Abel, each brought a different offering to God. Cain was a worker of the ground and Abel was a keeper of sheep. Cain's offering consisted of ***"some of the fruits of the soil as an offering to the Lord."*** His offering was rejected because it was based on works. In Genesis 4:4, we read, ***"And Abel also brought the firstborn of flock and of their fat portions."*** Hebrews 11:4 reads, ***"By faith Abel offered God a better sacrifice than Cain, through which he was commended as righteous. God commending him by accepting his gifts."*** What do you think was the difference? The writer of Hebrews reveals, Abel brought his offering out of faith. Some theologians believe Abel's was more acceptable because it was a blood sacrifice. Genesis chapter 4 does not reveal the reason that Abel's offering was more acceptable but the passage in Hebrews chapter 11 simply states that it was the better sacrifice.

Because Abel's offering was brought by faith is an insight to us that the condition of our heart is more important to God than the style of the offering. In 1 Samuel 15:22, we read, ***"To obey is better than sacrifice."*** God is looking for pure hearts and a life that has been completely surrendered to Him. He no longer requires an animal sacrifice because the Lamb of God, Jesus, shed His blood on the cross and became the blood sacrifice as the only payment needed for our sins. Abel's sacrifice foreshadowed the ultimate sacrifice of Jesus.

"For by grace you have been saved through faith. And this is not your own doing; it is the gift of God, not a result of works, so that no one may boast." Ephesians 2:8-9

"I appeal to you therefore, brothers, by the mercies of God, to present your bodies as a living sacrifice, holy and acceptable to God, which is your spiritual worship." Romans 12:1

"SIN IS CROUCHING AT THE DOOR"

CAIN & ABEL, DEVOTION 3

Kenny Hovis | *Prison Ministry Director*

Sacrifice is such an interesting word to me. It is a word that has many meanings and applications to so many different people. We, as parents, can *sacrifice* our time and finances for our children. A person in the military may offer up his or her life as a *sacrifice* in service to our country. A religious extremist may offer his or her life up as a *sacrifice*, as well as taking innocent lives in the process. Couples should *sacrifice* the tendency to focus on other people instead of the person they married. Philanthropists are said to *sacrifice* for others less fortunate out of their abundance. At our jobs, we *sacrifice* one of our most valuable commodities, our time, as a means of supporting ourselves and our families. Others may *sacrifice* their family and spouse by having an affair with another person. Someone may *sacrifice* their financial or physical health with some type of addiction. When it comes to defining the word *sacrifice*, the determining factor is motive.

In Genesis chapter 4, we have a detailed account of the sacrifice of two people, Cain and Abel. As the Bible shares the account of their sacrifice, we see a stark contrast between the two sacrifices. Cain, a farmer, or keeper of the land, gives a sacrifice out of the abundance of his crops. Abel, and tender of sheep gave of the firstborn and fat portions from his flock. God accepted Abel's sacrifice, but not Cain's. Why? I believe it was their motives.

Cain was unhappy and jealous of Abel as a result of God's approval of Abel's offering. God, being all-knowing says to Cain in Genesis 4:6, ***"The Lord said to Cain, 'Why are you angry, and why has your face fallen?'"*** God is telling Cain not to pout about Him not accepting his offering. It was Cain's fault. God even asked him a rhetorical question in the first part of verse 7 saying, ***"If you do well, will you not be accepted?"*** The answer is, of course, it will be accepted. But, He also gives Cain a warning in the second part of verse 7 saying, ***"And if you do not do well, sin is crouching at the door. Its desire is contrary to you, but you must rule over it!"*** He warns Cain that sacrifices given or submitted with sinful motives give an opportunity for sin to enter into our lives. We must resist the desire to keep the "best" for ourselves and give the leftovers to God.

Jesus taught the same concept. Luke 21:1-4 recounts how we should sacrifice to God. ***"Jesus looked up and saw the rich putting their gifts into the offering box, and he saw a poor widow put in two small copper coins. And he said, 'Truly, I tell you, this poor widow has put in more than all of them. For they all contributed out of their abundance, but she out of her poverty put in all she had to live on.'"*** Jesus is telling the disciples that the offering the rich people put in the box was an unacceptable sacrifice because they were giving out of their abundance. But, the widow giving much less, truly "sacrificed" and gave everything she had.

As Christians, we claim to have sacrificed our lives, everything that we have, and everything we are. We would do well to heed the warning God gave to Cain, and Jesus' teaching to His disciples on our sacrifices. We tend to be selfish and think we can give God small portions of all we value. Our desire must be to give all of our time, finances, possessions, family, or anything else we can lay at the feet of God as a sacrifice. We need to resist the tendency to keep the best or abundance for ourselves. It is not ours to keep anyway.

When we sacrifice with a pure motive and give of our best and all that we are and have, it gives God opportunity to receive that which we offer, or sacrifice, as something that pleases Him, and something He can use! Do not forget that sin is crouching at the door, waiting for the slightest opening to steal away our sacrifice, and make it unacceptable to God!

"AM I MY BROTHERS KEEPER?"

CAIN & ABEL, DEVOTION 4

Gareth Volz | *Senior (55+) Director*

"Am I my brother's keeper?" This question was first asked by Cain in Genesis 4:9. Cain argued with his brother Abel, and it got so heated that Cain killed his brother. In verse 8, God asks Cain, ***"Where is Abel your brother?"*** Cain responded with a lie – ***"I do not know; am I my brother's keeper?"***

In most families, brothers stick together and have each other's back, even if they have disagreements from time to time. The family is important, and family members look out for one another. As Christians, we are part of God's family, the Church, and we should look out for one another. God's Word has a lot to say about being our brother's keeper:

"Love one another with brotherly affection. Outdo one another in showing honor." Romans 12:10

"Repay no one evil for evil, but give thought to do what is honorable in the sight of all. If possible, so far as it depends on you, live peaceably with all." Romans 12:17-18

"For all the commandments, 'You shall not commit adultery, You shall not murder, You shall not steal, You shall not covet,' and any other commandment, are summed up in this word: 'You shall love your neighbor as yourself.' Love does no wrong to a neighbor; therefore love is the fulfilling of the law." Romans 13:9-10

"So then let us pursue what makes for peace and for mutual unbuilding." Romans 14:19

"Rather, speaking the truth in love, we are to grow up in every way into Him who is the head, into Christ, from whom the whole body, joined and held together by every joint with which it is equipped, when each part is working properly, makes the body grow so that it builds itself up in love." Ephesians 4:15-16

"For you were called to freedom, brothers. Only do not use your freedom as an opportunity for the flesh, but through love serve one another." Galatians 5:13

"Brothers, if anyone is caught in any transgression, you who are spiritual should restore him in the spirit of gentleness. Keep watch on yourself, lest you too be tempted. Bear one another's burdens and so fulfill the law of Christ." Galatians 6:1-2

"Now concerning brotherly love you have no need for anyone to write to you, for you yourselves have been taught by God to love one another." 1 Thessalonians 4:9

"Let brotherly love continue." Hebrews 13:1

"Finally, all of you, have unity of mind, sympathy, brotherly love, a tender heart, and a humble mind." 1 Peter 3:8

The Bible makes it clear: I am my brother's keeper!

SIN & CONSEQUENCES

CAIN & ABEL, DEVOTION 5

Isaiah Combs | *Worship Leader*

Nothing in life is free. I am sure you have heard this many times in your life. The older you get, the more you realize how true this is. Everything has a cost, whether it is now or later. It all costs something.

The same thing is true with our sin. There is a cost, and that cost is death and separation from God. Romans 6:23 says, ***"For the wages*** [cost] ***of*** [our] ***sin is death."*** Isaiah 59:2 adds, ***"But your iniquities*** [sin] ***have made a separation between you and your God, and your sins have hidden His face from you so that He does not hear."***

So the sin that we freely commit comes with a cost, and that cost is too great for us to repay. No one is innocent, no one lives sinless, and no one is free from the cost. Romans 3:23 says, ***"For all have sinned and fallen short of the glory of God."*** We were bound to sin and separation from God. Our cost follows us around and is bound to us like weighty chains.

"BUT" is such a small word, yet it is the difference maker. ***"For the wages of sin is death but the free gift of God is eternal life in Jesus Christ our Lord"*** (Romans 6:23). There is something in this life that is free, and that is the free gift of God. He paid our debt and wiped the slate clean. No longer are we a slave to our wages (cost) and death. No longer are we separated from God. The crazy thing is, all we have to do is accept the free gift.

"Because, if you confess with your mouth that Jesus is Lord and believe in your heart that God raised him from the dead, you will be saved. For with the heart one believes and is justified, and with the mouth one confesses and is saved" (Romans 10:9-10).

Who says there is nothing in this life that is free?

THE EFFECTS OF SIN ON OTHERS

CAIN & ABEL, DEVOTION 6

Matt Darden

"How did I get here?" With seven dollars in my pocket, two duffel bags, and the paranoia of a man on the run, I sat on a Greyhound bus. Rewind four years, I was 16 and on my own. I moved to Missouri in search of a new area and freedom. Freedom is not what I found. Being grounded to nothing, I became shackled to everything. In my search for the ultimate freedom, I became a slave to the fickle and ever-changing desires of my own heart. Jeremiah 17:9 (KJV) describes it, ***"The heart is deceitful above all things, and desperately wicked: Who can know it?"*** From within my haze, thoughts, and feelings of remorse continued to assault me. The question persisted, "How did I get here?" The answer can be found in the question. I got here because of me, because of me lying, manipulating, stealing, and the many other selfish things that I did.

I did not do these things to hurt those who hurt me. I did them because I always wanted the focus on me. My continued attempt to help myself left me lonely, bitter, and full of regret. But more importantly, how did it leave those who were on the receiving end of my wickedness? In my mess, I hurt my best friend, a man I had been friends with since third grade. I hurt him in many ways. I hurt him by lying. Just as Jacob hurt Esau by coming with deception, lying to receive the birthright from their father, I hurt Austin. As I hurt my brother, the very same things we see in the book of Genesis begin to echo into my own life. Distrust breeds distaste, and distaste breeds anger, and unchecked anger leads to the deterioration or dissolvent of the relationship.

Ecclesiastes 1:9 (KJV) says, ***"The thing that hath been, it is that which shall be; and that which is done is that which shall be done: and there is no new thing under the sun."***

Throughout the Bible and history as a whole, we see things repeat themselves. From the family feud of Cain and Abel to the lust of David after another man's wife, we see sin destroy other people. It can be heard through the struggle the Apostle Paul talks about in saying, "That which I would not, I do, but that which I would, I do not." It highlighted his humanity and the struggle that all Christians have. There is a struggle between the love we have for God and the sin that dwells within us. So in my actions, I hurt him, but I also hurt him in my lack of action.

Knowing the truth, I made little effort to communicate. It was due to my embarrassment and shame. I was ashamed of my infidelity to the Lord of hosts and to the life I knew He had planned for me. It is similar to Solomon's poor example and lack of instruction that left Rehoboam ill-equipped and weak ultimately resulting in the division of the kingdom into two groups. One group was cleaving to the laws of God, and another whose heart is after the things of the nations around them. This is parallel to the life of anyone who has the Spirit of God in them in that you must choose who you will serve.

1 Kings 18:21 (KJV) says, ***"How long halt ye between two opinions? If the Lord be God, follow him: but if Baal, then follow him. And the people answered him not a word."*** Just as when the people are confronted with their faults, they were speechless. I experienced that as I reflected on the hurt and havoc I had wreaked in the lives of so many lost souls. But that is not the end.

A verse that has helped me through my regrets and moving past my folly is found in the book of Jeremiah. The first verse of chapter three (KJV) says, ***"They say, if a man put away his wife, and she go from him, and become another man's, shall he return unto her again?... But thou hast played the harlot with many lovers; yet return again to me, saith the LORD."*** Now, in conclusion, I pose the following questions to you the reader.

Are you where you thought you would be in life? Why or why not?

Finally, are you halting between two opinions?

The goodness of God leads us to repentance as explained in the second chapter of the Book of Romans.

05

THE FLOOD

DR. RANDY T. JOHNSON,
GROWTH PASTOR

Red, orange, yellow, green, blue, indigo, and violet line up like a banner across the sky. It is the vibrant display of the rainbow. It often turns a gloomy morning into a bright and promising afternoon. Not only are our eyes brightened, but so is our outlook. We have seen rainbows since childhood, we know they visit after a rainfall, yet we still point them out to anyone around us. We pause and enjoy the moment. On certain very special occasions, we might even be treated to a "double rainbow." Look closely, the second rainbow is inverted as it proudly reverses the order of the colors.

Have you ever seen a double rainbow?

____

____

____

What thoughts does or should a rainbow bring to your mind?

____

____

____

Noah and the Ark is one of the most famous Bible stories. We speak of it with our children at an early age. We might even decorate their nursery with some aspect of its theme.

Genesis chapters 6-9 describe the story. Interesting enough, ten other books of the Bible reference Noah. His story is amazing. I want to give a basic portrait of him by using his name as an acronym.

1. Noble

The world was utterly wicked, yet Noah is described differently. I believe it is fair to call him a noble man. Genesis 6:9-10 says, ***"These are the generations of Noah. Noah was a righteous man,***

blameless in his generation. Noah walked with God. And Noah had three sons, Shem, Ham, and Japheth."

What descriptions are given about Noah?

___

___

___

What does it mean to walk with God?

___

___

___

Genesis 8:18-20 describes Noah's first actions after the flood, ***"So Noah went out, and his sons and his wife and his sons' wives with him. Every beast, every creeping thing, and every bird, everything that moves on the earth, went out by families from the ark. Then Noah built an altar to the Lord and took some of every clean animal and some of every clean bird and offered burnt offerings on the altar."***

What was priority number one for Noah once he exited the Ark?

___

___

___

How can worship become a part of our regular routine?

___

___

___

2. Obedient

Noah was a Noble man, and he was also Obedient. He had never experienced a flood or even rain, yet he follows directions in every detail. In Genesis 6:11-22, God lays some of the groundwork, ***"Now the earth was corrupt in God's sight, and the earth was filled with violence. And God saw the earth, and behold, it was corrupt, for all flesh had corrupted their way on the earth. And God said to Noah, 'I have determined to make an end of all flesh, for the earth is filled with violence through them. Behold, I will destroy them with the earth. Make yourself an ark of gopher wood. Make rooms in the ark, and cover it inside and out with pitch. This is how you are to make it: the length of the ark 300 cubits, its breadth 50 cubits, and its height 30 cubits. Make a roof for the ark, and finish it to a cubit above, and set the door of the ark in its side. Make it with lower, second, and third decks. For behold, I will bring a flood of waters upon the earth to destroy all flesh in which is the breath of life under heaven. Everything that is on the earth shall die. But I will establish my covenant with you, and you shall come into the ark, you, your sons, your wife, and your sons' wives with you. And of every living thing of all flesh, you shall bring two of every sort into the ark to keep them alive with you. They shall be male and female. Of the birds according to their kinds, and of the animals according to their kinds, of every creeping thing of the ground, according to its kind, two of every sort shall come in to you to keep them alive. Also take with you every sort of food that is eaten, and store it up. It shall serve as food for you and for them.' Noah did this; he did all that God commanded him."***

If a cubit is 18 inches, how large was the ark?

How does this passage describe Noah's obedience?

Genesis 7:5 repeats Genesis 6:22, ***"And Noah did all that the Lord had commanded him."***

Does this sentence describe you? How?

Hebrews chapter 11 is known as the Hall of Fame of Faith. Many mighty men and women are listed. In verse seven, Noah is included, ***"By faith Noah, being warned by God concerning events as yet unseen, in reverent fear constructed an ark for the saving of his household. By this he condemned the world and became an heir of the righteousness that comes by faith."***

What is ***"reverent fear?"***

It is believed that Noah may have taken close to 100 years to build the Ark. His obedience and faith were put on display daily before a hostile crowd. Genesis 7:7-10 describe part of the last steps, ***"And***

Noah and his sons and his wife and his sons' wives with him went into the ark to escape the waters of the flood. Of clean animals, and of animals that are not clean, and of birds, and of everything that creeps on the ground, two and two, male and female, went into the ark with Noah, as God had commanded Noah. And after seven days the waters of the flood came upon the earth."

After God closed the door of the Ark, how long was Noah and his family on the Ark before it started raining?

____

____

____

3. Active

Noah should be known for being Noble, Obedient, and Active. I wanted to use the word Assiduous describing his perseverance and his desire to show great care, but I thought it would not be as easy to remember as Active. He was hard-working and active. He did not have a lazy bone in his body.

Genesis 7:1-6 says, ***"Then the Lord said to Noah, 'Go into the ark, you and all your household, for I have seen that you are righteous before me in this generation. Take with you seven pairs of all clean animals, the male and his mate, and a pair of the animals that are not clean, the male and his mate, and seven pairs of the birds of the heavens also, male and female, to keep their offspring alive on the face of all the earth. For in seven days I will send rain on the earth forty days and forty nights, and every living thing that I have made I will blot out from the face of the ground.' And Noah did all that the Lord had commanded him. Noah was six hundred years old when the flood of waters came upon the earth."***

How many of each animal was taken on the Ark?

How old (young) was Noah through all of this?

Is God asking you to do something bigger than you?

4. Human

Even though Noah was Noble, Obedient, and Active, he was still Human. That might sound overly simplistic, but sometimes we place Bible heroes on a pedestal that feels unattainable for us.

Genesis 9:20-21 says, ***"Noah began to be a man of the soil, and he planted a vineyard. He drank of the wine and became drunk and lay uncovered in his tent."***

What sin is recorded about Noah?

It is not my intention to disgrace or belittle Noah. I am overly impressed by him. I want to remind all of us that through God we can do mighty things, but in ourselves, we can fall hard.

Bonus point: It would seem out of place to study the life of Noah and not examine God's covenant and symbol.

Genesis 9:8-17 says, ***"Then God said to Noah and to his sons with him, 'Behold, I establish my covenant with you and your offspring after you, and with every living creature that is with you, the birds, the livestock, and every beast of the earth with you, as many as came out of the ark; it is for every beast of the earth. I establish my covenant with you, that never again shall all flesh be cut off by the waters of the flood, and never again shall there be a flood to destroy the earth.' And God said, 'This is the sign of the covenant that I make between me and you and every living creature that is with you, for all future generations: I have set my bow in the cloud, and it shall be a sign of the covenant between me and the earth. When I bring clouds over the earth and the bow is seen in the clouds, I will remember my covenant that is between me and you and every living creature of all flesh. And the waters shall never again become a flood to destroy all flesh. When the bow is in the clouds, I will see it and remember the everlasting covenant between God and every living creature of all flesh that is on the earth.' God said to Noah, 'This is the sign of the covenant that I have established between me and all flesh that is on the earth.'"***

What does this covenant stipulate from God's side?

____

____

____

What is the visual reminder?

____

____

____

"While the Bible's account of the flood is one of judgment, it is also one of mercy and salvation." Ken Ham

It has been said that everything you need to know you can learn from Noah's Ark:

1. Do not miss the boat.
2. Remember that we are all in the same boat.
3. Plan ahead. It was not raining when Noah built the Ark.
4. Stay fit. When you are 60 years old, someone may ask you to do something really big.
5. Do not listen to critics; just get on with the job that needs to be done.
6. Build your future on high ground.
7. For safety's sake, travel in pairs.
8. Speed is not always an advantage. The snails were on board with the cheetahs.
9. When you are stressed, float awhile.
10. Remember, the Ark was built by amateurs; the Titanic was built by professionals.
11. No matter the storm, when you are with God, there is always a rainbow waiting.

METHUSELAH

THE FLOOD, DEVOTION 1

John Carter

It is really kind of interesting to see how God works through the meaning of people's names. Methuselah is only mentioned seven times in the Bible, and aside from a little bit of information in Genesis, he is primarily listed in genealogies. What can we learn about this man named Methuselah?

In Genesis 5:21-27, you can learn the most about Methuselah; he is the oldest man ever to live recorded in history. He was 969 years old. He was the Son of Enoch and the grandfather of Noah. When you dig a little deeper into the meaning of his name things start to get interesting.

For a meaning of the name Methuselah, *Jones dictionary of Old Testament Proper Names* translates the whole name, "When He Is Dead It Shall Be Sent."

"When He is dead it shall be sent!" kind of an ominous name to have as a kid I would think, but what is fascinating is that we see a prophecy given by Enoch through the name of his son. Often, we think it was just Noah that preached the judgment of the flood. However, there is evidence that Enoch and Methuselah would have known this day of judgment was coming as well. Consider this, God and Enoch where very close; they no doubt had conversations about where the world was at and where the world was going. In Genesis 6:6 you can read the thoughts of God, ***"And the Lord regretted that he had made man on the earth, and it grieved him to his heart."***

As I consider the meaning of Methuselah's name, I cannot help but link that the prophecy of judgment and his age are somehow directly linked. Can you imagine being 969 years old? Imagine the family reunion! We get excited when we see someone turn 100, imagine doing that eight more times! So, we can see that the world in which Methuselah lived in was a wicked world, God was heartbroken at the way man lived. God's patience was very long. I think what is incredible is that God had hope that man would change his ways, and He gave them every opportunity He could. In 2 Peter 3:9 we read, ***"The Lord is not slow to fulfill his promise as some count slowness, but is patient toward you, not wishing that any should perish, but that all should reach repentance."*** In the prophecy of Methuselah, we can see the same patience that God showed the people of Noah's time. God gave humanity the length of the oldest man ever recorded as a timeframe to turn their heart to God. Unfortunately, humanity in Noah's day did not heed the warning and repent; they kept on living as if God's patience would never run out.

Ironically, we have been given the same warning in Luke 17:26-27 where it says, ***"Just as it was in the days of Noah, so will it be in the days of the Son of Man. They were eating and drinking and marrying and being given in marriage, until the day when Noah entered the ark, and the flood came and destroyed them all."*** We can look around in our society and see a world that pays no attention to honoring God; there is little effort in trying to please Him. Jesus is coming again, this time to judge the world. I know we do not like to hear this message, but that does not make it any less true. What is incredible is that God is so patient with us. He does not wish that ***"any should perish, but that all should reach repentance."*** God is calling for repentance and a returning to Himself. Will you be like the people in Noah's day and miss it? Will you be willing to accept God's mercy and patience with you, and call to Him for forgiveness in repentance? The application of Methuselah's prophecy is clear;

judgment is coming. Will we ignore it and test God's patience with us or will we hear His message and repent?

NOAH "ONLY" RIGHTEOUS

THE FLOOD, DEVOTION 2

Pat MacDermaid | *Clothing Closet*

"These are the generations of Noah. Noah was a righteous man, blameless in his generation. Noah walked with God. And Noah had three sons, Shem, Ham, and Japheth." Genesis 6:9-10

God called Noah righteous, but that did not mean he was perfect and did not have sin in his life. Noah was righteous because he had a close relationship with God. He loved and trusted God, so when he was told by God to build an ark, he built an ark. The ark was not some little fishing boat. The ark he was told to build was, by today's standards, the size of an average World War II battleship and had three floors. It had plenty of room for all the creatures and people who would live in it during the flood.

Noah was obedient to God's will, so I think it is safe to say, he never grumbled, griped, or complained when God told him what He wanted him to do. He had three sons (Shem, Ham, and Japheth) who helped him build the ark. They must have been laughed at, teased, and called names, but they kept right on being obedient. Noah loved God and did what God told him to do. They walked in peace and harmony like a father and his son walking step and step, side by side. The son wanted to hear every word his father had to share with him. The father just wanted to spend time with his boy, to love him and be loved by him.

I lost my dad when I was 15 years old. I still miss him. I still remember Friday nights when I was a little girl of four or five years old. That was back when TV's were a new thing (yes, I am that old). I would climb onto my dad's lap and put my head on his chest right over his heart. He watched the Friday Night Fights. He loved to watch boxing, and I loved to listen to his heartbeat. I felt loved and safe.

I have come a long way since then. I know I have a Heavenly Father who loves me. He will never leave me. He always has time for me. He will forgive me for anything when I am truly sorry. He forgives and never holds it against me. He is good, kind, loving, and so much more. When I am in His will, I have peace.

I want and need a Noah kind of relationship with God. We all need it. I think we would all love to hear that God has called us righteous, blameless, and that we have found favor in His eyes. Take time to ask God what He would have you do for Him. Spend time alone with Him; you will be blessed. If you do not, you will miss so much.

OBEDIENCE

THE FLOOD, DEVOTION 3

Sue Harrington

Through Noah, the ark, the animals, and the flood, we can learn a lesson of obedience and protection. God chose to save Noah and his family because Noah was found to be a righteous man (obedient to God's commands), blameless in his generation (stood out), and walked with God (he had an obedient life).

The Lord commanded Noah to build the ark and then gather the animals and food. He said He was going to wipe out all mankind because they had become corrupt, violent, and wicked. It grieved His heart. Noah knew that because he was obedient that there was spiritual safety in following God's commands. Genesis 6:22 says, ***"Noah did this: He did all that God commanded him."*** Each time God gave him instruction, he did what God asked. He never concerned himself if it was convenient; he just followed in the act of obedience. God knows that it may go against the ways of the world to be obedient, but it brings us protection. It is our place of refuge from the floods of the world in which we live.

Just like God remembered Noah, his family, and the animals, He does not forget those who walk in obedience. We have to remain faithful when facing our storms. When Noah and his family were finally able to leave the ark, before doing anything else they built an altar to the Lord as an act of worship because they were grateful for God's protection, thanking Him. Our hearts need to always be in a state of worship and thankfulness for all that God does for us in this same manner. Noah was not exempt from a sinful nature because he could have perished in the flood as well but God's grace was upon Him, the same grace in which we are saved through faith in Jesus

Christ! Noah's life serves as a reminder to us all that judgment on sin is coming, the day of the Lord will come when He sends His Son. So, be an ambassador for Christ, obedient, and take His message of redemption to others.

TWO AND SEVEN

THE FLOOD, DEVOTION 4

Pat Bedell

The story of Noah's Ark begins in the early book of Genesis. God created the world, and sin had entered into it. With all of the violence and corruptness that was happening on earth, God wanted to restore the earth to its pre-creation state, so He was going to flood it with rain for forty days and forty nights. Noah was a strong follower of God, and God gave him instructions to build an ark. We first learn about Noah in Genesis 5:32 and that he was 500 years old. It took Noah and his three sons about 100 years to build the ark. Noah was 600 years old when he entered the ark. The ark was built so God could protect His creation.

Genesis 6:19-20 says, ***"And of every living thing of all flesh, you shall bring two of every sort into the ark to keep them alive with you. They shall be male and female. Of the birds according to their kinds, and of the animals according to their kinds, of every creeping thing of the ground, according to its kind, two of every sort shall come in to you to keep them alive."***

God called Noah to bring two animals into the ark with him to keep them alive. This was so the earth could repopulate after the flood subsides. Many interpret that God had only this instruction for Noah to keep His creation alive during the flood. But God also gave Noah some additional instructions in the following chapter.

Genesis 7:2-3 adds, ***"Take with you seven pairs of all clean animals, the male and his mate, and a pair of the animals that are not clean, the male and his mate, and seven pairs of the birds of the heavens also, male and female, to keep their offspring alive on the face of all the earth."***

God instructs Noah to bring seven pairs of clean animals as well. The reason becomes clear after the flood.

Genesis 8:20 exclaims, ***"Then Noah built an altar to the Lord and took some of every clean animal and some of every clean bird and offered burnt offerings on the altar."***

Noah used some of the clean animals to use as a sacrifice to God while allowing the unclean animals to be used to repopulate. He was able to worship God in sacrifices without making clean animals extinct.

I believe that it is God's message that everyone should know that God is the Creator, that sin has consequences, and judgment is coming. The Bible states that there was only one way onto the ark. Similarly, there is only one way to God. John 14:6 says, ***"Jesus said to him, 'I am the way, and the truth, and the life. No one comes to the Father except through me.'"*** For those who believe in Him, Jesus is our entrance into God's grace. This event may be very familiar to many of us, but we can always use a good reminder of what is to come. Are we living to please God? Are we representing a godly lifestyle? Are we giving glory to God for all of our blessings?

WALKING THEO

THE FLOOD, DEVOTION 5

Mary Jane Johns | *Worship Leader*

Theo is our chocolate lab. He is 79 pounds of pure muscle, slobber, and joy. Sometimes he sits and waits for us by looking longingly out the front window for either Steve or myself to pull in the driveway. In the process, he slimes my living room window. I still love him so much! Theo is a huge fan of daily walks through our subdivision. When walking, we generally take the same route every day, sunshine, snow, or wind. Theo has never met a pothole puddle he did not like. He is a very thankful and obedient pup. It is a sad day when it rains, and we cannot walk. Although Theo would be fine to walk in the rain, I am not a big fan.

In the Old Testament, God commanded Noah to build a huge boat. At that time, it was not even raining. The people around taunted and teased him relentlessly. Noah was obedient to God and did as he was told to the exact measurements. Noah brought his sons, their wives, a variety of animals, and birds into the boat.

God flooded the earth. His wrath was relentless on an ungodly, unholy, dismissive people who did not heed God's warning through His servant Noah. As the water continued to rise, it continued to rain. Then it rained some more! It was not small puddles (that Theo loves to run through), but huge amounts of water flooded the earth. It rained for 40 days and nights. God completely wiped the earth of people. Noah's family was safe inside the ark. After a series of tests to prove that the earth was dry enough to walk on, Noah, his family, all the animals, and birds exited the ark.

Genesis 8:20 says, ***"Then Noah built an altar to the Lord and took some of every clean animal and some of every clean bird and offered burnt offerings on the altar."***

Before Noah built a new home for himself, before he changed his clothes, before he even showered, He built an altar of sacrifice to the Lord. His greatest concern was not for himself, but to give honor to his holy and provisional God. Noah took the time to give God His very best which included clean animals to sacrifice.

Every day God is providing shelter for us in our deep waters. Noah showed a heart of thanksgiving through the pain of seeing the world wiped away. We can give honor to God for His provision for us through the rain and puddles that this life brings us.

Joy through pain is difficult; however, we can walk through the deep waters of life without reservation. Giving an offering of praise is showing obedience to a faithful and holy God. Your story will be so much richer. Is He worthy of your adoration and praise?

Take a moment and thank God for His continued provision and care for you while walking through the puddles and rainy moments.

RAINBOW

THE FLOOD, DEVOTION 6

Mark O'Connor | *Student Director*

There was a time not too long ago when I learned something that changed the way I viewed the Bible. For years, I had read the Bible, studied it, and grew close in my walk with Jesus. I knew the stories and events in the Old Testament, but only a small portion of it connected with me. Much of it at the time was downright painful and boring for me to read and study. As a result, I did a disservice to myself and those I was teaching.

I took an Old Testament Survey class for college, and it opened my eyes quite a bit to the amazing prefacing that was happening about the arrival of Jesus. This was quite interesting to me. I knew of much of the prophecy in the Old Testament that told of Jesus' coming to save the world. The book of Isaiah, throughout its sixty-six chapters, lays out in great detail the coming of Jesus and His life and reign. It tells us of John the Baptist coming before Him.

There is more to it than that. When we start to examine the fact that every event, story, and character in the Old Testament points back to Jesus, He is intertwined in every piece of Scripture. Jesus can be seen from Moses striking the rock, showing the pouring out of the living water, to the rainbow God showed Noah after the flood.

The rainbow you may be asking? Yep, before it became the sign of the LBGTQ community, the rainbow was, and still is, the picture of the promise made to Noah that God would never again flood the Earth. This is not even a short passing verse or two that is easy to skip over and miss. There are eleven verses that make up this new covenant that God makes with Noah. You can read it in Genesis 9:7-17.

My wife and I had the good fortune to spend a week in Maui, Hawaii this past January. I saw for the first time in my life, in all of its beauty, the entirety of a rainbow that stretched from end to end. We saw both ends touching the horizon. I wish I could put a picture here for you to see now. When I think back on it, I do not think of joking about the pot of gold at the end. I do not think of the rainbow flag filters that take up space on my Facebook page. I see Jesus. I see that, just like God sent the rainbow to Noah, for them to always be reminded of God's love and grace, He sent Jesus to us. He sent His Son to be an example of the love that He has for us. He lived a perfect life which included the sacrifice to carry a weight that I am not able to bear.

06

TOWER OF BABEL

DR. RANDY T. JOHNSON,
GROWTH PASTOR

I remember a specific day when I picked my daughter up from elementary school. I taught at the school; so we regularly went home together, but this time was different. My wife and son were not with us. It was a daddy and his little princess moment. I asked how her school day was. She said she learned a new language. The school was progressive, but I was still surprised. I asked her what it was and to say something in that language. She said, "lay ovlay ouyay; it is Latin." I chuckled as it was actually Pig Latin. It meant, "I love you." I was very careful not to burst her bubble.

The Linguistic Society of America reported in 2009 a list that included some 6,909 distinct languages. It is fun to see the words "I love you" listed in other languages.

Pig Latin: *lay ovlay ouyay*
Latin: *Te amo*
Spanish: *Te quiero / Te amo*
French: *Je t'aime, Je t'adore*
Mandarin: *Wo ai ni*
Japanese: *Aishiteru or Anata ga daisuki desu*
Arabic: *Ana behibak or Ana behibek*
German: *Ich liebe dich*
Italian: *Ti amo*
Korean: *Sarang Heyo or Nanun tangshinul sarang hamnida*
Portuguese: *Eu te amo*

For those who are fans of *The Lord of the Rings* by J.R.R. Tolkien, you would speak Elvish and say, "Amin mela lle."

What languages do you speak? Which would you like to speak?

____

____

____

How do you feel when you are around people who are speaking a different language?

____

____

____

Genesis 11:1 makes an interesting summary statement of the creation of Adam and Eve in the Garden of Eden, Cain killing his brother, and Noah and all the lost people, ***"Now the whole earth had one language and the same words."*** Everyone spoke the same language. Men and women may have even understood each other. All joking aside, everyone spoke the same language. Therefore, there is a common question, "Why do we have so many languages today?" Genesis chapter 11 gives the answer. It also records some problems from the past that resurface today if we are not careful.

Genesis 11:2-4 sets the stage, ***"And as people migrated from the east, they found a plain in the land of Shinar and settled there. And they said to one another, 'Come, let us make bricks, and burn them thoroughly.' And they had brick for stone, and bitumen for mortar. Then they said, 'Come, let us build ourselves a city and a tower with its top in the heavens, and let us make a name for ourselves, lest we be dispersed over the face of the whole earth.'"***

Why do you think they wanted to build a tower?

____

____

____

How does this break the command of God?

____

____

____

Three dangers and sins are listed or implied in this passage.

1. *"Let us build ourselves a city and a tower with its top in the heavens."*

They did not want a tower with its top being high, and in the sky, they wanted into to be right ***"in the heavens."*** They were right back in the earliest sins. The pride to be like God caused the downfall of Satan and then to mankind through Eve and Adam. Genesis 3:4-5 gives the dialogue between Eve and the serpent, ***"But the serpent said to the woman, 'You will not surely die. For God knows that when you eat of it your eyes will be opened, and you will be like God, knowing good and evil.'"*** They wanted to be like God. They wanted to be God.

How does this mindset resurface today?

____

____

____

2. *"Let us make a name for ourselves."*

They wanted to be known. They wanted to make a name for themselves. It was to be all about them. This is the epitome of selfishness.

What are some of the ways we exhibit selfishness today?

______

______

______

3. *"Lest we be dispersed over the face of the whole earth."*

They did not want to be scattered over the earth. They knew the command God had given in Genesis 1:28, ***"And God blessed them. And God said to them, 'Be fruitful and multiply and fill the earth and subdue it, and have dominion over the fish of the sea and over the birds of the heavens and over every living thing that moves on the earth.'"*** They were to fill the earth. After the Flood, God repeats the instructions in Genesis 9:1, ***"And God blessed Noah and his sons and said to them, 'Be fruitful and multiply and fill the earth.'"*** They were to separate. This would cause them to live on their own by faith. They could not control things or have the comfort of a large group. They were to step out in faith. Building a tower was not just prideful and selfish, it was an act of disobedience.

Where, what, or how has God called you?

______

______

______

Why have you not acted upon His direction?

______

______

______

Genesis 11:5-9 records how God kindly enforces His plan, ***"And the Lord came down to see the city and the tower, which the children of man had built. And the Lord said, 'Behold, they are***

one people, and they have all one language, and this is only the beginning of what they will do. And nothing that they propose to do will now be impossible for them. Come, let us go down and there confuse their language, so that they may not understand one another's speech.' So the Lord dispersed them from there over the face of all the earth, and they left off building the city. Therefore its name was called Babel, because there the Lord confused the language of all the earth. And from there the Lord dispersed them over the face of all the earth."

Do you view God as being harsh or gentle in His response?

____

____

____

Many have spoken and written on this passage with an emphasis on the power of unity. It is the synergy where one plus one equals more than two. It is the concept that "together we can accomplish more."

How is the unity at the tower different than a unity Christians are to have?

____

____

____

The whole struggle of the human soul is pictured in this tower. Are we trying to reach God by our means or are we going to reach Him by His means? The road to Hell is paved with selfishness, pride, and disobedience. Love is an antonym. We need to get out of our way and let Jesus step into the gap.

Jesus is love. He spoke the words, "I love you" in a universal language when He opened up His arms and died on the cross for you and me. His actions screamed love.

Other than some foreign language, what are some ways to express love to each other?

____

____

____

Does your life say, "I Love You" to God? How?

____

____

____

UNITY

TOWER OF BABEL, DEVOTION 1

Carole Combs | *Women's Ministry*

Disunity with God will never produce unity with man.

The word unity is a warm fuzzy word to me. When I think of unity, I picture a perfect tranquil utopia where everyone is living in perfect harmony and where there are no disagreements or conflicts. Nowhere in this world will you find this kind of unity. However, you can have unity with God in this life, and He has also prepared this perfect place for you to live for eternity with Him and with all those who have trusted His Son as their Savior. If there is disunity in this world, how then can you and I have unity with God and man in this world?

I believe it first begins with our unity with God. The people of Shinar (Genesis 11:1-9) seemed to be in perfect unity. They settled together, they had a plan together, they made bricks and mortar together, and they even built together. There was one problem; they did this all together without including God! They did not inquire or include the God that made them and all things into the construction of their lives or in the construction of their plans. God allowed them to continue for a time in their futility. Imagine God watching the whole process of their tower building. Imagine God watching you in the process of what you are doing in your life. God was watching them, as well as God is watching you. God is watching you and I as we make our plans, and as we build our lives. He wants to see if we include Him. Are you leaving God out of your plans? Do you find that there is disunity in your relationships?

Proverbs 3:5-6 says, ***"Trust in the Lord with all your heart and lean not unto your own understanding. In all your ways acknowledge***

him and he will make straight your paths." God is a holy and just God. He would not allow the people in Shinar to continue in their complete disregard of Him, nor will He allow us. We see nowhere in these verses that they inquired of God nor that He directed their paths. The decisions they made were on their own and without God. They thought they were in unity during this process, but sadly they were in disunity. God was not leading or guiding, only the "I, we, and us" were in charge. God allowed the language of the people to become completely different from one another. A father could not understand a son. A mother could not understand a daughter. God needs and wants to be placed in everything you do. Disunity with God will never produce unity with man. Fathers will be in disunity with sons, mothers will be in disunity with daughters, and husbands and wives will be in disunity. Neighbors will be in disunity with one another. The Church will be in disunity. The whole world will continue to be in disunity when God is not placed in the center. Go where God wants you to go. Make God's plans your plans. Build your life around His tower. ***"The name of the Lord is a strong tower; the righteous man runs into it and is safe."*** Proverbs 18:10

"GO TEAM"

TOWER OF BABEL, DEVOTION 2

Kenny Hovis | *Prison Ministry Director*

One of my favorite movies is from 1986; it is the movie *Hoosiers.* In the movie, Gene Hackman (one of the greatest actors of all time, in my humble opinion), plays the infamous basketball coach, Norman Dale. He is a tough, regimented disciplinarian that zealously preaches that there is only one way to play basketball. His mantra, "Team!" It is very much a David vs. Goliath plot, but the general theme is one of a small group of high school kids from very different situations in life coming together, learning to play and work together as a team to overcome impossible odds. In the Bible, we see examples of teamwork and how it can be used both negatively and the way it is supposed to be.

In Genesis chapter 11, we see the account of the descendants of Noah and how they were commanded by God to populate the earth. Instead of obeying the will of God, a large group came together in a place called Shinar and concluded that it would be a good idea to build a tower to reach up to the heavens, in an attempt, in my opinion, to elevate themselves to be on par with God. God in His infinite wisdom sees and knows the heart of man and says in Genesis 11:5-8, ***"And the Lord came down to see the city and the tower, which the children of man had built. And the Lord said, 'Behold, they are one people, and they have all one language, and this is only the beginning of what they will do. And nothing that they propose to do will now be impossible for them. Come, let us go down and there confuse their language, so that they may not understand one another's speech.' So the Lord dispersed them from there over the face of all the earth, and they left off building the city."*** Humanity was using teamwork to try and achieve a monument to their greatness. This is always a recipe for disaster.

The Apostle Paul writes to the church in Corinth and describes how we as Christians should view teamwork when it comes to our faith, and ministry. In 1 Corinthians 12:12-13, Paul says, ***"For just as the body is one and has many members, and all the members of the body, though many, are one body, so it is with Christ. For in one Spirit we were all baptized into one body—Jews or Greeks, slaves or free—and all were made to drink of one Spirit."*** Paul uses the analogy of us, believers of all ethnicities and positions, to be "one body." He goes on in verse 27 of chapter 12 to be more specific and says, ***"Now you are the body of Christ and individually members of it."*** A body is useless without a head, and Paul states that we, as the body, should have Christ at the head. All of the individual members working together in symphony and harmony, to achieve what we have each been gifted and called to do, to fulfill the leading of the Head of the body, Christ. All of our efforts and energies for His honor and glory alone!

Gene Hackman utters one of his famous quotes from the movie that is so true for us as the body of Christ as well. "Five players on the floor, functioning as one single unit. Team, Team, Team! No one more important than the other!" Let us remember as the body of Christ we are to work together, no one part more important than the other, no matter the gift set! We are to have the same goal and mindset. All we do, as well as all of the results, are done for His honor and His glory, not ours!

"GO TEAM!"

PRIDE

TOWER OF BABEL, DEVOTION 3

Josh Lahring | *Production Director*

I love to build and create. As a kid, I spent countless hours building with Legos. I can remember building something that made me feel so proud. Entering it into a contest, and yet did not receive any recognition for it. It was the greatest thing I had ever built; how could it not have been good enough? It is easy to become prideful and think that we are amazing when in reality, it is God who gave us the ability in the first place.

God gave man the ability to create. In Genesis chapter 11, man began to realize that there was nothing that they could not build. In verse 4, it says, ***"Then they said, 'Come, let us build ourselves a city and a tower with its top in the heavens, and let us make a name for ourselves, lest we be dispersed over the face of the whole earth.'"***

Pride had led man to want to build a city because they were worried about themselves. They did not want to be dispersed over the earth, so they came up with a way to solve that problem, and while doing it, they could bring glory to man. God, however, would not allow it. He confused their language, and they ended up being dispersed over the earth, the one thing they were trying to avoid.

James 4:6 says, ***"But he gives more grace. Therefore it says, 'God opposes the proud but gives grace to the humble.'"***

We, as man, in and of ourselves, are nothing. We are our Creator's masterpiece, and we are meant to be glorifying the Creator in all we do.

Are the things we do for our glory or God's?

DISOBEDIENCE

TOWER OF BABEL, DEVOTION 4

Philip Piasecki

The older my daughter gets, the more opinionated she is getting. Molly talks so much and is so loud. I do not know what Mary and I should have expected, seeing as both of us are very talkative people, but it has been a learning experience with her. She wants things her way, and when we do not allow that, she starts throwing things! She will grab anything within arm's length and throw it as far as she can. I think she may become a baseball player. She does not understand that when she behaves that way she is missing out on great plans that we have for her. When she throws a fit and does not eat her dinner, then she misses out on getting to have ice cream for dessert. When she tries to run out into the street at the playground, then she has to go home and does not get to play. Every time she behaves in this way, she is settling for less than what we had planned for her.

Genesis 11:2 says, ***"And as people migrated from the east, they found a plain in the land of Shinar and settled there."***

The sad thing is believers every day behave in the exact way my child does, and subsequently miss out on seeing God move. This Scripture is from the story of the Tower of Babel, and we see the people of God behaving in a disobedient way. After God saved Noah's family from the flood, His command to them was to "go fill the earth." Instead of listening to that command, the people disobeyed and instead, settled together in the land of Shinar. Very simply we can understand that disobedience causes us to miss out on plans that God has for us. More specifically, I think the word "settled" in this Scripture is so powerful. When we disobey God and settle in our safe and comfy life, we miss out on experiencing God in some incredible ways. The incredible thing about God's Kingdom is that He invites us to be a part of spreading it throughout this world. It is up to us if we are going to see God do amazing things through our lives, or if we are going to settle for hardly seeing Him move at all. God commands us to go into all the world and preach the Gospel, commands us to pray, commands us to worship, and the list is endless. All of these things are opportunities for us to be obedient to Christ and see Him doing incredible things in our lives, in the lives of others, and in this world. It is so easy to settle into disobedience, not daily seeking to follow the commands of Christ. This is not the life that He has called you to. We all would say we want to see God move, then be obedient and take action! Give Christ an opportunity to use you. Pray each day that the Holy Spirit would move in your heart to stir you to action. When we obey the commands of Christ, we will see Him move in mighty ways.

COMMUNICATION

TOWER OF BABEL, DEVOTION 5

Debbie Kerr | *Office Administrator*

When I was 17, our church choir went on a mission trip to Paris, France. Every evening we had the privilege to sing in a different church in the area. We learned to sing one song in French, but all other songs were sung in English. The Gospel message was preached in English with the help of an interpreter. The language barrier was real and evident but, the Spirit of God moved in spite of the barrier. I remember trying to communicate with the French people and how difficult it was; we often resorted to a game of charades. According to Google, there are roughly 6,500 different languages in the world. Have you ever wondered how all the different languages came to be?

In Genesis chapter 11, we read the account of the Tower of Babel, which is only mentioned in this one passage of Scripture. To build this tower out of brick and "slime" used for mortar required a great deal of communication. At the time of this historical event, the whole earth had only one group of people that spoke only one language. Genesis 11:4-9 says, ***"Then they said, 'Come, let us build ourselves a city and a tower with its top in the heavens, and let us make a name for ourselves, lest we be dispersed over the face of the whole earth.' And the Lord came down to see the city and the tower, which the children of man had built. And the Lord said, 'Behold, they are one people, and they have all one language, and this is only the beginning of what they will do. And nothing that they propose to do will now be impossible for them. Come, let us go down and there confuse their language, so that they may not understand one another's speech.' So the Lord dispersed them from there over the face of all the earth,***

and they left off building the city. Therefore its name was called Babel, because there the Lord confused the language of all the earth. And from there the Lord dispersed them over the face of all the earth."

This account in Genesis chapter 11 describes a very self-serving, prideful, and arrogant people. They wanted to make a name for themselves and make a tower to the heavens. They refused to disperse over all the earth as God had commanded. They stayed near each other to spread their wicked deeds and plan. God in His sovereignty intervened as He always knows our heart motive.

When we start hearing the word, "I," "we," or "us" too often we know we need to check ourselves; it is always a red flag that our hearts are veering off course into a dangerous place. It reminds me of another account in Scripture where the word "I" was the theme. In Isaiah 14:13-14, God is talking to Lucifer (aka Satan), who also wanted to be like God. The passage says, ***"You said in your heart, 'I will ascend to heaven; above the stars of God. I will set my throne on high; I will sit on the mount of assembly in the far reaches of the north; I will ascend above the heights of the clouds; I will make myself like the Most High.'"***

Have you had your "I's" checked lately? Are you communicating the language of Heaven or the language of Hell? Ask the Spirit of God to reveal who is on the throne of your life. Remember, our mouths reveal what our hearts conceal.

MAKE A NAME FOR OURSELVES

TOWER OF BABEL, DEVOTION 6

Richie Henson | *Production Director*

It seems like the greatest allure of the current generation is fame. I do not know many young people who would not like to be internet famous, myself included. I mean, who would not want a million strangers to watch videos about your life?

These desires for grandeur are not new to the current generation. In fact, they go all the way back to Babel. As civilization began to push East, a group of people came together to build a tower to the heavens. It seems strange to think that anyone might attempt to build a tower to heaven, but these people had convinced themselves the status of God was attainable.

As they began building the tower, an interesting statement is made in Genesis 11:4, ***"Then they said, 'Come, let us build ourselves a city and a tower with its top in the heavens, and let us make a name for ourselves, lest we be dispersed over the face of the whole earth.'"***

These people were looking to set themselves apart as important on the earth. I am not sure I could ever understand building a tower to heaven, but the feeling of wanting to be important is hard to shake. Beginning with Satan, the allure of being like God has led to destruction. For the people in Babel, they desired to be famous like God. They desired to have a name as known as God's. In what ways do we try to gain equality with God? Is it by accumulating wealth or possessions? Maybe we try to be equal with God by handling all of our problems or playing a large role in our community.

Whatever the case may be, we must always remember that no matter how tall we build our tower, God will always be bigger. No matter how famous we make our names, God's name will always be infinitely more famous.

Thankfully for us, we do not have to strive for equality with God. Instead, we can live in the grace of our Messiah, Jesus and have favor as God's children.

07

ABRAHAM'S CALL

DR. RANDY T. JOHNSON,
GROWTH PASTOR

My daughter is a prankster. She likes to take someone's phone and change the name to certain phone numbers so that when the person receives a call, it relays a different Caller ID. She changed a co-worker's phone so that when she called him, it read their boss' name. She had fun sending him on some random errands at 2:00 am.

Theodore Paraskevakos created Caller Identification in 1968. I am surprised it was that long ago. He was working in Athens, Greece as a communications engineer when he took an idea and made it happen. The next great invention was *67. That was the code you would use before typing the phone number if you did not want the call to have notification through Caller ID.

Do you like caller ID?

____

____

____

God "called" several men in Scripture. Abraham answered the call, Moses tried to ignore or postpone it, and Gideon wanted proof it was God. Peter and Isaiah did not leave God saying, "Can you hear me know?"

1. Abraham

God commanded Abraham to leave the comforts and safety of home. The destination was not listed. He was just told to start taking a step in the right direction. Instructions would follow. Abraham's calling sounds like Jesus' words in Matthew 19:29, ***"And everyone who has left houses or brothers or sisters or father or mother or children or lands, for my name's sake, will receive a hundredfold and will inherit eternal life."***

Genesis 12:1-3 records God's call to Abraham (Abram), ***"Now the Lord said to Abram, 'Go from your country and your kindred and your father's house to the land that I will show you. And I will make of you a great nation, and I will bless you and make your name great, so that you will be a blessing. I will bless those who bless you, and him who dishonors you I will curse, and in you all the families of the earth shall be blessed.'"***

What was Abraham giving up by leaving?

____

____

____

What promises were made to Abraham?

____

____

____

Genesis 11:30 says, ***"Now Sarai was barren; she had no child."*** How does this affect your thoughts on God's promises to Abraham?

____

____

____

Genesis 12:4-9 adds, ***"So Abram went, as the Lord had told him, and Lot went with him. Abram was seventy-five years old when he departed from Haran. And Abram took Sarai his wife, and Lot his brother's son, and all their possessions that they had gathered, and the people that they had acquired in Haran, and they set out to go to the land of Canaan. When they came to the land of Canaan, Abram passed through the land to the place at Shechem, to the oak of Moreh. At that time the Canaanites were in the land. Then the Lord appeared to Abram and said,***

'To your offspring I will give this land.' So he built there an altar to the Lord, who had appeared to him. From there he moved to the hill country on the east of Bethel and pitched his tent, with Bethel on the west and Ai on the east. And there he built an altar to the Lord and called upon the name of the Lord. And Abram journeyed on, still going toward the Negeb."

The first three words say a lot. What normally happens when we receive a drastic calling from God?

____

____

____

What do these verses say about Abraham's character?

____

____

____

2. Moses

God called Moses. It was as if Moses texted God saying, "Sorry I can't talk right now." Maybe it is like Caller ID, and Moses screened his calls. As you probably know, Moses was not excited about what God was saying. All he chose to do was mumble some excuses.

Exodus 3:11 says, ***"But Moses said to God, 'Who am I that I should go to Pharaoh and bring the children of Israel out of Egypt?'"***

Exodus 4:1 adds, ***"Then Moses answered, 'But behold, they will not believe me or listen to my voice, for they will say, 'The Lord did not appear to you.'"***

Exodus 4:10-17 continues, ***"But Moses said to the Lord, 'Oh, my Lord, I am not eloquent, either in the past or since you have spoken to your servant, but I am slow of speech and of tongue.' Then the Lord said to him, 'Who has made man's mouth? Who makes him mute, or deaf, or seeing, or blind? Is it not I, the Lord? Now therefore go, and I will be with your mouth and teach you what you shall speak.' But he said, 'Oh, my Lord, please send someone else.' Then the anger of the Lord was kindled against Moses and he said, 'Is there not Aaron, your brother, the Levite? I know that he can speak well. Behold, he is coming out to meet you, and when he sees you, he will be glad in his heart. You shall speak to him and put the words in his mouth, and I will be with your mouth and with his mouth and will teach you both what to do. He shall speak for you to the people, and he shall be your mouth, and you shall be as God to him. And take in your hand this staff, with which you shall do the signs.'"***

What excuses did Moses make?

____

____

____

What phrases did God use to refute Moses' (and ours) excuses?

____

____

____

Acts 7:22 says, ***"And Moses was instructed in all the wisdom of the Egyptians, and he was mighty in his words and deeds."***

How does this passage contradict Moses' excuses?

____

____

____

Moses was involved in some amazing feats of God. Think about what he would have missed out on if he would have rejected God's call. He saw the Red Sea opened, water come from a rock, manna, clothes that never wore out, and so much more.

3. Gideon

God called Gideon, and his response was similar to Moses (and all too often, us).

Judges 6:11-17 says, ***"Now the angel of the Lord came and sat under the terebinth at Ophrah, which belonged to Joash the Abiezrite, while his son Gideon was beating out wheat in the winepress to hide it from the Midianites. And the angel of the Lord appeared to him and said to him, 'The Lord is with you, O mighty man of valor.' And Gideon said to him, 'Please, my lord, if the Lord is with us, why then has all this happened to us? And where are all his wonderful deeds that our fathers recounted to us, saying, 'Did not the Lord bring us up from Egypt?' But now the Lord has forsaken us and given us into the hand of Midian.' And the Lord turned to him and said, 'Go in this might of yours and save Israel from the hand of Midian; do not I send you?' And he said to him, 'Please, Lord, how can I save Israel? Behold, my clan is the weakest in Manasseh, and I am the least in my father's house.' And the Lord said to him, 'But I will be with you, and you shall strike the Midianites as one man.' And he said to him, 'If now I have found favor in your eyes, then show me a sign that it is you who speak with me.'"***

What excuses does Gideon give?

____

____

____

Gideon was involved in some amazing feats of God. Think about what he would have missed out on if he would have rejected God's call. He saw God use 300 men take down 125,000 warriors. He was allowed to see God work miracles.

4. Peter

Who walked on water?

____

____

____

The obvious answer is Jesus, but Peter would have been a good answer, too. Jesus called out to the disciples. Peter trusted Him and stepped out of the boat.

Matthew 14:28-33 says, ***"And Peter answered him, 'Lord, if it is you, command me to come to you on the water.' He said, 'Come.' So Peter got out of the boat and walked on the water and came to Jesus. But when he saw the wind, he was afraid, and beginning to sink he cried out, 'Lord, save me.' Jesus immediately reached out his hand and took hold of him, saying to him, 'O you of little faith, why did you doubt?' And when they got into the boat, the wind ceased. And those in the boat worshiped him, saying, 'Truly you are the Son of God.'"***

What kind of conversation do you think Peter and the other disciples had later about Peter on the water?

People often criticize Peter's lack of faith causing him to sink. However, I think they miss a point. Twelve disciples were there, and only one stepped out of the boat. Think about what Peter would have missed out on if he would have just sat back and done nothing. God is calling us to an amazing life. He is offering front row seats to His miracles.

5. Isaiah

As God "contemplates" who He can trust, Isaiah gives the response we all should consider.

Isaiah 6:8 says, ***"And I heard the voice of the Lord saying, 'Whom shall I send, and who will go for us?' Then I said, 'Here I am! Send me.'"***

"God did not direct His call to Isaiah - Isaiah overheard God saying, '. . . who will go for Us?' The call of God is not just for a select few but for everyone. Whether I hear God's call or not depends on the condition of my ears, and exactly what I hear depends upon my spiritual attitude." Oswald Chambers

God has a plan for you and your life. The Caller ID reads, "God." Have you answered? What has He called you to do?

____

____

____

"God does not choose people because of their ability, but because of their availability." Brother Andrew

THE ART OF LISTENING

ABRAHAM'S CALL, DEVOTION 1

Ryan Story | *Location Pastor - Burton*

We are all born with an innate ability to listen. Babies have the ability to recognize their parent's voice from the moment they are born. I remember how foolish I felt talking to my wife's stomach for nine months, but I will never forget when my son's both looked at me. There were some odd feeling as even little mush balls of adorable, they understood what I said. As children grow, listening becomes a skill. Language comprehension, linguistics, and vocabulary are all things that children are learning as they grow. As time goes on, a child grows to understand who "mama" is for no other reason than the praise and excitement parents get when that child repeats the word that has been said to them millions of times before the age of one. The child does not have the ability to know that "mama" is the informal way of saying "mother;" all the baby knows is when they say something, people react.

Listening is a key part of communication. Communication is a key part of any relationship. There are so many times when I have had my head buried in my phone playing Clash Royal and my wife or sons were trying to get my attention. There is nothing that is so disheartening as when you are saying something and no one is listening. I have learned in the few years of being married and as a parent, that when a person is talking to you, they generally want to see an action out of you. If my wife says, "I need you to get Zeke a cup of milk," and my response is "heard you," that is doing little to help the situation. Be honest, you have lost it on one of your children, your spouse, or a co-worker because they "heard you" but did nothing after it. Since we all have the ability to listen, the issue that we all face is simple, do we act, do we respond after we hear something?

Genesis chapter 12 is the beginning of Abram's calling from God. The story starts when one day God called a man named Abram. Genesis 12:1 says, ***"Now the Lord said to Abram."*** This is the beginning of Abram's story. God told Abram to leave his comfort zone and go. God is an amazing communicator, He is able to speak to anyone and can be heard even when no one is listening. The amazing golden nugget of truth is in Genesis 12:4 that says, ***"So Abram went."*** The beauty is, I do not think it would of mattered what God said to Abram, he would have listened; he would have obeyed.

Obedience is linked to listening. My oldest son is a maniac and has not one ounce of fear. He is strong willed as one can be, and he knows how to get his way. I have learned that in order for him to be obedient to the rules of my house, I cannot expect him to do so unless he listens. I learned early that just spanking him when de does wrong was not correcting his behavior. I had to get on his level and re-communicate what his expectations where. If by chance Broly hits his little brother, if I correct him and he does it again, I take Bro in another room, sit down, make him look me eye to eye and make sure he is listening to what he is doing wrong. I call these "dude chats." Once I was able to teach my son that he needed to listen to his father's rules, the obedience came. Not all the time, but he listens better than he did.

Our walks with God are like that. We all know we need to live obediently to God. We all know we should not sin, we all know we should love those who are hard to love, and we all know we must be the light of the world. Sometimes life is not always just an "I am not being obedient issue" it is a "I am not listening" problem. If you are looking to be recklessly obedient to Jesus, you may have to learn how to listen to Him before you get to obeying Him.

BEING A BLESSING

ABRAHAM'S CALL, DEVOTION 2

James Clouse | *Student Pastor*

My grandparents were a huge blessing to my brother and I growing up. There was a little while where my mom was trying to raise us on her own. I remember the impact that my grandparents had on me. I remember the morning my grandfather taught me how to cut pancakes with a fork and knife to my grandmother took us out to the garden to get vegetables. They were a blessing to us when we needed it. Not only were they a blessing to us but the things that we had learned from them will continue to our children and grandchildren.

This relates to the call of Abram. If you have never heard of this name before, you may be surprised. God called Abram, or Abraham, out of his home country to take his family to the Promised Land. God tells Abram in Genesis 12:2, ***"And I will make of you a great nation, and I will bless you and make your name great, so that you will be a blessing."***

The Lord here is telling Abram that he will be the father of great nations. God later in Genesis tells Abraham that he will have more descendants then the stars in the sky. The influence that Abraham will have on his descendants will be a blessing to more than he realized at this moment.

I think this is important for us to remember for our own lives. We need to allow God to use us in His amazing ways. We need to take that step of faith and leave our own comfort zone to let God use us to influence people around us. Abraham would never have been a blessing to his family and to other people if he did not first listen to God and leave his home.

When we now read through the Bible, we see the history of Abraham and the amazing influence his descendants had on history. My grandparents had an amazing influence on me by helping my mother out when she needed it most. How are you letting God use you as an influence to others around you? How have you taken a step to let God use you as a blessing to others? Sometimes you may not ever see the blessing that you have given to other people.

PROMISES

ABRAHAM'S CALL, DEVOTION 3

Gareth Volz | *Senior (55+) Director*

In Genesis 12:1, we read, ***"Now the LORD said to Abram, 'Go from your country and your kindred and your father's house to the land that I will show you.'"*** Then in the next few verses, He makes three promises to Abraham:
Verse 2: ***"I will make of you a great nation."***
Verse 3: ***"In you all the families of the earth shall be blessed."***
Verse 7***: "To your offspring I will give this land."***

These promises were given to Abraham (Abram) when he was 75 years old, and he and his wife Sarah were childless. I am sure that at first Abraham wondered if he had heard God correctly. Sometimes when God tells us to do something it seems hard, beyond what we can envision. But we need to remember what God said in Isaiah 55:8-9, ***"For my thoughts are not your thoughts, neither are your ways my ways, declares the Lord. For as the heavens are higher than the earth, so are my ways higher than your ways and my thoughts than your thoughts."***

Each one of the promises in Genesis chapter 12 is important to fulfill God's plan for the nation of Israel, but today I would like us to focus on the promise in verse 7. The promise is repeated in Chapter 13:14-17, where Abraham is told to survey the land God was giving to him and his descendants. In chapter 15:18-20, we are told that it is the entire area from the river of Egypt to the Euphrates river. The last part of verse 7 tells us that Abraham built an altar to the Lord who had appeared to him. Abraham heard God's promise and immediately worshipped God.

God tells us how Abraham responded to God's promise in Hebrews 11:8-10, ***"By faith Abraham obeyed when he was called to go out to a place that he was to receive as an inheritance. And he went out, not knowing where he was going. By faith he went to live in the land of promise, as in a foreign land, living in tents with Isaac and Jacob, heirs with him of the same promise. For he was looking forward to the city that has foundations, whose designer and builder is God."*** Abraham's life is a great example of how God fulfills His promises, and God gives us a promise, if we follow Abraham's example.

God promises in Galatians 3:23-29, ***"Now before faith came, we were held captive under the law, imprisoned until the coming faith would be revealed. So then the law was our guardian until Christ came, in order that we might be justified by faith. But now that faith has come, we are no longer under a guardian, for in Christ Jesus you are all sons of God, through faith. For as many of you who were baptized into Christ have put on Christ. There is neither Jew nor Greek, there is neither slave nor free, there is no male or female, for you are all one in Christ Jesus. And if you are Christ's, then you are Abraham's offspring, heirs according to promise."***

We can study God's Word to learn the Lord's will for every situation in our lives.

WORSHIP

ABRAHAM'S CALL, DEVOTION 4

Philip Piasecki

The older I get, the more I realize how difficult it is to remember everything that I have to do. When I was in college, I never had to write anything down. I could just remember what I was supposed to do and do it! After graduating, getting married, having a kid, and Mary getting pregnant again, we have so much more going on now. I have gotten in trouble multiple times by double booking us because I did not put the event in the calendar. Calendars and to-do lists are so important. Unless Siri reminds me that I put the clothes in the washing machine, they are going to sit there wet all night. I could go on and on about different situations where I just forgot and needed someone to remind me.

Genesis 12:7 says, ***"Then the Lord appeared to Abram and said, 'To your offspring I will give this land.' So he built there an altar to the Lord, who had appeared to him."***

Why did Abram build an altar? He built an altar so that he could remember. Anytime, for the rest of his life, as he walked by that altar, he would be reminded of what the Lord had promised him and what the Lord had done for him. Why do we worship? Why do we sing and praise God? It is so that we can remember. Our world is built on being busy, it is so easy to get swept up in that and forget about Christ. We get so bogged down by what the Lord "has not done for us" that we so easily forget the amazing gifts that He has given us. We get so focused on who we are that we forget who Jesus Christ is. This is why we need to worship God; this is why we sing on a Sunday morning. When we finally get through the doors of the church building, we can exhale, sing the words on the screen, and start remembering who Christ is. We get to sing about how He has never failed us, about His reckless love for us, how He is our only King, and about the glorious day that our sins were forgiven. All of these things help us remember.

Our praise and worship is an altar to Christ. It is on this altar that we sacrifice our selfishness, forgetfulness, and our sinfulness, and we remember who Christ is and what He has done for us. There is power in God's people coming together, proclaiming the truth of Scripture in song, and together celebrating who Christ is. Do not let it become something that is an afterthought, or you may find yourself forgetting. Worship and remember what Christ has graciously done for you.

FIRST THING TO DO

ABRAHAM'S CALL, DEVOTION 5

John Hubbard | *Worship Leader*

Have you ever been sure that God was moving right in front of you? Maybe you have witnessed a group of people putting their faith in Jesus shortly after a Pastor has preached, or you have heard that someone whose health had been failing is doing inexplicably better.

What is your first reaction in those moments? "The preacher must be good. Well they have got the right doctor, or maybe they have got the right combination of medication." We have all played the "if I win the lottery, the first thing I would do" game, what is your first move? Would you pay off your mortgage, buy a new car, or get your mother something nice?

In Genesis, Abram is instructed by God to gather up his family and all his belongings and move to a foreign land that he will inherit. As he arrives in the land of Canaan, it is interesting to see what will be the first thing he does.

Genesis 12:7-8 says, ***"Then the Lord appeared to Abram and said, 'To your offspring I will give this land.' So he built there an altar to the Lord, who had appeared to him. From there he moved to the hill country on the east of Bethel and pitched his tent, with Bethel on the west and Ai on the east. And there he built an altar to the Lord and called upon the name of the Lord."***

As Abram followed God obediently through the land of Canaan, he continuously prioritized worshiping the Lord. When Abram had heard from God that his descendants would inherit the land, he stopped there and built an altar. In those days a burnt sacrifice was the way you worshipped God. Abram's first move was not to plan his new house, or to think much of himself for earning his inheritance. He knew that everything that was happening was because God had done it. We like to put the credit where it often does not belong - in a pastor, a doctor, or our own hard work, but it all belongs to God.

ABRAHAM & SARAH LIE

ABRAHAM'S CALL, DEVOTION 6

Wes McCullough | *Production Director*

A few weeks ago I watched a special on Netflix called *The Push.* The premise of this social experiment is this: can an ordinary person be coerced to kill someone in 90 minutes? The entire situation is scripted and directed with actors, props, special effects, and filmed with hidden cameras. Dozens of people were involved in the social experiment but only the subject was unaware of the goal. Starting with small compromises the subject of the experiment is influenced with peer pressure and strong suggestions that were less than moral. This social experiment was conducted five times, only one person refused the final "push" to take a life.

When I read of Abram and Sarai's journey to Egypt in Genesis 12:10-20, my thoughts were of principles. Principles are foundational to our character. We should not violate them for any reason. I wonder why Abram would trust his own cunning over God's protection. God had just directed Abram towards the Promised Land with this assurance, ***"And I will make of you a great nation, and I will bless you and make your name great, so that you will be a blessing. I will bless those who bless you, and him who dishonors you I will curse, and in you all the families of the earth shall be blessed"*** (Genesis 12:2-3). Much like ourselves, Abram's focus on God's impending blessings was quickly lost. He let the situation be more important than God's will.

God's faithfulness to His promise shines in this story. God promised Abram and Sarai's offspring would be too numerous to count. When Abram gave up his wife for his safety, God orchestrated a reunion so they could one day receive the promised blessing. Once again we see that God can not be caught off guard and His plan can not be distorted by our failures.

Are your principles set in stone? If someone asks you to lie, cheat, steal, or kill will you be ready to answer? Make the Christ-like choice and let God sort it out. It is much worse to offend God than man.

08

LOT'S LIFE

DR. RANDY T. JOHNSON,
GROWTH PASTOR

I have been to Cedar Point, Six Flags, Disney World, and a host of carnivals, but I am not a "ride's" person. However, I do like people-watching. It is reported that there are over 400 amusement parks and attractions in the United States with about 375 million guest annually. It is a billion-dollar industry.

Rides can give the sense that you are living on the edge of life and death. Fear turns to thrill as you raise your arms in the middle of the ride as a sign of courage. We have all seen the news footage or heard the reports of fatal or near-fatal accidents. I do not want to be hanging upside down one thousand feet in the air for 40 minutes while a high school student tries to fix the problem.

The International Association of Amusement Parks and Attractions tries to comfort us by reporting that the chance of being seriously injured on a fixed-site ride at an amusement park is 1 in 17 million. They go on to document that the number of deaths on America's roadways in 2014 was 32,675 and that the chance of being struck by lightning in the U.S. is 1 in 775,000. Hence, amusement parks must be safer than driving or dancing in the rain.

Do you like amusement parks? If so, what is your favorite ride?

____

____

____

In the Old Testament, they did not have amusement parks. However, Lot went on the most dangerous ride. He experienced the deadly "slippery slope."

Psalm 1:1 gives the progression of one who is headed down the slippery slope, ***"Blessed is the man who walks not in the counsel of the wicked, nor stands in the way of sinners, nor sits in the seat of scoffers."***

Notice the verbs. What is the progression?

___

___

___

How does this happen today?

___

___

___

Lot's life is recorded in Genesis chapters 13, 14, and 19. Each chapter shows a different aspect of the progression of Psalm 1:1.

1. *"Blessed is the man who walks not in the counsel of the wicked."*

Abraham has always been viewed as a man of God. Lot left home to go with his uncle. He saw something special in Abraham and wanted to be with him. He did not know what it would entail or where they would go, but he felt it was his best choice. However, after awhile, things are not as smooth as one would hope.

Genesis 13:8-13 records some discord and the proposed solution, ***"Then Abram said to Lot, 'Let there be no strife between you and me, and between your herdsmen and my herdsmen, for we are kinsmen. Is not the whole land before you? Separate yourself from me. If you take the left hand, then I will go to the right, or if you take the right hand, then I will go to the left.' And Lot lifted up his eyes and saw that the Jordan Valley was well watered everywhere like the garden of the Lord, like the land of Egypt, in the direction of Zoar. (This was before the Lord destroyed Sodom and Gomorrah.) So Lot chose for himself all the Jordan Valley, and Lot journeyed east. Thus they separated from each other.***

Abram settled in the land of Canaan, while Lot settled among the cities of the valley and moved his tent as far as Sodom. Now the men of Sodom were wicked, great sinners against the Lord."

What do you think caused the strife?

____

____

____

How can this happen today?

____

____

____

2. *"Blessed is the man...nor stands in the way of sinners."*

In the Genesis chapter 13 passage, we read that ***"the men of Sodom were wicked, great sinners against the Lord."*** When Lot moved away from Abraham, he chose to move toward Sodom. It gets worse.

In Genesis 14:11-12, we find that not only did Lot move near Sodom, but it was also not long before he lived in Sodom. The passage says, ***"So the enemy took all the possessions of Sodom and Gomorrah, and all their provisions, and went their way. They also took Lot, the son of Abram's brother, who was dwelling in Sodom, and his possessions, and went their way."***

Why would Lot want to live in Sodom?

____

____

____

First Corinthians 15:33 says, ***"Do not be deceived: 'Bad company ruins good morals.'"***

How does this passage relate to Lot?

___

___

___

How does the passage relate to today?

___

___

___

Is there someone in your life that you are allowing to pull you down?

___

___

___

"Taking it easy is often the prelude to backsliding. Comfort precedes collapse." Vance Havner

3. *"Blessed is the man...nor sits in the seat of scoffers."*

If you study the life of Boaz in the Book of Ruth or the life of Mordecai in the Book of Esther, you will find that major transactions took place at the gates of the city. This is where the city officials or judges would position themselves. Genesis 19:1 shows us how engrained Lot had become in the wicked city of Sodom, ***"The two angels came to Sodom in the evening, and Lot was sitting in the gate of Sodom. When Lot saw them, he rose to meet them and bowed himself with his face to the earth."***

Why would Lot be at the city gates of Sodom?

____

____

____

How does this apply to today?

____

____

____

"Prayer is the way you defeat the devil, reach the lost, restore a backslider, strengthen the saints, send missionaries out, cure the sick, accomplish the impossible, and know the will of God." David Jeremiah

The Book of Proverbs warns to avoid the street of the evil woman. Unfortunately, too many men have driven by her street, stopped to say Hi, and eventually took a step past the bed of roses to pushing up daisies. Sex outside of marriage steers a relationship down a dead end. It reminds me of the college student who wants to be accepted. They first walk by the party, eventually stop to see what is happening, and then do things they never thought they would as part of being "sworn in" to a new group of "friends."

We regularly hear of embezzlement. I am sure it started small "out of necessity," and then progressed or digressed to extremes. First Timothy 6:10 warns about the love of money, ***"For the love of money is a root of all kinds of evils. It is through this craving that some have wandered away from the faith and pierced themselves with many pangs."***

How can the love of money lead to evil?

___

___

___

Demas is only mentioned three times in Scripture. Colossians 4:14 says, ***"Luke the beloved physician greets you, as does Demas."*** Philemon 1:24 adds, ***"And so do Mark, Aristarchus, Demas, and Luke, my fellow workers."*** Both of these passages show that he was serving with Paul and known by other believers. Unfortunately, he makes a bad life decision. Second Timothy 4:10 says, ***"For Demas, in love with this present world, has deserted me and gone to Thessalonica. Crescens has gone to Galatia, Titus to Dalmatia."***

What does it mean that he was ***"in love :vith this present world?"***

___

___

___

How does this happen today?

___

___

___

"The Christian life is very much like climbing a hill of ice. You cannot slide up. You have to cut every step with an ice axe. Only with incessant labor in cutting and chipping can you make any progress. If you want to know how to backslide, leave off going forward. Cease going upward and you will go downward of necessity. You can never stand still." Charles Spurgeon

Remember, we are all only one bad choice from the deadly ride down the slippery slope.

LOT WITH ABRAHAM

LOT'S LIFE, DEVOTION 1

Isaiah Combs | *Worship Leader*

Have you ever heard a story that starts really good and then goes from bad to worse? These stories are like train wrecks. You do not want to see it, but you cannot look away. The story of Lot is one of those train wrecks. Lot's story is one of the saddest stories in the Bible. His story started out so good with a great decision to follow his uncle.

We first meet Lot in Genesis chapter 13; he is traveling with his uncle, Abraham.

Abraham is arguably the most influential man in the Bible besides Jesus. Abraham was a man God blessed and promised (made a covenant) to make him a great nation. His offspring would be so great in number it would be like the sand on the beach and the stars in the sky.

Genesis 12:2 says, ***"And I will make of you a great nation, and I will bless you and make your name great, so that you will be a blessing."***

Genesis 22:17 adds, ***"I will surely bless you, and I will surely multiply your offspring as the stars of heaven and as the sand that is on the seashore."***

One of the crazy things about this story is that Abraham and his wife did not have children. So Abraham decided to bring his nephew Lot along on the journey that God was sending him. God had given Abraham a land called Bethel. Abraham ended up splitting this land with Lot. Lot by choice took the land closest to the cities of Sodom and Gomorrah. That choice was the beginning of the end for Lot.

You would think that with this investment from this great man of God (Abraham) on Lot's life, it would set him up for some serious success. Sadly, it did not. Lot made bad decision after bad decision that led to some serious pain in Lot's life. He fathered two children that became the fathers of the Moabites and the Ammonites. These two nations that were constantly at war with the Israelites (the chosen people of God and Abrahams descendants). This is only part of Lot's chaotic life.

Genesis 19:36-38 shows how although someone has a great start in life, their decisions can lead others to bad choices, ***"Thus both the daughters of Lot became pregnant by their father. The firstborn bore a son and called his name Moab. He is the father of the Moabites to this day. The younger also bore a son and called his name Ben-ammi. He is the father of the Ammonites to this day."***

SEPARATION OF LOT FROM ABRAHAM

LOT'S LIFE, DEVOTION 2

James Clouse | *Student Pastor*

Have you ever made a decision and instantly regretted it? I know that many times in life I have made decisions that I soon regretted. Whether it was a sin in my life or buying a house at the top of the housing market, I have made some poor choices. Life presents many decisions that we need to seek answers to. Whether the question is which college to go to, which house to buy, or whom to marry there are always important questions that need to be answered. It may not surprise you, but this is nothing new. Through the Bible, we can see numerous times where there is a choice that needs to be made. Abram and Lot had to separate from each other for logistical and peacekeeping reasons.

Genesis 13:8-13 says what happened, ***"Then Abram said to Lot, 'Let there be no strife between you and me, and between your herdsmen and my herdsmen, for we are kinsmen. Is not the whole land before you? Separate yourself from me. If you take the left hand, then I will go to the right, or if you take the right hand, then I will go to the left.' And Lot lifted up his eyes and saw that the Jordan Valley was well watered everywhere like the garden of the Lord, like the land of Egypt, in the direction of Zoar. (This was before the Lord destroyed Sodom and Gomorrah.) So Lot chose for himself all the Jordan Valley, and Lot journeyed east. Thus they separated from each other. Abram settled in the land of Canaan, while Lot settled among the cities of the valley and moved his tent as far as Sodom. Now the men of Sodom were wicked, great sinners against the Lord."***

Spend a moment focusing on the situation in front of Lot. Lot and Abram have both left their home. They have left everything that is familiar to them to go to a place where the Lord has promised them. But there is strife amongst the families and Lot ends up having to separate from Abram. Abram offers up a choice to Abram of which land to go to. Genesis offers up a detailed situation on how Lot chose which direction to go in where it mentions that ***"Lot chose for himself."*** Lot chose his path on his own and without the Lord's direction. Lot saw what options were in front of him and which looked more appealing to him. He also saw that the land he chose was closer to Sodom, a very sinful city.

Things do not go too well for Lot after this poor decision. How often do we as Christians decide on our own what is going to happen next in our lives without God's direction? Go to God for which direction to go in your life. If you are presented with multiple paths in your life, seek God first.

ABRAHAM RESCUES LOT

LOT'S LIFE, DEVOTION 3

Ben Kirkman | *Director of Facilities*

Looking at the life of Lot can be pretty depressing and frustrating. You see a man who is placed by God into the same family as Abraham (what a cool uncle to have); you see a man with wealth and riches and incredible opportunity; you see a man with so much seemingly throw it all away. Lot chooses to surround himself with wickedness, and it has horrific results for him and his family. It is easy when reading about Lot to focus solely on his terrible choices and the horrible situations into which he willingly walks. When you focus on Lot's failures, you can unintentionally overlook God's working. When studying Lot's life, it is evident that even amidst his poor choices, God is at work! You can see "El Elyon," "the Most High God," extending grace, mercy, patience, and tenderness time and time again.

In Genesis chapter 14, we find the kings of Sodom and Gomorrah, along with three other kings, rebelling against the four kings to which they had been subject for twelve years. This rebellion led to war. Five kings against four seemed like good odds for Sodom and Gomorrah, but they lost. They lost badly: they lost their possessions and provisions, and many people were taken captive.

Genesis 14:12 adds, ***"They also took Lot, the son of Abram's brother, who was dwelling in Sodom, and his possessions, and went their way."*** Lot, who chose to move into Sodom, who chose to associate himself with the wickedness of Sodom, just lost everything, including his freedom. He went from a man who had everything to a prisoner of war over a hundred miles from home. I can imagine him wondering, "What just happened? How did I end up here? How did my life fall apart so quickly?" (Have you ever been there?)

It is theoretically possible that this is the last we ever hear about Lot. God could leave Lot and those that ignored the LORD to be judged according to their wickedness, and He could do so righteously. The Gracious Redeemer steps in and brings Uncle Abraham to the rescue. Do you see God's grace and mercy at work? God has a rescue planned. Abraham takes his private militia of 318 men, along with trained warriors from his allies, he travels over one hundred miles, he defeats the army that five kings could not handle, and he brings Lot and his possessions home.

Genesis 14:16 says, ***"Then he brought back all the possessions, and also brought back his kinsman Lot with his possessions, and the women and the people."***

I am thankful that the Bible records stories of God's patient dealings with humanity. It is so wonderful to be reminded that even though we may struggle and falter in our decision-making, we have a loving Savior that is full of grace and mercy. I know that I need God's tender mercies daily!

"Oh Give thanks unto the LORD, for He is good; for his steadfast love endures forever!" Psalm 118:1

LOT AT THE CITY GATES

LOT'S LIFE, DEVOTION 4

Ryan Story | *Location Pastor - Burton*

Lot is one of the most exciting characters in the Bible. Lot was Abram's (eventually God named him Abraham) nephew. When God initially called Abram, Lot joined Abram in his travels. Eventually, God's blessing was so vast that Abram's workers and Lot's workers began to fight and cause strife within those traveling to Canaan. Abram and Lot decided to split up, and each took an area of land. Lot chose the land that would be located in the Jordan Valley. Lot was living in the Jordon Valley which was full or rich fertile soil, water, and many cities that were full of sinful people groups including Sodom and Gomorrah. While Lot was living in this area, a war broke out, and Lot was captured by a group of people that were fighting against the kings of the Jordon Valley area. Eventually, Abram heard of this and sent 318 trained men to save his nephew. Genesis 14:16 says, ***"Then he brought back all the possessions, and also brought back his kinsman Lot with his possessions, and the women and the people."***

After Abram restored Lot, the next time we see Lot is five chapters later. Most Bible scholars would say that the gap of time between Genesis chapter 14 and Genesis chapter 19 would be about 17-30 years. Lot went from being rescued and restored to sitting in the gates of one of the most sinful cities that has ever existed. Genesis 19:1 says, ***"The two angels came to Sodom in the evening, and Lot was sitting in the gate of Sodom."*** The people who hung out at the city gates where the people of influence. The people who hung out there were there to conduct business and other political matters. The people who hung out at the city gates were there to welcome new people to the cities. If a person was hanging out at the city gate, they were most likely a person who represented the city in some way. That is where Lot was. Lot went from following Abram on the journey God had given him, to serving a city that would be destroyed by God.

Here is the part that I cannot quite explain. What happened to all of the wealth, people, livestock, and other blessings that Lot had in Genesis chapter 14? I have studied my Bible for about two weeks looking for any evidence of what Lot had. The only thing that can be found is Lot had a home, a wife, and two daughters. We can make assumptions that he did have more family, but nothing is crystal clear. The thing I see here is Lot traded up what God had given him to have a worldly position and worldly status. Lot traded in his blessing to be something in the world's eyes.

I watch husbands and fathers trade their family, the thing with which God blessed them, in for a career. I have watched wives and mothers trade in all the blessings that God has given them so they can have "me time." I have watched parents allow their child to trade in "church" for sports and other extracurricular activities and wonder why their child walks the path that the devil has given them. While I write this my wife and two sons are sleeping. Every morning I awake; I am in complete awe of what God has given me. I never thought I would have a family, and I never thought I would have a wife or children. I cannot imagine ever trading what God has blessed me with for anything. My wife will be loved and led to being closer to God. My sons will be loved, disciplined, and encouraged to live for Jesus. I cannot fathom what was going on in Lot's mind that would make him trade in everything he had for trivial success. Lot sold out on what God had for him. If there is something we can learn from Lot, it is this, do not trade in the things that God has given you, because you may not get them back. Lot lost everything because he wanted to be what he wanted to be, not what God wanted him to be. Take a moment tonight to figure out the things that God has blessed you with and cherish them, protect them, and never consider trading them.

WICKEDNESS & MIRACLE

LOT'S LIFE, DEVOTION 5

Gareth Volz | *Senior (55+) Director*

The wickedness and miracle described in Genesis 19:4-11 centers on the household of Lot. Lot is an interesting character, and in many ways, typical of many Christians today. Lot was raised in the godly home of his Uncle Abraham, and he was able to observe Abraham's walk with God. We know that Lot was a child of God because he is described in 2 Peter 2:8 as a "righteous man."

As Lot grew in years, he went into business with his uncle, and between them, they owned large flocks of sheep. Their herds became so large that Lot's herdsmen began to feud with Abraham's herdsmen over where their sheep should graze. Abraham did not want this to cause trouble in the family, so he told Lot they needed to separate their herds and selflessly gave Lot the first choice of land. Lot saw how lush the Jordan Valley was and chose that for his herd. Unfortunately, the cities of Sodom and Gomorrah were located in that region.

Lot got his focus off God and on himself and what pleased him. He went from looking toward Sodom (Genesis 13:10) to moving his tents near Sodom (Genesis 13:12) to living in Sodom (Genesis 14:12). Sodom is a picture of the world, and the world is full of sin (Genesis 13:13). God tells us that we are to live for Him, separate from the world. But to do that, our focus must be on Jesus and what pleases Him, not on the things of the world. Thus, as we get to Genesis chapter 19, Lot has compromised his testimony. He did not like the sin of homosexuality that was rampant in the city, but he liked the lifestyle Sodom provided him. He even became a city official.

In Genesis chapter 19, God decided to bring judgment on the sins of Sodom and its sister city Gomorrah, by destroying them with fire. However, because Lot was one of God's people, and because of Abraham's pleading with God, He sent two angels to rescue Lot, his wife, two daughters and their husbands before judgment came. Verses 4-11 show how much Lot's compromise with sin affected his testimony. The men of the city demanded that Lot turn over the two men (they did not know they were really God's angels) so they could have sex with them. To his credit, Lot stood up to them and refused to turn them over to the men to be defiled. To his discredit, he offered to let the men of Sodom have sex with his daughters instead. The men of the city were so into homosexuality that this offer did not interest them. Nor did they have any respect for Lot. When they got ready to storm Lot's house and take the two angels and Lot, the angels pulled Lot inside and struck the men of the city with blindness.

What lessons can we learn from this tragic episode in the life of Lot? First, keep our eyes on God, not the world or the things of the world. Second, flirting with sin has disastrous results. In 1 Corinthians 15:33, Paul says, ***"Do not be deceived: 'bad company ruins good morals.'"*** We need to love God, focus on the things of God, fellowship with His people, and speak the truth in love to those who do not know God. Third, just as Lot was spared from God's judgment on the sins of Sodom, Christians are spared from sin judgment because Jesus has already paid the penalty for our sins on the cross.

DON'T LOOK BACK

LOT'S LIFE, DEVOTION 6

Donna Fox | *Assistant to the Growth Pastor*

"Flee for your lives! Don't look back... But Lot's wife looked back, and she became a pillar of salt." Genesis 19:17, 26 (NIV)

The cities of Sodom and Gomorrah had become evil. Terrible, unspeakable things were happening there, and God was going to destroy them and all the people there. An angel appeared to tell Lot to take his family and flee immediately. Lot, his wife, and daughters hesitated, so the angel had to grab their hands and force them to flee. Once out, Lot's wife turned and looked back. She looked back at what she left behind. She fondly looked back at where her heart was. She disobeyed. She died because of it.

Worldly things ensnare us. They tempt us day and night. If we give in to temptation, we sin. Sodom and Gomorrah had become very sinful cities. God had sent two angels to warn of destroying the cities and the evil people. But He chose to save Lot and his family. The angels said, "Go now, don't look back."

Lot's wife disobeyed. She showed where her heart truly was, in the sinful city. She did not want to leave that behind. First, she had to be forced to leave, taken by the hand and forcefully removed. Then she turned around to look back in direct disobedience. She lost her life that day because of her disobedience.

I remember another story in Genesis 2:16-17, the story that started it all – sin, disobedience, and death. Adam and Eve were in the Garden. Everything was perfect. God had said, ***"You may surely eat***

of every tree of the garden, but of the tree of the knowledge of good and evil you shall not eat, for in the day that you eat of it you shall surely die." Enter Satan in the form of a serpent, to tempt them. Eve, and Adam, disobeyed. The consequence was death. Their demise was not immediate as was Lot's wife, but nonetheless, it led to death which had not existed before.

God desires our obedience and will not tolerate any less. There are consequences for our behavior, for our disobedience. Sin cannot be hidden and will lead to repercussions, if not in this lifetime then we will have to answer for them on the Judgment Day.

If you do not guard your heart now, each day, and flee from worldly, evil things, your heart becomes harder and harder, and obedience becomes harder and harder.

How can you guard your heart? Have a relationship with Jesus that is every minute of every day, not just Sunday morning for an hour. Be in the Word. Fellowship with other believers. Grow in the Word in a Growth Community. Pray. Immerse yourself in the love of Jesus, and He will help you flee from temptation and sin. Of course, you will still sin, no one is perfect but Jesus. But when you do sin, repent, ask Him for forgiveness, and the sin will be forgiven. It is when your heart stays in Sodom that you will run into trouble!

09

ABRAHAM, HAGAR, & ISHMAEL

DR. RANDY T. JOHNSON,
GROWTH PASTOR

One of my favorite songs is *My Way* by Frank Sinatra:

And now, the end is near
And so I face the final curtain
My friend, I'll say it clear
I'll state my case, of which I'm certain
I've lived a life that's full
I traveled each and ev'ry highway
And more, much more than this, I did it my way

Did you catch yourself singing along with the words?

Do you have a favorite song? Do you have an "our song?"

____

____

____

As I was reading Genesis chapter 16 studying the interaction of Abraham (Abram) and Sarah (Sarai), I thought about that song. My cozy feelings of hearing Ol' Blue Eyes sing, changed as I realized we too often do it our way and miss God's perfect plan.

In Genesis chapter 15, Abraham is wondering if a relative will be classified as his offspring to continue his family line and fulfill God's promise. Verse 4 says, ***"And behold, the word of the Lord came to him: 'This man shall not be your heir; your very own son shall be your heir.'"***

Genesis chapter 16 continues the dilemma. Verses 1-3 say, ***"Now Sarai, Abram's wife, had borne him no children. She had a female Egyptian servant whose name was Hagar. And Sarai said to Abram, 'Behold now, the Lord has prevented me from bearing children. Go in to my servant; it may be that I shall obtain children***

by her.' And Abram listened to the voice of Sarai. So, after Abram had lived ten years in the land of Canaan, Sarai, Abram's wife, took Hagar the Egyptian, her servant, and gave her to Abram her husband as a wife."

How long had it been since God promised an offspring for Abraham?

___

___

___

Is it significant that ***"Abram listened to the voice of Sarai?"***

___

___

___

Culturally, this was an accepted practice for a man to obtain a male heir. However, instead of going to God, they do it "their way." They probably viewed it as if God needed help in keeping His promise.

How do we make the same mistake today?

___

___

___

Genesis 16:4-6 continue the story, ***"And he went in to Hagar, and she conceived. And when she saw that she had conceived, she looked with contempt on her mistress. And Sarai said to Abram, 'May the wrong done to me be on you! I gave my servant to your embrace, and when she saw that she had conceived, she looked on me with contempt. May the Lord judge between you and me!' But Abram said to Sarai, 'Behold, your servant is in your power;***

do to her as you please.' Then Sarai dealt harshly with her, and she fled from her."

How was their plan successful and unsuccessful?

____

____

____

The word "contempt" is used twice in this passage. What feelings come to mind when you hear that word?

____

____

____

In verses 1-3, Sarah blames God that she is barren. In these verses, she blames Abraham that Hagar is pregnant. How do we distinguish when it is God's plan, someone else's fault, or our responsibility?

____

____

____

Hagar fled and is on her own. Her name means "stranger." She must have felt like one at that point. Verses 7-12 record the beautiful truth of how God visits us when we are in our dark places: ***"The angel of the Lord found her by a spring of water in the wilderness, the spring on the way to Shur. And he said, 'Hagar, servant of Sarai, where have you come from and where are you going?' She said, 'I am fleeing from my mistress Sarai.' The angel of the Lord said to her, 'Return to your mistress and submit to her.' The angel of the Lord also said to her, 'I will surely multiply your offspring so that they cannot be numbered for multitude.' And the angel of the Lord said to her,***

'Behold, you are pregnant
and shall bear a son.
You shall call his name Ishmael,
because the Lord has listened to your affliction.
He shall be a wild donkey of a man,
his hand against everyone
and everyone's hand against him,
and he shall dwell over against all his kinsmen.'"

What instructions were given to Hagar? Why?

___

___

___

What promise was given to Hagar?

___

___

___

Ishmael means "God has heard." How does this relate to the passage?

___

___

___

How does this relate to our lives today?

___

___

___

Who are Ismael's offspring? Has the prophecy of this passage held true?

____

____

____

Genesis 16:13-16 concludes the chapter giving Hagar's response, ***"So she called the name of the Lord who spoke to her, 'You are a God of seeing,' for she said, 'Truly here I have seen him who looks after me.' Therefore the well was called Beer-lahai-roi; it lies between Kadesh and Bered. And Hagar bore Abram a son, and Abram called the name of his son, whom Hagar bore, Ishmael. Abram was eighty-six years old when Hagar bore Ishmael to Abram."***

What does this passage reveal about Hagar's view of the angel?

____

____

____

"Beer-lahai-roi" means "Well of the Living One Who Sees Me." What does this say about Hagar's faith?

____

____

____

How does this relate to our lives today?

____

____

____

They were in the land for ten years before Ishmael was born. It will be another thirteen years until Sarah actually gets pregnant. What are some reasons why God allows His blessings to be prolonged?

____

____

____

God had a plan for Abraham to have a son and it included Sarah. I think we can feel their struggle with time and trying to understand everything, but they still tried to do things "their way."

Proverbs 14:12 and 16:25 say, ***"There is a way that seems right to a man, but its end is the way to death."***

How do these verses relate to Abraham, Sarah, and Hagar?

____

____

____

What problems were caused then and now due to their poor choice?

____

____

____

"Remember this. When people choose to withdraw far from a fire, the fire continues to give warmth, but they grow cold. When people choose to withdraw far from light, the light continues to be bright in itself but they are in darkness. This is also the case when people withdraw from God." Augustine

ABRAHAM & MELCHIZEDEK

ABRAHAM, HAGAR, & ISHMAEL, DEVOTION 1

Philip Piasecki

It is time to open up and be honest. I really like "stuff." I am sure if you take a good look at yourself, you will be able to identify "stuff" that you really like as well. I put "stuff" in quotations because it can be interchangeable with a lot of different things. For me, "stuff" is technology and electronics. I am a sucker for the latest and greatest tech inventions. I have slowly accumulated some smart home tech, added a couple of nice speakers, and sometimes I am still not satisfied. The Lord has convicted me on this, that I need to be more content with what I have. Then, I read Genesis 14:17-24 and I was even more convicted!

Genesis 14:17-24 says, ***"After his return from the defeat of Chedorlaomer and the kings who were with him, the king of Sodom went out to meet him at the Valley of Shaveh (that is, the King's Valley). And Melchizedek king of Salem brought out bread and wine. (He was priest of God Most High.) And he blessed him and said, 'Blessed be Abram by God Most High, Possessor of heaven and earth; and blessed be God Most High, who has delivered your enemies into your hand!' And Abram gave him a tenth of everything. And the king of Sodom said to Abram, 'Give me the persons, but take the goods for yourself.' But Abram said to the king of Sodom, 'I have lifted my hand to the Lord, God Most High, Possessor of heaven and earth, that I would not take a thread or a sandal strap or anything that is yours, lest you should say, 'I have made Abram rich.' I will take nothing but what the young men have eaten, and the share of the men who went with me. Let Aner, Eshcol, and Mamre take their share.'"***

In this passage, we see the interaction between Abraham, Melchizedek the king of Salem, and the king of Sodom after Abraham returned from a great victory in battle. Abraham had just fought a hard battle, he had his army with him, and Melchizedek meets him with the gift of bread and wine and blesses him. The king of Sodom greets Abraham by offering for him to take whatever goods he desires from the spoils of the victory. The contrast between these two gifts became more and more evident as I studied this passage. Melchizedek gave a gift that would take care of essential needs, while the king of Sodom tried to ensnare Abraham with gifts of material things. Abraham was not a covetous person; he understood that everything he needed God had given to him, so he refused the king of Sodom's offer. This way, he was protecting himself from the king of Sodom ever claiming that he made Abraham rich, as we see in verse 23.

We clearly can see how Melchizedek is a picture of Jesus in this Scripture. Jesus meets our essential needs, while the world tries to distract us with the desire for material things. I always like to add a disclaimer in these type of discussions; there is nothing wrong with having things or being rich. Abraham was very rich, and he was still able to be a godly man. Issues arise when we desire riches more than the things of Christ and when we rely on our belongings more than we rely on Christ. This Scripture shows us what Abraham's mindset was, and what our mindset should be as well. We need to be satisfied with how the Lord provides for us and trust in Him only for our needs. Fight and pray against the constant desire to get more and more "stuff." This is something that I find myself needing to do daily. Our whole world is built around the accumulation of wealth and things. Our Christian mindset should be built around becoming more like Christ and being satisfied in our relationship with Him. Ask God to allow you to recognize all the incredible ways that He has blessed you and be thankful for those things!

PROMISE TO ABRAHAM

ABRAHAM, HAGAR, & ISHMAEL, DEVOTION 2

Roger Allen | *Recovery Director*

In the summer of 1981, Kayla and I became husband and wife. We were married in a small church on the outskirts of Clare, Michigan. We were excited to begin our new life and the challenges we would face. Through many trials and hardships, we have remained together, and we are more in love than ever before. Our individualism is slowly evaporating and becoming as the Bible says ***"one flesh"*** (Genesis 2:24). Through a miscarriage and a failed adoption, our marriage has persevered. We are now in that stage of life where we no longer dream of children. The circle of life looks different to us than most couples.

In Genesis chapter 15, we find a similar situation. Abram, while still childless, asks what the Lord would have for him. With no child, his only successor is Eliezer of Damascus, who is at best a surrogate for an heir. Possibly a servant or extended family member, he was the only suitable successor. At least he would be one who would take care of them in their old age (and inherit their wealth). Led outside, the Lord shows Abram the heaven overhead and says; ***"And he brought him outside and said, 'Look toward heaven, and number the stars, if you are able to number them.' Then he said to him, 'So shall your offspring be'"*** (Genesis 15:5).

To a man as old as Abram (possibly in his eighties), this must have seemed a bold yet comforting promise. Abram and Sarai's wish to have a legitimate heir would ultimately be fulfilled. Genesis 15:6 says, ***"And he believed the Lord, and he counted it to him as righteousness."***

Because of his belief, Abram became the "father of many nations." The Lord became his protector and shield. His reward was great. What does that mean to us? How do we see the promise of God in our lives? I remember when I was first saved, I read most of the Bible within the first seven to ten days. I had an insatiable desire to learn the Word of God. One of the first verses I read was Romans 8:29 (CSB), which says, ***"For those he foreknew he also predestined to be conformed to the image of his Son, so that he would be the firstborn among many brothers and sisters."***

The moment I read this verse, I realized what the Lord had promised. That through me, many in my family would be saved and come to know Him. To see that unfold in my life is a comforting example of the Lord's promise. I am so glad that the prayers of my faithful wife were heard those many years ago. You see, it was not until I was forty-six years old when I accepted Christ, and I received the great reward.

"And now I am about to go the way of all the earth, and you know in your hearts and souls, all of you, that not one word has failed of all the good things that the Lord your God promised concerning you. All have come to pass for you; not one of them has failed."
Joshua 23:14

ABRAHAM BELIEVES

ABRAHAM, HAGAR, & ISHMAEL, DEVOTION 3

Wes McCullough | *Production Director*

"And behold, the word of the Lord came to him [Abraham]***: 'This man shall not be your heir; your very own son shall be your heir.' And he brought him outside and said, 'Look toward heaven, and number the stars, if you are able to number them.' Then he said to him, 'So shall your offspring be.' And he believed the Lord, and he counted it to him as righteousness."*** Genesis 15:4-6

When God told Abraham he would have more descendants than he could count, Abraham was childless and more than 75 years old. His wife was approaching 70, but he believed the promise of God without hesitation. That is pretty incredible.

It is helpful to contrast this story to another found in Judges 6:36-40. Gideon, in seeking God's favor in battle, asks that a wool fleece, left out overnight, be wet amongst dry ground. God does exactly that, but then Gideon curiously asks God the next day to keep the fleece dry amongst wet ground. God again provided the sign of His favor to Gideon in battle. There are many times in Scripture where people asked God for a specific sign to confirm their faith. Asking twice, as Gideon humbly did, strikes me as an instance where I expected God to be unhappy for being tested and untrusted.

Abraham was different. He received God's promise and believed without question, without tangible confirmation. It is an inspiring and encouraging example of unconditional faith. The New Life translation says that Abraham's unquestioning belief in this promise ***"made him right with God"*** (Genesis 15:6 NCV). I find it so satisfying when people do the right thing as Abraham did in this case. In my book, it ranks close to the quality of David being a man after God's heart (Acts 13:22).

Looking back, God has always kept His promises. Sometimes they seemed impossible or took years to be fulfilled, but God always kept His word. If God tells you He will do something you should have no doubts, only patience.

"Now faith is the assurance of things hoped for, the conviction of things not seen. For by it the people of old received their commendation." Hebrews 11:1-2.

BITTERNESS

ABRAHAM, HAGAR, & ISHMAEL, DEVOTION 4

Dani Reynolds | *Graphic Designer*

"Now Sarai, Abram's wife, had borne him no children. She had a female Egyptian servant whose name was Hagar. And Sarai said to Abram, 'Behold now, the Lord has prevented me from bearing children. Go in to my servant; it may be that I shall obtain children by her.' And Abram listened to the voice of Sarai. So, after Abram had lived ten years in the land of Canaan, Sarai, Abram's wife, took Hagar the Egyptian, her servant, and gave her to Abram, her husband as a wife. And he went in to Hagar, and she conceived. And when she saw that she had conceived, she looked with contempt on her mistress. And Sarai said to Abram, 'May the wrong done to me be on you! I gave my servant to your embrace, and when she saw that she had conceived, she looked on me with contempt. May the Lord judge between you and me!' But Abram said to Sarai, 'Behold, your servant is in your power; do to her as you please.' Then Sarai dealt harshly with her, and she fled from her." Genesis 16:1-6

When I first read this message, I could not figure out who was bitter, who carried the bitterness in their heart. I tried reading a few chapters before this one and a few after and yet I still was not able to catch who was guilty of being bitter. I decided to start writing in hopes of something popping out at me. I decided to start writing about bitterness and how I could relate something to it. After I wrote that version, I asked for folks to review it and let me know if it made any sense. Surprise, nope! I had a lot to say but nothing that really was relatable to Genesis 16:1-6. Back to square one. I reread the passage, and I read other devotions based on bitterness, I prayed, "God, please use me to be your voice. Please show me what I am missing." I started to dig deeper than just these six verses. I started to research each party involved in this story. I had to look at the big picture to understand these six verses. All of a sudden, God revealed a ton of things and man I was not able to write it all down quick enough. The information was flowing over, and my hand could not keep up.

Matthew 19:26 says, ***"But Jesus looked at them and said, 'With man this is impossible, but with God all things are possible.'"*** Thank you, Jesus! Thank you for answering my prayer and helping find the bitterness in this passage.

Sarai decided to take matters into her own hands by giving her servant girl to her husband. She wanted a child to be conceived. Sarai did not wait for God's timing. When we take matters into our own hands, chaos erupts. I think that maybe Sarai was upset that her servant girl was able to conceive and she was not. She became bitter because I think she thought that Hagar thought she was better than Sarai. Sarai is the one who started the mess. Hagar was the servant girl and did as she was told to do. There is so much more to this story than just these six verses. Sarai got bent out of shape towards Hagar and complained to her husband, Abraham. In verse five we read, ***"Sarai said to Abram, 'May the wrong done to me be on you! I gave my servant to your embrace, and when she saw that she had conceived, she looked on me with contempt. May the Lord judge between you and me!'"***

Sarai opened that can of worms and then when she realized that she made a mistake, she blamed her husband. If she had just trusted God and His timing, Sarai would have had a son of her own, but she became impatient and tried to play God.

Sarai went on a power trip and started to treat Hagar badly. Hagar was like, "I am out of here. You made me do this, but then you got mad because I succeeded in getting pregnant as you wanted, but now you are mad at me. I am out!" Hagar fled.

I can say when I have taken things into my own hands and did not ask God for help, I have made a mess; for instance, this devotion. I wasted so much time in writing what I thought I was to write about instead of going to the One who has all the information. Once I prayed, asked God to help me, stepped out of the way, and allowed God and His perfect timing to be exposed, I reaped the benefits. God directed my path and opened my eyes to realize that Sarai was the bitter one. Try to look at the big picture and rely on God. He knows everything.

"'I am the Alpha and the Omega,' says the Lord God, 'who is and who was and who is to come, the Almighty.'" Revelation 1:8

NO MOCKING ZONE

ABRAHAM, HAGAR, & ISHMAEL, DEVOTION 5

Ryan Story | *Location Pastor - Burton*

I feel that every third devotion, I write something along these lines, "I love reading the Bible." I will also confess there are many chapters in the Bible that are super difficult for me to understand completely. I always struggle to comprehend exactly why God does something. The story of Abraham, Hagar, and Ishmael is one of them. I truly hope you have been reading through the book of Genesis with us as a church. I spent some time researching this family's relationship and discovered an amazing truth. If you do not understand something in the Bible, always keep digging! God has an amazing way of showing up in your life when you search for Him.

To get to where we are trying to go, we have to understand God's story on how He used Abraham. Abram was picked by God to be the patriarch of God's people, unbeknownst to Abram that this meant a name change, a lot of walking, and a crazy family to lead. When God told Abraham that he would have children, Abraham's wife laughed at the idea of her bearing children at such an old age. Eventually, sadness, grief, and guilt overtook Sarah, Abraham's wife. Sarah offered Abraham her servant girl to be a surrogate of sorts. This is where everything gets a bit messy. Hagar, the servant girl, does have a child. Genesis16:16 says, ***"Abram was eighty-six years old when Hagar bore Ishmael to Abram."***

Whenever man tries to interject into God's plan, situations never get better. In this case, things start to get super dicey. Fast forward fourteen years and Abram (now Abraham) has another child, ***"Abraham was a hundred years old when his son Isaac was born to him"*** (Genesis 21:5). Family dynamics can be difficult to navigate.

When you have a mixed family, things become even more difficult. There is little mention of what life was like for Abraham's family until one pivotal moment recorded in Genesis chapter 21.

Genesis 21:8-13 says, ***"And the child grew and was weaned. And Abraham made a great feast on the day that Isaac was weaned. But Sarah saw the son of Hagar the Egyptian, whom she had borne to Abraham, laughing. So she said to Abraham, 'Cast out this slave woman with her son, for the son of this slave woman shall not be heir with my son Isaac.' And the thing was very displeasing to Abraham on account of his son. But God said to Abraham, 'Be not displeased because of the boy and because of your slave woman. Whatever Sarah says to you, do as she tells you, for through Isaac shall your offspring be named. And I will make a nation of the son of the slave woman also, because he is your offspring.'"***

In this one moment, a teenager felt it was appropriate to mock an infant. Ishmael was 14 years older than Isaac. For the longest time, I always struggled with this part. I always felt Sarah's insecurity got the best of her. I always felt bad how Abraham packed up his one son and sent him and his mother on his way. I never understood why God blessed and was with Hagar and Ishmael. Watching God bless what would eventually become a future generation of people who would oppose God's people is mind-boggling. So how do we piece all of this together?

To fully understand this story, you will have to jump to the letter to the Galatian church. In chapter four, Paul explains the allegory of the two boys. Isaac was the promised child that God told Abraham he was going to have. From Isaac eventually came Jesus and because of Jesus came the church, this includes you and me. Ishmael was a child from the flesh. He was conceived because Abraham did not have faith in the promises of God. Yes, Sarah had her part in this as well. However, men of God are meant to lead. The reason Ishmael was sent out was not just for mere teasing; it was flesh mocking spirit. This moment was when the devil and the dominion of darkness were mocking promises and the Spirit. Galatians chapter six tells us that God will not be mocked. This moment is larger than just two children bickering. Ishmael was in direct conflict with Isaac and God said he had to go.

This was when I had my hair blown back with what I learned. Dispose of the fact that God did take care of Hagar and Ishmael; He did not tolerate him mocking the promise. How often do we mock the promises of God; how often do we look down from which God can deliver us? How often do we mock churches, pastors, or other leaders in the church? For Ishmael, it probably seemed like mere banter between older brother and little brother; however, I believe that the mocking was rooted in bitterness, hurt, and ultimately sin which is rooted in the devil. God protects His family, His works, and ultimately His name. In all of this theology and study, remember that God is with us. He is with us in the hurt, brokenness, and rebellion. Please realize and remember, God will not allow His promises to be mocked, slandered, or perverted.

"GOD OF SEEING"

ABRAHAM, HAGAR, & ISHMAEL, DEVOTION 6

Pat Bedell

In Genesis 16:13, Hagar says something profound about God, ***"So she called the name of the Lord who spoke to her, 'You are a God of seeing,' for she said, 'Truly here I have seen him who looks after me.'"***

When I was three years old, my mom started bringing me to the Catholic church where I began my Christian walk. I started my Catechism classes when I was around five, and I began to learn who Jesus was and what He did for us. It was the year after that my younger sisters began to attend church as well, but as all siblings do when they are younger, we began to cause mischief during mass and shortly after that, my mom took us out of the church due to behavioral issues.

Fast forward to high school, and early college days, I had done more than my fair share of sinning. From lying and disobeying my parents to making immoral decisions, I was in quite a mess. My second year of college, I came to know Christ as my Savior, and I started to live my life for Him.

As I read the Bible and listened to sermons more often, I began to learn that God was watching over me and seeing everything I had done while I was not seeking Him. Hebrews 4:13 says, ***"And no creature is hidden from his sight, but all are naked and exposed to the eyes of him to whom we must give account."*** When I understood what that meant in my life, I was heartbroken. More importantly, I realized that I was disobeying and hurting Christ with all of my actions and decisions in the past. Proverbs 5:21

adds, ***"For a man's ways are before the eyes of the LORD, and he ponders all his paths."*** I was embarrassed and shameful, but I was also grateful that He had His eyes on me the whole time. He thought of the paths to set me on and ultimately led me to Him. Romans 6:14 says, ***"For sin will have no dominion over you, since you are not under law but under grace."*** To live under God's grace is so amazing and gratifying.

Now that I know the Lord is watching me, it keeps me accountable for my actions and decisions. It helps me to repent of sin and live only for Him. It also gives me inspiration and a responsibility to lead my family and friends to live likewise. Do you have anyone in your life who might need to know that God is watching over them? I challenge you to be a light in their world and to show them that the grace of God is real and that He is watching over them with love and grace.

Our Lord is "the God of seeing." This should challenge us, but it is also the most comforting concept. God sees you.

10

ABRAHAM, SARAH, & ISAAC

DR. RANDY T. JOHNSON,
GROWTH PASTOR

The Guinness World Record book has some fascinating information:

Feodor Vassilyev of Russia has the record of having the most children. She bore a record-breaking 69 children. She gave birth to an astonishing 16 pairs of twins, seven sets of triplets, and four sets of quadruplets. It has been said that it is *Cheaper by the Dozen.*

Maria del Carmen Bousada Lara of Spain is credited as the oldest lady to give birth. Not only did this senior citizen give birth, but she also had twin boys, Christian and Pau, at the age of 66 years 358 days.

The information must be outdated as CBS News reported that Daljinder Kaur of India, gave birth to her first child at the age of 70.

What thoughts go through your mind when you hear how many children one lady had or how old one was when she had a child?

____

____

____

This information is also faulty as the Book of Genesis records the story of Abraham, Sarah, and eventually Isaac. As we examine this miracle birth, there is an underlying theme of laughter. God's promise of Abraham becoming a great nation through his heir by Sarah is recorded in three key chapters of the Bible.

1. Abraham laughed.

Laughter is a language of its own. Whether it is a chuckle or full-out belly-buster, it can be very contagious. When someone puts out a roar or embarrassing snort, others will often smile without even knowing the cause of the amusement. Abraham laughed first.

Genesis 17:15-21 says, ***"And God said to Abraham, 'As for Sarai your wife, you shall not call her name Sarai, but Sarah shall be her name. I will bless her, and moreover, I will give you a son by her. I will bless her, and she shall become nations; kings of peoples shall come from her.' Then Abraham fell on his face and laughed and said to himself, 'Shall a child be born to a man who is a hundred years old? Shall Sarah, who is ninety years old, bear a child?' And Abraham said to God, 'Oh that Ishmael might live before you!' God said, 'No, but Sarah your wife shall bear you a son, and you shall call his name Isaac. I will establish my covenant with him as an everlasting covenant for his offspring after him. As for Ishmael, I have heard you; behold, I have blessed him and will make him fruitful and multiply him greatly. He shall father twelve princes, and I will make him into a great nation. But I will establish my covenant with Isaac, whom Sarah shall bear to you at this time next year.'"***

What does God promise Abraham in this passage?

____

____

____

How did Abraham respond? Why?

____

____

____

For whom did he express concern? Why?

____

____

____

Who is your Ishmael that you want to see blessed?

____

____

____

Abraham laughed. He knew God was mighty and could do anything, but he was caught off-guard by God's promise. He laughed with God. It is good to remember the words of Proverbs 17:22, ***"A joyful heart is good medicine, but a crushed spirit dries up the bones."***

"Laughter is the most beautiful and beneficial therapy God ever granted humanity." Chuck Swindoll

However, it is important to realize there is laughing, and then there is laughing. Not all laughter is the same.

2. Sarah laughed.

Laughter is not always positive. Who is laughing, when they are laughing, and why they are laughing are all important aspects of whether the laughter is positive or negative. It can make the difference between someone laughing with you or at you.

Genesis 18:9-15 records Sarah's laughter, ***"They said to him, 'Where is Sarah your wife?' And he said, 'She is in the tent.' The Lord said, 'I will surely return to you about this time next year, and Sarah your wife shall have a son.' And Sarah was listening at the tent door behind him. Now Abraham and Sarah were old, advanced in years. The way of women had ceased to be with Sarah. So Sarah laughed to herself, saying, 'After I am worn out, and my lord is old, shall I have pleasure?' The Lord said to Abraham, 'Why did Sarah laugh and say, 'Shall I indeed bear a child, now that I am old?' Is anything too hard for the Lord? At***

the appointed time I will return to you, about this time next year, and Sarah shall have a son.' But Sarah denied it, saying, 'I did not laugh,' for she was afraid. He said, 'No, but you did laugh.'"

What news did Sarah hear? How did she respond?

___

___

___

How did God view her laughter?

___

___

___

How does this correspond to today?

___

___

___

3. God laughed.

Laughing can be fun. It can be healthy. Most of us have experienced the other extreme when it does not feel good. People will laugh as a form of mockery. Few things are as rewarding as getting the last laugh.

Part of God getting the last laugh involved names. Changing names can distinguish a new stage or assignment in life. A little boy named Jimmy might become known as Jim or Jimbo in his teens and James as an older man. Abram's new calling had him become Abraham and Sarai's new stage in life brought her to the point of being known as Sarah. However, the humor comes in being told to name the son Isaac which means "He who laughs" or "He laughs." While blessing them, God got the last laugh and always will.

Genesis 21:1-7 records the birth of Isaac, ***"The Lord visited Sarah as he had said, and the Lord did to Sarah as he had promised. And Sarah conceived and bore Abraham a son in his old age at the time of which God had spoken to him. Abraham called the name of his son who was born to him, whom Sarah bore him, Isaac. And Abraham circumcised his son Isaac when he was eight days old, as God had commanded him. Abraham was a hundred years old when his son Isaac was born to him. And Sarah said, 'God has made laughter for me; everyone who hears will laugh over me.' And she said, 'Who would have said to Abraham that Sarah would nurse children? Yet I have borne him a son in his old age.'"***

Has your name evolved through time?

How old were Abraham and Sarah when Isaac was born?

What miracle are you praying for from God?

God laughed. We know He has a sense of humor and He likes seeing us enjoy His creation. However, we need to learn when to laugh. Timing is everything. Our humor should never come across as disbelief in God's Word or character.

"Laughter is the closest thing to the grace of God." Karl Barth

"Then our mouth was filled with laughter, and our tongue with shouts of joy; then they said among the nations, 'The Lord has done great things for them.'" Psalm 126:2

ABRAHAMIC COVENANT

ABRAHAM, SARAH, & ISAAC, DEVOTION 1

Chuck Lindsey | *Reach Pastor*

"After these things the word of the Lord came to Abram in a vision, saying, 'Do not be afraid, Abram. I am your shield, your exceedingly great reward.' But Abram said, 'Lord God, what will You give me, seeing I go childless, and the heir of my house is Eliezer of Damascus?' Then Abram said, 'Look, You have given me no offspring; indeed one born in my house is my heir!' And behold, the word of the Lord came to him, saying, 'This one shall not be your heir, but one who will come from your own body shall be your heir.' Then He brought him outside and said, 'Look now toward heaven, and count the stars if you are able to number them.' And He said to him, 'So shall your descendants be.' And he believed in the Lord, and He accounted it to him for righteousness. Then He said to him, 'I am the Lord, who brought you out of Ur of the Chaldeans, to give you this land to inherit it.' And he said, 'Lord God, how shall I know that I will inherit it?' So He said to him, 'Bring Me a three-year-old heifer, a three-year-old female goat, a three-year-old ram, a turtledove, and a young pigeon.' Then he brought all these to Him and cut them in two, down the middle, and placed each piece opposite the other; but he did not cut the birds in two. And when the vultures came down on the carcasses, Abram drove them away. Now when the sun was going down, a deep sleep fell upon Abram; and behold, horror and great darkness fell upon him. Then He said to Abram: 'Know certainly that your descendants will be strangers in a land that is not theirs, and will serve them, and they will afflict them four hundred years. And also the nation whom they serve I will judge; afterward they shall come out with great possessions. Now as for you, you shall go to your fathers in peace; you shall

be buried at a good old age. But in the fourth generation they shall return here, for the iniquity of the Amorites is not yet complete.' And it came to pass, when the sun went down and it was dark, that behold, there appeared a smoking oven and a burning torch that passed between those pieces. On the same day the Lord made a covenant with Abram, saying: 'To your descendants I have given this land, from the river of Egypt to the great river, the River Euphrates—the Kenites, the Kenezzites, the Kadmonites, the Hittites, the Perizzites, the Rephaim, the Amorites, the Canaanites, the Girgashites, and the Jebusites.'"
Genesis 15:1-21 (NKJV)

Abraham is the father of the Hebrew people. But the story of how he became a father is nothing short of a miracle from God. Their story begins in the city of Haran where Abraham and Sarah are married. Like any newly married young couple, they (and everyone else) expected children to come along soon after. A year went by, and they have no children. "No problem, we will just be patient, it is God's timing." Two years pass, still no children. "Well, the Lord is in control, maybe we will have the doctor take a look." Three years come and go, still nothing. "This is getting serious." Soon five years had passed. "We have tried everything." Five years stretched into ten, ten languished into twenty, twenty years painfully became thirty, until finally, all hope had diminished.

Over the years, I have met many Abraham's and Sarah's. They are couples who begin with great hope and expectation but have watched the years tick by them. The hope they once had, has disappointed and has finally been abandoned. By the time we see them in Genesis chapter 15, they are nearly 90 years old. Abraham and Sarah had given up hope of having children long before this age. It is realistic to say that the dream had been dead for 40 years!

So then God came to Abraham and said, ***"Do not be afraid, Abram. I am your shield, your exceedingly great reward."*** Is it any wonder that in pain we heard Abraham cry out, "I know I have You, but I do not have children!" The dream may have died, but the pain had not.

Abraham goes on to say in verse 3, ***"Look YOU have given me no offspring."*** Then came the promise from God. Verse 4 says, ***"...one who will come from your own body shall be your heir."*** Understand what is happening here. God is promising Abraham that he and Sarah are going to have a child. Not only that but in verse 5, God tells Abraham that an entire nation and race of people are going to come from him. Abraham, with one promise from God, went from being both childless and having no heir, to have a son and an entire nation of people as his posterity. One promise from God changed everything.

The importance of what happens next cannot be overstated. Verse 6 simply says, ***"And he believed in the Lord, and He accounted it to him for righteousness."*** Abraham believed, not just in what God was promising to do, Abraham believed in the God who was making the promise. The promises of God always require a decision. It is to believe or disbelieve. But that decision is always a decision about God Himself. Abraham at that moment, was faced with a choice. Is God, GOD? Is He true? Is He good? Is He able? All of this was decided in a moment until we read, ***"and he believed in the Lord."*** He trusted the God who was making the promise and the result was Abraham's eternal salvation. The way verse 6 is written in the Hebrew language (original language of the Old Testament), it literally says, "and God put righteousness/sinlessness into Abraham's account." To illustrate exactly what happened here, think about it this way: Abraham's "spiritual" credit cards were completely maxed out, he was drowning in the debt of his own "righteousness" (or lack thereof), he was losing everything, and was headed to prison for all that he owed. But God made a deposit into Abraham's spiritual bank account. In one moment of belief, God deposited billions and billions of dollars, here called "righteousness" into Abraham's eternal account. Not only was his debt paid, but he had been gifted the righteousness of God. Abraham was saved simply because he believed. He believed in the God who made the promise and salvation was given to him.

From that moment forward God spoke about Abraham's future as though it had already happened and treated Abraham like a son. Every promise from God came to pass. The Jewish nation is the result. Amazing!

What God did for Abraham, He will do for you. Abraham's story is the prototype story of how God saves men and women; by merely believing. We are saved when we believe the God who makes these promises. Abraham was not saved by his righteousness, his "goodness," or his efforts. We will not be either. Like you and I, because of sin, Abraham owed an incredible debt that would have sent him to a debtor's prison (Hell) forever. But he believed God. Do you? The Lord says, ***"Whoever calls on the name of the Lord shall be saved."*** There is your choice. Believe or disbelieve. Do you need to be saved? Will God save? Is He good? Is He able? If you will admit your need, confess your sin to God, and believe, then you, like Abraham will have salvation deposited into your eternal account.

ABRAHAM'S NAME CHANGED

ABRAHAM, SARAH, & ISAAC, DEVOTION 2

Noble Baird | *Community Center Director*

For as long as I can remember, people have always questioned my name. Whenever I meet someone new and introduce myself, I always look forward to their reaction. They usually give me one of two reactions, that of disbelief or surprise because they think its a cool name. Noble is not a typical name by any means. I have found this to be true over the past 26 years as I have never met anyone else with the same name. However, I have also come to understand that for some reason it is a difficult name to spell as well. Whenever I walk into Starbucks or a sandwich shop to place an order the name on the order or cup will be: Mobile, Nobel, Noel, Noah, or Nable. It truly feels like I win the lottery whenever someone actually spells my name right on the first try!

In Genesis chapter 17, God appears before Abram and makes a new covenant with him. It is within this covenant that God promises to multiply Abram's offspring and bless them as long as they continue to follow after God as their one and only God. As part of this covenant, Abram receives a name change. In Genesis 17:4-5 it reads, ***"Behold, my covenant is with you, and you shall be the father of a multitude of nations. No longer shall your name be called Abram, but your name shall be Abraham, for I have made you the father of a multitude of nations."*** This name change is not only signifying the promise of the covenant with which Abram enters with God, but it is also a reminder of what his legacy will now be.

A question that I am often asked is why did your parents name you Noble? To which I give a two-fold answer. The first is that my father was reading a Louis L'Amour book and Noble was one of the characters in his novel. Secondly, my parents wanted to give me a name that they had hoped one day I would live up to and fulfill. Boy did they give me a tall order! However, I am grateful for the name my parents gave me. Yes, the misspelling can sometimes become annoying, but I would not change my name for anything. You see, Abram was given a new name. It was a name that he would have to live up to, and that would leave a legacy for generations to come. Translated literally, Abraham means "father of many nations." God did not give him this name to simply help the questions and, I am sure, the misspelling of Abram; but He gave him this name to signify the new covenant that was promised.

Abraham left behind a legacy to his children, grandchildren, great-grandchildren, and so many more as he truly become the father of many nations. However, more importantly, he left a legacy of faith and obedience in the one true God. It is God that would fulfill the promise He made to Abraham. As you continue on in your week, I challenge you to think about your name. Maybe the actual meaning of your name is not significant, but what is more important is what your legacy will be. How will you be remembered? Abraham is remembered for his faith and obedience. Because of that, God made a covenant with him and made a great nation out of his family. What legacy will your name leave behind?

SARAHS'S NAME CHANGED

ABRAHAM, SARAH, & ISAAC, DEVOTION 3

Holly Boston | *Women's Ministry Director*

Have you ever wished you could change your name? Several years ago my daughter Mackenzie was complaining about her name. I told her that originally our favorite girls name was Andrea but by the time she was born Mackenzie was the up and coming name, unique. Her response, "You should have stuck with Andrea."

According to Proverbs 22:1, ***"A good name is to be chosen rather than great riches."*** In biblical times, there was more to choosing a name than googling the top ten baby names. A person's name was a reflection of their character, their reputation. Throughout the Bible we see God change names: Abram to Abraham, Jacob to Israel, Cephas to Peter, and Saul to Paul to name a few. Sarai, wife to Abram, was the only woman in the Bible whose name was changed by God. Sarai, meaning "my princess" was changed to Sarah, meaning "princess to all" which reflected God's plan for her life. Genesis 17:15-16 records, ***"As for Sarai your wife, you shall not call her name Sarai, but Sarah shall be her name. I will bless her, and moreover, I will give you a son by her. I will bless her, and she shall become nations; kings of peoples shall come from her."***

In addition to reflecting God's plan, I found this citing in a commentary by James Garlows, "The Hebrew letter H is the sound of breath and generally signifies the breath or presence of God." But this was the wife of Abraham, "father of Israel," she had to have known God before this.

A review of Sarai's life helped me to understand. In Genesis 12:1-2, Abram her husband was called to leave his home, ***"To the land that I will show you. And I will make of you a great nation, and I will bless you and make your name great, so that you will be a blessing."*** Sarai followed her husband to this new land and by Genesis 13:14-16, God's promise becomes more specific, ***"Lift up your eyes and look from the place where you are, northward and southward and eastward and westward, for all the land that you see I will give to you and to your offspring forever. I will make your offspring as the dust of the earth, so that if one can count the dust of the earth, your offspring also can be counted."***

The Bible does not tell us what their conversations were, but I am confident that Abram shared these promises with Sarai. By Genesis chapter 16, we see a wife committed to her husband and fully in support of God's calling on her husband's life. There was just one problem: she was aging, barren, and unable to see her part in God's plan. As a young Christian, I was so encouraged by the testimony of other believers, how God was speaking to them, working in their lives, and directing them. I was not experiencing these things, and I began to question if I knew Christ.

I would imagine this might have been how Sarai was feeling. After all, God was speaking to Abram, not her. With no child in sight and time passing, Sarai takes matters into her own hands and has her husband sleep with her maidservant. She opened the door to a season of personal pain as well as centuries of embattlement as we see in the history of the Arab people.

In Genesis chapter 17, God speaks profoundly and changes the landscape of Sarai's life. We see her name changed to Sarah and so much more. God specifically names Sarah as the woman He would use to build the nations (See 17:15 above). For the first time, Sarah experiences God's Word for herself, ***"The Lord said, 'I will surely return to you about this time next year and Sarah your wife shall have a son.' And Sarah was listening at the tent door behind him"*** (Genesis 18:10).

It is after Sarah hears her name and has a personal experience with God that we see God's incredible plan come to fruition. Shortly after, Sarah conceived and bore Abraham's son, Isaac. Generations later Jesus Christ the Messiah would be born.

Like Sarah, when our experience with God is second hand, limited to a great sermon or the testimony of others, our view will be limited by our perspective and our resources which always results in us going our way to our destination. But a personal walk with Christ, grounded in daily prayer and studying the Word of God, will open our eyes and ears to His perspective, give us access to His resources, and ultimately take us to His destination.

If you know Jesus as your Savior, your name has been changed, ***"See what great love the Father has lavished on us, that we should be called children of God"*** (1 John 3:1-2 NIV).

You are His, and His plan for you is perfect. Jeremiah 29:11 says, ***"For I know the plans I have for you, declares the Lord, plans for welfare and not for evil, to give you a future and a hope."*** It is time for each of us to go beyond hearing about the amazing Savior we serve and see Him for ourselves.

Job 42:5 adds, ***"I had heard of you by the hearing of the ear, but now my eyes see you."***

"I want you to do more than just hear about what God is doing, to be part of something that is bigger than you." Pastor Jim Combs

ABRAHAM'S RESPONSE

ABRAHAM, SARAH, & ISAAC, DEVOTION 4

Joshua Combs | *Lead Pastor*

Genesis 17:19 says, ***"…Sarah your wife shall bear you a son."***

God brings to Abraham what is probably the strangest news the Father of Faith could possibly imagine. God says of Sarah, Abraham's wife, ***"I will bless her, and moreover, I will give you a son by her. I will bless her, and she shall become nations; kings of peoples shall come from her"*** (Genesis 17:16). God explains to Abraham, who is 100 years old, that his 90-year-old wife, Sarah, will be giving birth to a son next year. God leaves no room for doubt or questions: Abraham will be the father, Sarah will be the mother, and the child, Isaac, will be the son of promise, with whom God will fulfill His covenantal relationship with Abraham.

Sadly, Abraham's reaction is less than what we might expect or imagine from this great saint. He outright laughs at God. His human mind is unable to imagine fathering a child at 100, but the audacity of God to suggest that Sarah will give birth just seems comical. Abraham may have not been laughing at God, so much as he was laughing at Sarah. Ironically, that is exactly what God had planned, announced, and would accomplish. Sarah would give birth. The scorn she felt as a childless woman would be removed.

This announcement is the first time God would reveal to Abraham that his wife, Sarah, would be the mother of the promised child. Abraham and Sarah had sought other means of providing an heir, but that was not God's plan or His design. God was honoring marriage. The holiness of one man and one woman for life was and still is God's design. Abraham broke that covenant. He violated the sanctity of His marriage with Sarah. But God honored their marriage by choosing to miraculously bless this aging couple with a child. What Abraham did was culturally acceptable, but is never honored by the Lord. First Peter 3:7 states, ***"Likewise, husbands, live with your wives in an understanding way, showing honor to the woman as the weaker vessel, since they are heirs with you of the grace of life, so that your prayers may not be hindered."***

God warns husbands not to dishonor their wives because the consequences are that God refuses to accept our prayers. Do not laugh at God. Do not laugh at your wife. As God did in Genesis chapter 17 and confirms in Hebrews 13:4, ***"Let marriage be held in honor among all..."***

SARAH'S RESPONSE

ABRAHAM, SARAH, & ISAAC, DEVOTION 5

Jen Combs | *Women's Ministry*

"They said to him, 'Where is Sarah your wife?' And he said, 'She is in the tent.' The Lord said, 'I will surely return to you about this time next year, and Sarah your wife shall have a son.' And Sarah was listening at the tent door behind him. Now Abraham and Sarah were old, advanced in years. The way of women had ceased to be with Sarah. So Sarah laughed to herself, saying, 'After I am worn out, and my lord is old, shall I have pleasure?' The Lord said to Abraham, 'Why did Sarah laugh and say, 'Shall I indeed bear a child, now that I am old?' Is anything too hard for the Lord? At the appointed time I will return to you, about this time next year, and Sarah shall have a son.' But Sarah denied it, saying, 'I did not laugh,' for she was afraid. He said, 'No, but you did laugh.'" Genesis 18:9-15

The story of the Lord coming to Abraham and telling him that Sarah will become pregnant and have a child are what make for my nightmares. Josh and I have five kids ranging from 14 to 4. We had babies young, and I am now 36, I cannot even imagine having a child at the age Sarah was in this story. You hear people talk of little "surprises" happening when they are in their late 40's. Guys, these are the things that keep me up at night. People constantly ask us if we are going to have any more kids, my standard answer is, "No, Lord willing. But I also know, He has a sense of humor."

All joking aside, this is such a real-life example of what the Lord does in our lives. There is so much in just these few short verses. It would take a few devotions to pick it all apart. You have a lady who was told by the Lord that she would be fruitful and multiply. Now she is 90 years old, and it has not happened. I am sure she was questioning whether or not she heard the Lord right. I am sure she had lost hope. I am sure she was heartbroken. I am sure she lost faith a time or two. Ever lose hope before? Have you questioned whether or not what God said was true? Have you found yourself heartbroken over something you could not change? Did you lose faith?

Now the Lord came and told her what she had wanted for years is finally going to happen, and she laughs! I do not judge her at all for this response. She is thinking to herself, "It is a complete impossibility." Read the verses, it says right there, she does not have her period, and she is too old for sex with her husband. I would be laughing, too. Then I think the seriousness of her denial sinks in a bit, and she is afraid. She has seen firsthand what the Lord can do and realized that it is, in fact, a possibility. It was not in her timing. It definitely was not convenient. It definitely caused some anxiety.

Why do you think the Lord waited until she was 90 to fulfill this promise to Abraham and Sarah? The Bible talks about everything happening for the glory of the Lord. He chose to perform an outright miracle for this couple. There was no other way that this pregnancy was going to be explained except that the Lord made it happen. I know that we all have had times in our lives, where the Lord does not exactly work in our timing, He does not always choose to do things the way we would like. But we have to rest in knowing that He knows best, He has got it all under control, He receives glory in some funky ways (90-year-old pregnant lady?), and that He does, in fact, love us.

ABRAHAM INTERCEDES FOR SODOM

ABRAHAM, SARAH, & ISAAC, DEVOTION 6

Kenny Hovis | *Prison Ministry Director*

In the past four years, I have been on all but one prison trip that we have scheduled with the prison ministry. Most of the trips I went as a volunteer, the rest while I have been on staff. I have a passion for going on these trips to share the Gospel with the people who are behind bars and are desperately in need of someone to show them Christ-like love. This whole process has made me more effective sharing my faith at home as well. It has given me the opportunity to pray with and for many people, which I consider an honor.

One of the interesting dynamics of going into the prisons is when we have an opportunity to pray with the inmates. They may want you to pray for family, a case they have coming up, their own safety and health, and in some cases, you get the distinct privilege of showing them how to throw their lives to God. I often ask the person if it is something they have been praying for themselves and almost every time they say "yes!" This is the perfect opportunity for me to segue to the Gospel. In the second part of James 5:16 it says, ***"The prayer of a righteous person has great power as it is working."*** I always ask them if they think God hears their prayers.

We see an example of this in Genesis 18:22-33. Abraham is praying for the righteous people that may be left in Sodom as God is going to destroy the city because of its wickedness. He is asking God to spare the city if He can find 45 righteous people, then continuing to ask five more times all the way down to if He can find ten righteous people. Abraham finds favor with God as he petitions on behalf of the supposed righteous, each time lowering the standard for when He will bring judgment on the people of Sodom. He hears the righteous man, and He puts value to Abraham's cries for mercy.

We give God reason to listen to our prayers when we are following in His will. He is thrilled when our lives are surrendered to His leading and guiding. I go back to the example of speaking with the inmates. After I ask them if they think God hears their prayers, then generally say yes. I then ask them how their relationship is with their Heavenly Father. If they are not living a life that is pleasing to God, in His will, they do not give God opportunity to hear their prayer. It is like when we were children, and we did not do what our Dad wanted us to do. When we were disobedient, our father surely did not say, "Thanks for not doing what you were supposed to do. Here is your allowance and some money for ice cream!" That logic does not carry forward into our relationship with our Heavenly Father. We want Him to bless us, hear us, and do as we ask even though we do not perform the act He wants most from us, obedience.

Let us pursue a holy, righteous life, full of obedience. Much like the example of Abraham, when God finds us righteous, He is pleased with us, and it gives Him reason to listen to our petitions. He hears even the utterances and concerns that we cannot put into words!

11

ABRAHAM "SACRIFICES" ISAAC

DR. RANDY T. JOHNSON,
GROWTH PASTOR

When I think through some of the greatest examples of faith in the Bible, Abraham's trust in God to the point of being willing to sacrifice his son, ranks near the top of my list. He heard God and obeyed. He did not argue, make excuses, or procrastinate. He knew his job was obedience; God's job was to keep His word and raise up a nation through Isaac.

I like acronyms. I started researching acronyms for FAITH. "For All Is Through Him" is a good reminder that God is active in the world today. "Forsaking All I Trust Him" and "For Answers, I Trust Him" are both strong definitions of faith. I enjoy "Fantastic Adventure In Trusting Him" because life is an amazing journey when we allow Him to steer. However, I think my favorite acronym is "Fear Ain't In This House." It might sound a little like street-talk, but it reminds us that we do not need to live in fear because God is in control.

Is there an acronym you enjoy?

____

____

____

Abraham did not fear because he knew God was in control and He would keep His word. Genesis chapter 22 records a powerful statement in faith. The story has four key sections.

1. God Called

God answered His promise as Abraham and Sarah have a son. Isaac has just become a teenager when God calls him.

Genesis 22:1-2 says, ***"After these things God tested Abraham and said to him, 'Abraham!' And he said, 'Here I am.' 2 He said, 'Take your son, your only son Isaac, whom you love, and go to the***

land of Moriah, and offer him there as a burnt offering on one of the mountains of which I shall tell you.'"

What does God tell Abraham to do?

____

____

____

How would you expect Abraham to respond to God's instructions?

____

____

____

2. Abraham Responded

God called, and Abraham responded. It sounds very simple. Although it is the right thing to do, it does not appear to be the easiest, popular, or most comfortable choice. Genesis 22:3-4 states Abraham's response, ***"So Abraham rose early in the morning, saddled his donkey, and took two of his young men with him, and his son Isaac. And he cut the wood for the burnt offering and arose and went to the place of which God had told him. On the third day Abraham lifted up his eyes and saw the place from afar."***

How soon does Abraham respond?

____

____

____

What excuses would most people give for waiting before they responded?

____

____

____

3. Abraham Called

I am sure Abraham was preoccupied the whole trip up the mountain as he was talking with God. It reminds me of the statement, "As long as there are tests in school, there will be prayer." This was a test, and there was prayer.

Genesis 22:5-10 says, ***"Then Abraham said to his young men, 'Stay here with the donkey; I and the boy will go over there and worship and come again to you.' And Abraham took the wood of the burnt offering and laid it on Isaac his son. And he took in his hand the fire and the knife. So they went both of them together. And Isaac said to his father Abraham, 'My father!' And he said, 'Here I am, my son.' He said, 'Behold, the fire and the wood, but where is the lamb for a burnt offering?' Abraham said, 'God will provide for himself the lamb for a burnt offering, my son.' So they went both of them together. When they came to the place of which God had told him, Abraham built the altar there and laid the wood in order and bound Isaac his son and laid him on the altar, on top of the wood. Then Abraham reached out his hand and took the knife to slaughter his son."***

What statements show Abraham's faith in God?

____

____

____

Why do you think Abraham did not have his servants climb the mountain with him?

How was Abraham like God?

How are Jesus and Isaac similar in their "sacrifice?" (i.e. Mount Moriah)

Hebrews 11:17-19 adds, ***"By faith Abraham, when he was tested, offered up Isaac, and he who had received the promises was in the act of offering up his only son, of whom it was said, 'Through Isaac shall your offspring be named.' He considered that God was able even to raise him from the dead, from which, figuratively speaking, he did receive him back."***

How does this passage relate to the scenario?

4. God Responded

This story has a beautiful ending. We often miss the miracle because we do not obey the call. By ignoring God's direction, we miss the supernatural. Genesis 22:11-19 says, ***"But the angel of the Lord called to him from heaven and said, 'Abraham, Abraham!' And he said, 'Here I am.' He said, 'Do not lay your hand on the boy or do anything to him, for now I know that you fear God, seeing you have not withheld your son, your only son, from me.' And Abraham lifted up his eyes and looked, and behold, behind him was a ram, caught in a thicket by his horns. And Abraham went and took the ram and offered it up as a burnt offering instead of his son. So Abraham called the name of that place, 'The Lord will provide'; as it is said to this day, 'On the mount of the Lord it shall be provided.' And the angel of the Lord called to Abraham a second time from heaven and said, 'By myself I have sworn, declares the Lord, because you have done this and have not withheld your son, your only son, I will surely bless you, and I will surely multiply your offspring as the stars of heaven and as the sand that is on the seashore. And your offspring shall possess the gate of his enemies, and in your offspring shall all the nations of the earth be blessed, because you have obeyed my voice.' So Abraham returned to his young men, and they arose and went together to Beersheba. And Abraham lived at Beersheba."***

How do you think this situation affected Abraham's faith?

____

____

____

How do you think Isaac viewed this situation in years to come?

____

____

____

The key phrase is ***"The Lord will provide."*** There are other passages of Scripture that promise the same truth.

David said in Psalm 23:1, ***"The Lord is my shepherd; I shall not want."***

In Philippians 4:19, Paul said, ***"And my God will supply every need of yours according to his riches in glory in Christ Jesus."***

Paul covers it again in 2 Corinthians 9:8, ***"And God is able to make all grace abound to you, so that having all sufficiency in all things at all times, you may abound in every good work."***

How is God testing you right now?

____

____

____

What do you need to do and when will you start?

____

____

____

"God is able to accomplish, provide, help, save, keep, subdue... He is able to do what you can't. He already has a plan. God's not bewildered. Go to Him." Max Lucado

James also reminded us of this story in James 2:20-24, ***"Do you want to be shown, you foolish person, that faith apart from works is useless? Was not Abraham our father justified by works when he offered up his son Isaac on the altar? You see that faith was active along with his works, and faith was completed by his works; and the Scripture was fulfilled that says, 'Abraham believed God, and it was counted to him as righteousness'—and he was called a friend of God. You see that a person is justified by works and not by faith alone."***

"Though troubles assail, And dangers affright,
Though friends should all fail, And foes all unite;
Yet one thing secures us, Whatever betide,
The Scripture assures us, the lord will provide." John Newton

"GOD TESTED ABRAHAM"

ABRAHAM "SACRIFICES" ISAAC, DEVOTION 1

Richie Henson | *Production Director*

Life is lived on a vast spectrum of emotion. For some of us, we experience certain emotions more than others. For instance, I struggle with anxiety. For those of you who may be less familiar, simply put, I worry all the time about everything. Often, this worry can be crippling. Being that anxiety is a very real part of my life, I think my favorite feeling is relief. There is little as sweet as walking through a period of anxiety only to reach a resolution and gain a sense of relief.

Although not everyone deals with such strong anxiety, I know we all can think of times in our lives when we felt overwhelmed in our circumstances. As we finish Genesis chapter 21, Abraham is coming to the end of a very challenging portion of his life. Abraham made the terrible mistake of not trusting God for a son and had a child through Sarah's handmaid. Now, at the age of 100, Sarah is finally bearing a son, and it seems that things are getting back on track and Abraham can finally have some relief from the stress of his situation.

We then come to the next chapter, and the very first verse says, ***"After these things God tested Abraham and said to him, 'Abraham!' And he said, 'Here I am'"*** (Genesis 22:1). Abraham has just come through a very difficult time in life, and God turns around and decides to test Abraham. What would the purpose of this be? Why would God choose to test Abraham right after Abraham just completed a test?

This seems like a difficult question, but I think there is a simple answer. God is not content for us to stay the same. God wants us to continue to grow and become the people He desires us to be. The best way to grow is to be tested and stretched. As imperfect people, we always want things to be easy, but if we are willing to embrace the difficult, God will work to make us more like Jesus.

I think at this point in his life, Abraham understood this as he immediately responds to God's call. My prayer for us is that we would be willing to answer the call of God even when we would rather take the easy road.

ABRAHAMS'S RESPONSE

ABRAHAM "SACRIFICES" ISAAC, DEVOTION 2

John Hubbard | *Worship Leader*

"After these things God tested Abraham and said to him, 'Abraham!' And he said, 'Here I am.' He said, 'Take your son, your only son Isaac, whom you love, and go to the land of Moriah, and offer him there as a burnt offering on one of the mountains of which I shall tell you.' So Abraham rose early in the morning, saddled his donkey, and took two of his young men with him, and his son Isaac. And he cut the wood for the burnt offering and arose and went to the place of which God had told him." Genesis 22:1-3

It is important to remember that Abraham's story does not begin here. He had already been through so much with God, waiting year after year for God to give him a son through Sarah. When I see just this part of the story, I am shocked at Abraham's willingness to, for lack of a better word, execute this command. Keep in mind that already Abraham has made mistakes in his walk with God. He had tried to do things his own way in the past when he felt God was taking too long for his wife, Sarah, to bear him a son. So, Abraham had a son through Hagar called Ishmael. This plan of Abraham and Sarah did not work out as well as they had hoped. How often do we make our own plans in place of God's plans?

Whenever I read this chapter I cannot decide if Abraham knew God was testing him or not, Abraham had already been told that he would become a great nation through Isaac, so surely he will not have to kill him. Isaac is now old enough to comprehend and speak to his father about the process of building an altar.

Genesis 22:7-8 says, ***"And Isaac said to his father Abraham, 'My father!' And he said, 'Here I am, my son.' He said, 'Behold, the fire and the wood, but where is the lamb for a burnt offering?' Abraham said, 'God will provide for himself the lamb for a burnt offering, my son.' So they went both of them together."***

Again, is Abraham lying to his son or is he sure that God will provide? Either way, I think the most important thing Abraham did was to respond immediately. He did not know how it would turn out, but he knew that he would do what God commanded. He did not just head out and rush through this command; he equipped himself to succeed in his task. He prepared his donkey, and he gathered and cut wood for the fire.

What has God commanded us to do now? In our day and age, we like to have the best-laid plans. We desire no surprises, no variables, and no failure. We love to prepare ourselves, but are we fulfilling our task?

HEBREWS 11:17-19

ABRAHAM "SACRIFICES" ISAAC, DEVOTION 3

Philip Piasecki

When I look back at my four years of college, I have a lot of really great memories. I remember meeting my wife on my first day of classes during my junior year. I remember winning the intramural dodgeball and basketball championships. I remember meeting our Waterford Worship Leader, John Hubbard, on our first day of freshman orientation. The one thing I do not look back fondly on is all the exams and tests. I never enjoyed taking tests; if someone tells you that they do enjoy tests, suggest they see a counselor because something is wrong with them. However, tests are there for a reason; it is a way to find out if you actually learned what you were supposed to. I can say I understand a subject completely, but if I cannot pass a test on it, then odds are I did not actually comprehend it.

One of the greatest tests we see in the Bible was when Abraham was commanded by the Lord to sacrifice his son Isaac. Why did God give Abraham this test? It was to see if he had learned what he was supposed to about the nature of God. Abraham passed with flying colors, and because of that we see an account of this story in Hebrews 11:17-19, ***"By faith Abraham, when he was tested, offered up Isaac, and he who had received the promises was in the act of offering up his only son, of whom it was said, 'Through Isaac shall your offspring be named.' He considered that God was able even to raise him from the dead, from which, figuratively speaking, he did receive him back."*** Abraham knew that even if God let him go through with the sacrifice of Isaac, God could raise him from the dead. Abraham understood God's promises and fully trusted Him, even when God's commands did not make sense to him.

Hebrews chapter 11 holds story after story of amazing acts of faith from throughout Scripture. Abraham's faith is so inspirational and so deeply convicting. I know that personally, I lack that level of faith every day. I know that there are tests from God of my faith that I fail daily. There are basic things that I struggle to trust God with when in contrast Abraham trusted God to raise his son from the dead. I am sure you can think of areas in your life where you constantly lack faith. The remedy to this is to gain a better understanding of the promises of God. When our faith is lacking, we can remember the words of Scripture and be encouraged.

Romans 8:28 says, ***"And we know that for those who love God all things work together for good, for those who are called according to his purpose."***

Philippians 4:6-7 adds, ***"Do not be anxious about anything, but in everything by prayer and supplication with thanksgiving let your requests be made known to God. And the peace of God, which surpasses all understanding, will guard your hearts and your minds in Christ Jesus."***

Matthew 6:31-34 continues the thought, ***"Therefore do not be anxious, saying, 'What shall we eat?' or 'What shall we drink?' or 'What shall we wear?' For the Gentiles seek after all these things, and your heavenly Father knows that you need them all. But seek first the kingdom of God and his righteousness, and all these things will be added to you. 'Therefore do not be anxious about tomorrow, for tomorrow will be anxious for itself. Sufficient for the day is its own trouble.'"***

For the rest of the day, meditate on these verses, let them remind you of the goodness of God. Let these verses encourage you to have faith in every situation just like the faith of Abraham that we see in Hebrews chapter 11.

CONFIDENCE

ABRAHAM "SACRIFICES" ISAAC, DEVOTION 4

Mary Jane Johns | *Worship Leader*

My son-in-law, Chris is an exceptional human being. He is a geologist (the study of rocks) in North Dakota. Chris has been part of our family for about four years now, we love him to pieces, and he is a rock star! We also have the world's greatest grandchildren, Calvin and baby ToriKate. But, I digress. When our daughter, Kaili Mae was expecting Cal, we were all elated! She was having a baby boy. What would this boy child look like? Whom would he favor in appearance, disposition, coloring, and eye color? What I failed to share with you is that Chris is an only child. Chris is adopted as well. His genetic history is somewhat of a mystery. However, we do know that Chris was and is very loved and very wanted.

There is a child in the Bible that was also very loved and very much wanted. Although Isaac was not adopted, he was the only child of Abraham and Sarah. For years they had longed for a babe to love and hold. God kept His promise to Abraham and Sarah (after a series of mishaps on both parts) by allowing Sarah to conceive at the age of 90 years old. I can not even imagine how she must have felt knowing at the age of 90 she was going to have a baby! How crazy is that? God showed complete and utter grace in this situation. Sarah is one of only two females listed in the Hall of Fame of Faith listed in Hebrews chapter 11. Verse 11 (NIV) says, ***"And by faith even Sarah, who was past childbearing age, was enabled to bear children because she considered him faithful who had made the promise."***

Genesis 22:2 adds, ***"Take your son, your only son, Isaac, whom you love, and go to the land of Moriah, and offer him there as a***

burnt offering on one of the mountains of which I shall tell you." God continued on to command him to take two servants, a donkey, and set off on the 50-mile journey to the region of Moriah. God was asking Abraham for the ultimate sacrifice. What was God thinking? Asking Abraham to give his only son as a sacrifice instead of a clean lamb was just too much! Yet, in John 3:16 God did that very thing, ***"For God so loved the world that He gave His only son that whoever believes in Him should not perish but have eternal life."*** Jesus, God's Son was the ultimate sacrifice. He was offered up for us.

To make his son, Isaac, an offering was a test of character, will, and faith of Abraham. Earlier in Genesis, God specifically said that the promise would be through Isaac (Genesis 21:12). Abraham remained obedient. There was hope.

Genesis 22:8 says, ***"'God will provide for Himself the lamb for the burnt offering, my son.' So they went both of them together."*** Abraham, Isaac's dad, was proceeding in faith toward the sacrifice and trusted that God would provide for them. That my friend is real faith. God did provide. God always provides. Whether it is a ram in the bushes, extra money to cover a bill, a child that a desperate couple desires, or a husband for your eldest daughter (Chris), He is faithful. Will you be obedient and trust God to provide for you, too?

FAITH

ABRAHAM "SACRIFICES" ISAAC, DEVOTION 5

Josh Lahring | *Production Director*

In Genesis chapter 22, we see Abraham being told by God to take his only son, Isaac, and sacrifice him on an altar made of wood. Genesis 22:6-8 (NIV) records, ***"Abraham took the wood for the burnt offering and placed it on his son Isaac, and he himself carried the fire and the knife. As the two of them went on together, Isaac spoke up and said to his father Abraham, 'Father?' 'Yes, my son?' Abraham replied. 'The fire and wood are here,' Isaac said, 'but where is the lamb for the burnt offering?' Abraham answered, 'God himself will provide the lamb for the burnt offering, my son.' And the two of them went on together."***

Here we see a couple of things. First, Isaac had faith in his father and second, that Abraham had faith in God that He would provide even though he did not know what the outcome would actually be. In both cases we see the child obeying his father.

After I graduated from high school, I did what every student did and tried to figure out what I should do for a career. I decided that I would go to the University of Michigan Flint to study Music. After a year of that, I realized that there was no way I would make a career out of music and that I had to change to something different. After reviewing the degrees they offered, I started the fall semester in computer science. I knew quite a bit about computers so I thought it would be a good fit and there would be a lot of jobs available. I was consumed with being in control of my future, as everyone tells you, you have to have a plan.

Three weeks into the program, I was at a church event, and God made me realize that I could not live my life that way. When I got home, I told my mom I was dropping out and transferring to a Christian college to study Music and Bible Theology. I was nervous about it, but yet at peace that I knew it was what God had called me to do. Years later, I was asked to come work at the River Church in Goodrich full-time and every day I am able to use all my gifts for His purpose.

Imagine the fear Abraham had while heading up that mountain to sacrifice his son. He knew he had to do what God had called him to do even though it did not make sense. Yet, he knew that God would provide. When he was about to kill his son, an amazing thing happens. Verses 12-13 (NIV) record, ***"'Do not lay a hand on the boy,' he said. 'Do not do anything to him. Now I know that you fear God, because you have not withheld from me your son, your only son.' Abraham looked up and there in a thicket he saw a ram caught by its horns. He went over and took the ram and sacrificed it as a burnt offering instead of his son."***

Sometimes what we are called to do does not make logical sense, but we must have faith that God will provide and that His ways are perfect. Trust God, have confidence, walk in faith, and look for God to provide.

"THE LORD WILL PROVIDE"

ABRAHAM "SACRIFICES" ISAAC, DEVOTION 6

Caleb Combs | *Gathering Pastor*

The story in Genesis chapter 22 is one with which I have always struggled. God had just blessed Abraham and Sarah with a baby when all signs pointed to them being too old. Yet, now God challenged Abraham with the blessing. He told him to take Isaac to Moriah and offer him as a sacrifice. Now, this is where I struggle. This seems totally opposite of the character of God. Yet, Abraham was obedient. He took his only son, some supplies, and headed to the mountain. On the way, Isaac asked his father, "Where is the sacrifice?" Abraham responded that God would provide. Several times Isaac asked his father on the journey, and every time the response was the same, "God will provide!" I am not sure if you have children, but if God asked this of me, I am not sure I would have responded the same way Abraham did. I would ask, "Really God? I prayed for years that you would give us a child, and now you want to take him away?" Abraham had to be thinking all of these thoughts, yet his actions showed a resilient faith. When they reached the top of the Moriah, Isaac built the altar and then his father laid him on it. The Bible tells us that when Abraham lifted the knife, God called to him, "Abraham, Abraham, Abraham, don't lay a hand on Isaac, I have provided the sacrifice." Just as God said, there was a ram stuck in a bush nearby, and Abraham and Isaac made a sacrifice to God. Genesis 22:14 says, ***"So Abraham called the name of that place, 'The Lord will provide;' as it is said to this day, 'On the mount of the Lord it shall be provided.'"***

This is an incredible story of God's provision and testing, yet I have always struggled with understanding the desperation in which God put Abraham. Ultimately, it was a calling by God to Abraham for him to trust Him. Recently, I was able to travel to Durban, South Africa to serve at Key of Hope. Key of Hope is a ministry that works with children throughout Durban. It is an incredible ministry, founded and run by Dan and Rachel Smither. Before we went to South Africa, I thought it would be a great idea to bring some supplies. We brought suitcases packed with school supplies to be distributed by Dan and Rachel. I also know how big soccer is there, so I called in a favor. My friend, Caleb Stanko, plays professional soccer in Germany and he has a huge love for missions, and so he provided soccer equipment and jerseys for me to take with us.

On our first day in South Africa, we dumped all of the bags out in Dan's office, and he was excited about all of the supplies. That same day the director of his soccer programs came to him with a dilemma. He had spent most of his soccer supply budget on something other than supplies. He came to Dan and explained that his team had been unable to train and even play in games because they had not eaten. You see, most of them barely have enough money to eat once a day, and that was not close to enough nourishment for them to be able to play games or practice. The soccer director decided to use the supply of money to feed them and now was not sure how he was going to supply the needed soccer equipment. In the same response Abraham responded to Isaac, Dan responded, "God will provide!" Dan told him to turn around and see the very equipment he needed had already been provided by God. The young man was absolutely amazed at how real God was and is.

As I sit typing this devotion, I am challenged by that exact statement, "Do you realize how real God is?" I am ashamed of my unwillingness to trust that God will provide. I want to take control of situations myself and not trust that God will intervene. Maybe you are just like me and are a "control freak." Or maybe you have no issues in trusting God. I know in the easy situations, I have no problem trusting. But when the rubber meets the road, and our situations turn dire, that is when we truly see the extent of our faith. Do you trust that God will provide? I can say definitively that God will provide! It may not look the way you thought or imagined, but we have a real and active God working for our favor.

12

ISAAC & REBEKAH

DR. RANDY T. JOHNSON,
GROWTH PASTOR

"Arranged marriages" are still practiced in India and the Oriental culture. It is the concept of parents finding the right mate for their child. The idea is that children are too young and impulsive to make lasting choices. The other design is "love marriages" with an individual who they will marry. Some studies have shown that "love marriages" are stronger for the first five years, but that "arranged marriages" are stronger for the next 30 years.

Would you have been willing to let your parents pick your spouse?

____

____

____

Do you think you could have been more helpful in helping your children or some other younger friends in choosing their mate if they would have let you?

____

____

____

The story of Isaac and Rebekah is a beautiful love story that not only started as an arranged marriage but is also a story about trust. Genesis chapter 24 shows the value of trusting older, wiser people and also trusting God. Everything is contained in this 67 verse chapter.

1. Trust Older or Other People

Genesis 24:1-9 starts the story of trusting others, ***"Now Abraham was old, well advanced in years. And the Lord had blessed Abraham in all things. And Abraham said to his servant, the oldest of his household, who had charge of all that he had, 'Put your hand under my thigh, that I may make you swear by the Lord, the***

God of heaven and God of the earth, that you will not take a wife for my son from the daughters of the Canaanites, among whom I dwell, but will go to my country and to my kindred, and take a wife for my son Isaac.' The servant said to him, 'Perhaps the woman may not be willing to follow me to this land. Must I then take your son back to the land from which you came?' Abraham said to him, 'See to it that you do not take my son back there. The Lord, the God of heaven, who took me from my father's house and from the land of my kindred, and who spoke to me and swore to me, 'To your offspring I will give this land,' he will send his angel before you, and you shall take a wife for my son from there. But if the woman is not willing to follow you, then you will be free from this oath of mine; only you must not take my son back there.' So the servant put his hand under the thigh of Abraham his master and swore to him concerning this matter."

What kind of trust is Abraham showing?

___

___

___

How important is marrying someone of the same faith? Why?

___

___

___

Does the passage say anything about Isaac's trust? If so, how?

___

___

___

"Show me a successful individual and I'll show you someone who had real positive influences in his or her life. I don't care what you do for a living—if you do it well I'm sure there was someone cheering you on or showing the way. A mentor." Denzel Washington

It is important to find people we can trust. Proverbs 15:22 says, ***"Without counsel plans fail, but with many advisers they succeed."*** Getting advice from godly people can help us avoid horrible pitfalls. Paul points out the importance of older people helping the younger ones navigate through life. Titus 2:3-5 says, ***"Older women likewise are to be reverent in behavior, not slanderers or slaves to much wine. They are to teach what is good, and so train the young women to love their husbands and children, to be self-controlled, pure, working at home, kind, and submissive to their own husbands, that the word of God may not be reviled."***

Who do you trust for godly advice?

___

___

___

"If I have seen further it is by standing on the shoulders of giants." Isaac Newton

In 2 Timothy 2:2, Paul tells Timothy to invest into others, ***"And what you have heard from me in the presence of many witnesses entrust to faithful men, who will be able to teach others also."***

Are you intentionally investing in anyone?

___

___

___

"We make a living by what we get, we make a life by what we give."
Winston Churchill

It is important to trust others; however, it is more important to trust God first.

2. Trust God

Trusting God is at the heart of Christianity. Proverbs 3:5-6 says, ***"Trust in the Lord with all your heart, and do not lean on your own understanding. In all your ways acknowledge him, and he will make straight your paths."***

Genesis 24:10-14 shows the servant's obedience and faith, ***"Then the servant took ten of his master's camels and departed, taking all sorts of choice gifts from his master; and he arose and went to Mesopotamia to the city of Nahor. And he made the camels kneel down outside the city by the well of water at the time of evening, the time when women go out to draw water. And he said, 'O Lord, God of my master Abraham, please grant me success today and show steadfast love to my master Abraham. Behold, I am standing by the spring of water, and the daughters of the men of the city are coming out to draw water. Let the young woman to whom I shall say, 'Please let down your jar that I may drink,' and who shall say, 'Drink, and I will water your camels'—let her be the one whom you have appointed for your servant Isaac. By this I shall know that you have shown steadfast love to my master.'"***

How does this section show the servant's faith?

____

____

____

What did the servant pray?

Gideon prayed for God to give him a sign. Judges 6:36-40 records the story, ***"Then Gideon said to God, 'If you will save Israel by my hand, as you have said, behold, I am laying a fleece of wool on the threshing floor. If there is dew on the fleece alone, and it is dry on all the ground, then I shall know that you will save Israel by my hand, as you have said.' And it was so. When he rose early next morning and squeezed the fleece, he wrung enough dew from the fleece to fill a bowl with water. Then Gideon said to God, 'Let not your anger burn against me; let me speak just once more. Please let me test just once more with the fleece. Please let it be dry on the fleece only, and on all the ground let there be dew.' And God did so that night; and it was dry on the fleece only, and on all the ground there was dew."***

What does Gideon request of God?

When is praying for a "sign" (Gideon's fleece) a good thing to do?

When is praying for a "sign" (Gideon's fleece) an indicator of a lack of faith?

____

____

____

One of my favorite sermons is by Andy Stanley. The main point of the message centers on prayer and the mindset, "If you don't, it won't." It is the statement that we should be praying for God to show up big time in our lives. We need to pray for things bigger than ourselves. We need to pray that if God does not intervene, we are in trouble. It is total trust in God. Philip Yancey said it well, "I have learned that faith means trusting in advance what will only make sense in reverse."

"Never be afraid to trust an unknown future to a known God." Corrie Ten Boom

Before the servant finished praying, the attractive Rebekah approached him and offered water for him and his camels. She was an answer to a specific prayer (Genesis 24:15-21). The servant gave her gifts and went to meet her family (verses 22-28). Rebekah had a brother, Laban, who appeared to be her protector and advisor. The servant and Laban have a lengthy discussion as the servant stays for dinner and a place to spend the night (29-49). Laban gives Rebekah his blessing, and she leaves the next day to marry Isaac (50-61). The chapter closes with Isaac and Rebekah getting married (62-67).

How did Rebekah trust others?

____

____

____

Isaiah 26:3 says, ***"You keep him in perfect peace whose mind is stayed on you, because he trusts in you."***

Psalm 9:10 adds, ***"Those who know your name trust in you, for you, LORD, have never forsaken those who seek you."***

MAKING PROMISES

ISAAC & REBEKAH, DEVOTION 1

Jill Osmon | *Assistant to the Lead Team*

I am not the most patient person; when I know something is going to happen, I want it immediately. That is pretty normal in the instant gratification culture in which we live. Abraham and Sarah went through the same thing. God promised them a great nation from their offspring, but they were older, to the point that they found it funny when they received God's Word that they would conceive. ***"And he brought him outside and said, 'Look toward heaven, and number the stars, if you are able to number them.' Then he said to him, 'So shall your offspring be'"*** (Genesis 15:5).

Time and again Abraham and Sarah doubted God's promise and tried to provide it themselves. We have all been there, right? We know God promises us many things (peace, comfort, joy), but we fail to be patient in waiting for those things. We sometimes miss them because they do not come in packages, places, and people we think they will come, and in doing so, we failed to embrace God's promises when He does bring them. We waste many years trying to create what God has promised us and through that create messes of our lives. Abraham and Sarah took it upon themselves to provide an offspring, and those decisions and repercussions are still felt today. That is a pretty epic disaster of a plan that we can all understand. What epic disaster have you had in your life because you did not trust God?

One of my favorite themes of the Bible is the redemption of our human failings. We go through the pain and the hurt so that we can recognize and appreciate the redemption and grace that God offers. If we learn and grow from these, we get another chance to hold onto His promises, and wait and see God do some epically amazing things. That leads us to Genesis chapter 15.

Genesis chapter 15 is the culmination of Abraham embracing God's plan, and trusting that God would provide what He promised in His timing. Abraham sends his servant to find a wife for Isaac believing and trusting that God would provide. ***"The Lord, the God of heaven, who took me from my father's house and from the land of my kindred, and who spoke to me and swore to me, 'To your offspring I will give this land,' he will send his angel before you, and you shall take a wife for my son from there"*** (Genesis 24:7). In the end, he believed. My prayer is that we learn from Abraham and Sarah. We should not wait our entire lives to finally embrace God's promises in His timing. Instead, we should live a life defined by our radical faith, believing in a God who provides in His perfect timing.

PRAY SPECIFICALLY AND PRAY BIG

ISAAC & REBEKAH, DEVOTION 2

Joshua Combs | *Lead Pastor*

Setting aside all of the cultural contexts of the Ancient Near East for a brief moment, simply put, we meet a man in Genesis chapter 24 who is looking for a wife. Strangely, he is looking for a wife for his boss' son, Isaac. I am sure as the son of the extravagantly wealthy Abraham, Isaac had had many ladies (with their father's prodding) vying for his affection and hand in marriage. Marrying Isaac would have equaled wealth, servants, and great herds. But Isaac had submitted to his father, who had dispatched the head of his household to the land of Mesopotamia in the city of Nahor at the well. The sun was beginning to set, so the scorching heat began to subside, and that was the time when the women of the city would come to the well to draw water. The servant knew this was a great place to meet all of the ladies of the city and Lord willing, find a bride for Isaac. The servant, however, does not simply rely on his own understanding or knowledge but begins to pray. The specificity and boldness of this prayer in inspiring. Abraham's servant realizes that without the Lord's blessing, this could be a waste of a trip. As he is finishing his prayer, Genesis 24:15 says, ***"Before he had finished speaking, behold, Rebekah..."***

The servant had yet to finish praying, and the Lord was answering. As we pray, we must never forget that we are approaching a royal throne. ***"Let us then with confidence,"*** the writer of Hebrews states, ***"draw near to the throne of grace, that we may receive mercy and find grace to help in time of need"*** (Hebrews 4:16). Our prayers need not be small or timid. We approach God's throne, not as uninvited, intruding guests, but children approaching our Father who has repeatedly invited us to test the limits of His power, the vastness of His resources, and the depth of His love.

As a secondary application and challenge, we see a biblical framework for finding a wife or a husband. Here are a few guidelines we see here in the Scripture:

1. Honor your parents/spiritual leaders (24:1-11)
2. Pray – Ask God to direct your steps (24:12-14)
3. Look for someone with a servant's heart (24:14-27)
4. It is ok to look for someone you think is beautiful (24:16)
5. Watch for consistency in the person's life (24:21)
6. Honor their family (24:22-53)
7. Do not force it (24:58)

REBEKAH'S HARD WORK

ISAAC & REBEKAH, DEVOTION 3

Sierra Combs | *Women's Ministry Director*

I am going to be really honest and candid with you and share some things about myself that you may not know. Though if you have ever met me, or maybe even seen me, it might not be a big surprise. The first thing is, I am not very strong. Shocker! I guarantee I can probably beat you when it comes to who has longer arms, but as for their strength, I will lose every time. My family still likes to remind me of the time when I could not even bench the bar (with no weights on it). Of course, my niece who was eleven at the time could do it, so that made for a hilarious afternoon for everyone but me. The second thing, and I probably should just keep this to myself, I do not like hard work. I particularly do not like it if it involves manual labor. It goes along with my long weak arms. I am convinced my body was just not made for it. Some people are just natural worker bees, and unfortunately, I am not one of them. Of course, the Bible (and sometimes my husband) reminds me to do everything without grumbling and complaining, and to do all things for the glory of God, and so I try my best. When asked to write this devotion, I found it slightly ironic and also kind of convicting, because I know that this is a character trait I need to keep working on and developing in myself. I encourage you to open up the Word today to Genesis chapter 24, where we find the story of the search for a perfect wife for Isaac, the son of Abraham. In verse 15, we meet a beautiful and godly girl named Rebekah.

Here is a little backstory. Abraham knew it was time for Isaac to marry, but he could not just marry anyone. This woman needed to be special. There were a few specific requirements she must fulfill, most importantly that she be a pure, godly woman who worshiped the one true God. Abraham sent his trusted servant off on a mission to find her with ten camels in tow. Yes, there were ten camels! I once rode one camel in the wilderness of Israel, and let me tell you something, they are feisty and temperamental creatures. I can only imagine having to deal with ten of them. But these camels actually came in quite handy in helping find the perfect wife for Isaac, because what better way to find a good woman than to use the "camel test." This was an important mission and the servant did not want to mess it up. He asked God to give him success and laid out his test. After his long journey, he would go to the spring and ask a woman for a drink of water, and if she obliged and also offered (on her own accord) to give water to the camels, she would be the one! I imagine that the servant was stunned to find that before he even finished telling God his plan, the beautiful Rebekah entered the scene with her water jar on her shoulder. Genesis 24:17-20 tells us what happens next, ***"Then the servant ran to meet her and said, 'Please give me a little water to drink from your jar.' She said, 'Drink, my lord.' And she quickly let down her jar upon her hand and gave him a drink. When she had finished giving him a drink, she said, 'I will draw water for your camels also, until they have finished drinking.' So she quickly emptied her jar into the trough and ran again to the well to draw water, and she drew for all his camels."*** Notice that not only does Rebekah offer to give a little water to the camels, she offers to water them until they are no longer thirsty. Back to me being honest, I would have totally failed this test, because this was some serious hard work. Camels drink a ton of water. One thirsty camel could easily finish off 20 gallons of water in less than a half hour. Multiply that by ten and consider that water jugs at this time held around two to three gallons. Even if the camels were only a little thirsty and drank 30 gallons each, that is 300 gallons of water. If we estimate the jugs held three gallons each (about 24 pounds), that is at least 100 trips back and forth to the spring! It would take an extremely kind and hardworking woman to offer to do this for a stranger on her own accord. This is exactly the kind of wife Abraham would have had in mind for his son. She was one who not only did what she was asked but would go completely out of her way to serve others. She could have easily given the man a drink and then just walked away, or begrudgingly offered her help and then complained when the work became too hard. Instead, out of the goodness of her heart, Rebekah put herself through extremely hard work for no apparent gain. She did not know that she was being tested, and yet her godly character was impossible to miss. It was this godly character that opened the door to her destiny, and God blessed her greatly.

It is unlikely I will ever have to rely on my ridiculously weak arms to give water to a bunch of thirsty camels (and if so, hopefully, I am strong enough to twist the hose spout), but I am reminded that every day brings opportunity for us to go out of our way to serve others. One of the greatest investments we can make in this life is developing a godly character and letting it shine for the world to see. Even when it is extra hard, or when there is seemingly nothing in it for us, the blessing is always waiting on the other side.

DO NOT DELAY

ISAAC & REBEKAH, DEVOTION 4

Ryan & Cathy Story | *Location Pastor - Burton*

Could you imagine buying a house without seeing it first? Would you consider getting a new car without looking it over? How about choosing the person you will spend the rest of your life with, would you be willing to jump into marriage sight unseen? Chances are you answered "no" in regards to each of those questions. We live in a time where online purchases are the norm. You can order just about anything you can think of having, knowing that if it does not actually fit the way you wanted, work the way you expected, or is the actual color you imagined, you can simply return it. No commitment is necessary.

In Genesis chapter 24, Abraham sent his servant to find a bride for his son Isaac. Verses 1-53 give the account of Abraham's charge to his servant, the travels, meeting of a young woman, Rebekah, and the servant's request for her to return back to his master with him. These verses portray the goodness of God and his faithfulness in provision. In verses 54-56 the servant showed no delay in wanting to leave and return to Abraham and Isaac with Rebekah. In verse 58, ***"And they called Rebekah and said to her, 'Will you go with this man?' She said, 'I will go.'"*** When reading, I pause here because I cannot imagine the boldness it took to say those three simple words. Rebekah is going to marry a man she has never met, sight unseen.

Personally, I struggle with this. I cannot even decide if I want to move the couch in my living room without actually seeing it first! I do not do well with being told to picture something; I need to see it to really picture that idea in my mind. Even more than a concept, I struggle with spontaneity. I am definitely a planner and thrive off of routines. I want to know as many details as possible before jumping into a major decision. I am challenged as I look at Rebekah. God had clearly orchestrated the meeting between her and the servant, and she recognized that. Prior to Rebekah's statement that she would go, verse 55 shows Rebekah's mother and brother saying, ***"Let the young woman remain with us a while, at least ten days; after that she may go."*** How easy would it have been for Rebekah to tell the servant that despite all of the ways they could see this had been God's plan, she was going to listen to her family and wait just a few more days before leaving? How often do I do this in my own life? How often do you do it in yours? You know God has called you to make that move, finalize that decision, or make that call, but you would really rather wait just a few more days. We like to ask and wait for just one more sign, one more indication that those choices are truly what God is asking of us. We find ourselves lacking Rebekah's boldness in saying "I will go."

Hebrews 11:1 states, ***"Now faith is the assurance of things hoped for, the conviction of things not seen."*** Sometimes our faith is making moves, sight unseen. Now, there certainly are times where planning is important, but there are also times where we are being called to trust and show our faith in our willingness to do what God is asking of us.

We are all called to go, to share Christ's love and the Good News with the world. Isaiah 6:8 writes, ***"And I heard the voice of the Lord saying, 'Whom shall I send, and who will go for us?' Then I said, 'Here I am! Send me.'"*** It can be easy to think that we would say, "Here I am Lord! I am willing to go!" but in reality, are you willing to be like Rebekah and actually go? The rest of Genesis chapter 24 recounts the servant and Rebekah traveling back to Canaan. She met and became one with Isaac. This all happened because she was willing to say, "I will go."

Today, what is God asking you to do? Where is He calling you to go that you have been delaying? As the servant says to Rebekah's family in verse 56, ***"But he said to them, 'Do not delay me…'"*** It is time to stop delaying and do what is being asked of us!

IMMEDIATE RESPONSE

ISAAC & REBEKAH, DEVOTION 5

Philip Piasecki

These days, we want everything fast. We want our food immediately once we order it. We want someone to respond to our text message the second that they receive it. We even get mad if our Amazon package takes longer than two days to arrive! It is incredible to think about this for a second, an item that you were able to order on the internet, from your couch, that is shipped from across the country, took longer than two days to show up on your porch and you are upset? The technology we have today, to have everything instantaneously is almost magic, and yet we still want it to be faster. We treat God like this in our prayer lives as well. He asks us to have patience, wait on Him, and we will see Him move. Other times, however, we are blessed to see an immediate response to our prayer. We see an example of this immediate response to prayer in the story of Isaac and Rebekah.

The last couple days we have been looking at different aspects of the story of Isaac and Rebekah from Genesis chapter 24. Abraham sends his servant with a seemingly impossible task, go to a different country, find a wife for my son, and bring her back here. I love verse 12, ***"And he said, 'O Lord, God of my master Abraham, please grant me success today and show steadfast love to my master Abraham.'"*** I imagine the servant sitting there thinking unless God shows up this is going to be impossible, so he goes to the Lord in prayer. As we have seen the last couple of days, the Lord brings Rebekah to the servant, and he accomplishes the goal Abraham gave him. In verse 26 we see the servant's response, ***"The man bowed his head and worshiped the Lord."*** He had his prayer answered, and he immediately worshiped the Lord to thank Him.

There is so much to learn from this Scripture when we look at it from the perspective of the servant. Daily we will find ourselves in situations that seem impossible unless God steps in the middle of it. It is at those moments that we need to bring our situation before God and ask Him to bless. So often, we do not see answers to prayer because we do not even ask Him to do something! You are mistaken if you think that God does not step in during your day-to-day life. He wants to, He is willing, and He wants us to ask Him to help. Abraham's servant prayed and saw God immediately answer that prayer. We too can see God do incredible things like that in our life; we just need to commit to asking Him.

NO EXCUSES

ISAAC & REBEKAH, DEVOTION 6

Ryan Story | *Location Pastor - Burton*

People are interesting. People in group settings are even more interesting. While I am no sociologist, I have always been fascinated with one concept. Whenever a group of people are working together in any facet, family, work, or school, more often than not, one group seems to work just above the least active person. This may not be in every case but think about your life. For the majority of people, people like to work within the status quo. No one wants to be known as "the try hard," and no one wants to be known as the low man on the totem pole. Sadly, we sometimes have that mentality when it comes to living for Jesus. We may not say it publicly, but we often think, that someone is living for Jesus a "little bit too much" or thinking, well I may not be a perfect parent, but at least my kid did not turn out like that kid. We live in a unique culture; we live in a culture that does not like pushing each other to achieve a goal. Since we live in such an individualistic society, we tend to only look out for ourselves. This is not what the Bible tells us to do. We are meant to push each other to live for Jesus more and more. We should want others to succeed more than us in our walk with God. But it seems like we tend to try to slow others down, so we do not look bad.

There is one character I have never really liked in the Bible, and it is Isaac. I have never seen him as anything more than a dweeb. In Genesis chapter 24, Abraham sends a servant to find his son a wife. Again, dweeb, a man is meant to find his wife, but I will relent. Abraham told his servant to look for a woman with particular qualities, and she needed to do something particular. Take some time to read the story to figure out what those are. Eventually, the servant finds Rebekah. When the servant goes and asks Rebekah to leave with her to do what God wants of Rebekah, her family says something interesting. In Genesis 24:55-56, it says, ***"Her brother and her mother said, 'Let the young woman remain with us a while, at least ten days; after that she may go.' But he said to them, 'Do not delay me, since the Lord has prospered my way. Send me away that I may go to my master.'"*** Even though Rebekah's family agreed that God had a plan for her, they still tried to slow her down! For Rebekah to say, "do not delay me" is something I wish I were able to have in my walk with God.

My favorite thing about living for Jesus is there is no ceiling for how far we want to take it. If you want to read the Bible, do it. You cannot say that someone delayed you. If you do not read, game is on you. If you want to pray with someone at work or school, do it. Do not let situational awkwardness delay you. If you want to serve, do it. Do not let your schedule hinder you from being used by God. So often we live to the level of the lowest level of expectation. We all know times when people have slowed us down, but we also know that we tend to slow ourselves down more than anyone else. Stop making excuses for living for Jesus. Stop letting people, schedules, excuses, or past hurt slow you down.

13

JACOB & ESAU

DR. RANDY T. JOHNSON,
GROWTH PASTOR

Through the years, I have collected a variety of sports and entertainment memorabilia. I have an autographed baseball by Babe Ruth, a signed picture by the Olympian Jesse Owens, and personalized Ping-Pong paddles by Lady Antebellum. However, my most unique piece is probably an autographed 8" x 10" movie photo. Arnold Schwarzenegger (6' 3" and 230 pounds) and Danny Devito (4' 10" and 150 pounds) were on set for their 1988 film entitled "Twins." It is obviously a comedy seeing those two together as twins.

Twins seem to have a unique bond. In middle school, I played basketball with twin brothers. At first, the only way I could tell them apart was that Lyle had part of a finger missing due to a lawnmower accident. Later, I realized Louis had a slight mark on his nose. Eventually, it got much easier. When they teamed up, they were tough.

The Bible records at least three sets of twins. First, Genesis 38:27-30 speaks of Perez and Zerah (there is an interesting story about a scarlet thread). Second, the disciple Thomas who is often known as "Doubting Thomas" was also called "Twin" (John 11:16). Finally, the most famous twins in the Bible are Jacob and Esau (Genesis chapters 25-33).

Were you raised knowing any twins? Do you have any funny stories about them?

___

___

___

Although Jacob and Esau were twins, they were about as similar as Arnold Schwarzenegger and Danny Devito. Their interests, personalities, and parental favoritism are displayed in Scripture.

There are three noteworthy situations that happened while they both still lived at home. Each aspect lasted less than 24 hours, but still impacts the world today.

1. Determined at Birth

Even before day one, the boys were wrestling. This was more than the exciting "Oh, I felt him kick" feeling. The boys were wreaking havoc for mom, and it carried over into their birth.

Genesis 25:19-26 records MMA season one, ***"These are the generations of Isaac, Abraham's son: Abraham fathered Isaac, and Isaac was forty years old when he took Rebekah, the daughter of Bethuel the Aramean of Paddan-aram, the sister of Laban the Aramean, to be his wife. And Isaac prayed to the Lord for his wife, because she was barren. And the Lord granted his prayer, and Rebekah his wife conceived. The children struggled together within her, and she said, 'If it is thus, why is this happening to me?' So she went to inquire of the Lord. And the Lord said to her, 'Two nations are in your womb, and two peoples from within you shall be divided; the one shall be stronger than the other, the older shall serve the younger.' When her days to give birth were completed, behold, there were twins in her womb. The first came out red, all his body like a hairy cloak, so they called his name Esau. Afterward his brother came out with his hand holding Esau's heel, so his name was called Jacob. Isaac was sixty years old when she bore them."***

How long did Isaac and Rebekah have to wait to have children? Why do you think God had it this way?

____

____

____

What prophecy did the Lord give Rebekah concerning the boys?

___

___

___

What unique thing happened at their birth and what could that signify?

___

___

___

2. Deal for Birthright

God had a plan for both boys right from their birth. His plan did not match up well with the traditions of the day. However, we see how they started to unfold in Genesis 25:27-34, ***"When the boys grew up, Esau was a skillful hunter, a man of the field, while Jacob was a quiet man, dwelling in tents. Isaac loved Esau because he ate of his game, but Rebekah loved Jacob. Once when Jacob was cooking stew, Esau came in from the field, and he was exhausted. And Esau said to Jacob, 'Let me eat some of that red stew, for I am exhausted!' (Therefore his name was called Edom.) Jacob said, 'Sell me your birthright now.' Esau said, 'I am about to die; of what use is a birthright to me?' Jacob said, 'Swear to me now.' So he swore to him and sold his birthright to Jacob. Then Jacob gave Esau bread and lentil stew, and he ate and drank and rose and went his way. Thus Esau despised his birthright."***

Describe Esau.

___

___

___

Describe Jacob.

Which son represents you best? How?

What happened in this story concerning the birthright?

Who do you think is in the wrong?

3. Disguise for Blessing

The birthright gave the oldest son a double portion of the inheritance when dad died. Jacob now owned that claim. The blessing was when the father spoke truth into the lives of his sons. The oldest son tended to be "dad's favorite" and would receive the best blessing. Jacob not only received the birthright, but Genesis chapter 27 shows how he was able to get the better blessing, too.

Genesis 27:1-4 says, ***"When Isaac was old and his eyes were dim so that he could not see, he called Esau his older son and said to him, 'My son'; and he answered, 'Here I am.' He said, 'Behold, I am old; I do not know the day of my death. Now then, take your***

weapons, your quiver and your bow, and go out to the field and hunt game for me, and prepare for me delicious food, such as I love, and bring it to me so that I may eat, that my soul may bless you before I die.'"

How does this section try to undermine God's voiced plan given to Rebekah at the birth of the boys?

____

____

____

Rebekah plots against her husband and for her favored son in Genesis 27:5-17, ***"Now Rebekah was listening when Isaac spoke to his son Esau. So when Esau went to the field to hunt for game and bring it, Rebekah said to her son Jacob, 'I heard your father speak to your brother Esau, 'Bring me game and prepare for me delicious food, that I may eat it and bless you before the Lord before I die.' Now therefore, my son, obey my voice as I command you. Go to the flock and bring me two good young goats, so that I may prepare from them delicious food for your father, such as he loves. And you shall bring it to your father to eat, so that he may bless you before he dies.' But Jacob said to Rebekah his mother, 'Behold, my brother Esau is a hairy man, and I am a smooth man. Perhaps my father will feel me, and I shall seem to be mocking him and bring a curse upon myself and not a blessing.' His mother said to him, 'Let your curse be on me, my son; only obey my voice, and go, bring them to me.' So he went and took them and brought them to his mother, and his mother prepared delicious food, such as his father loved. Then Rebekah took the best garments of Esau her older son, which were with her in the house, and put them on Jacob her younger son. And the skins of the young goats she put on his hands and on the smooth part of his neck. And she put the delicious food and the bread, which she had prepared, into the hand of her son Jacob."***

What was Rebekah's plan?

Was Jacob more concerned with doing something wrong or getting caught?

Who is at fault the most in this story – Isaac, Rebekah, Esau, or Jacob? Why?

Verses 18-25 record Jacob's success in deceiving his father. Genesis 27:26-29 gives the blessing for Jacob, ***"Then his father Isaac said to him, 'Come near and kiss me, my son.' So he came near and kissed him. And Isaac smelled the smell of his garments and blessed him and said, 'See, the smell of my son is as the smell of a field that the Lord has blessed! May God give you of the dew of heaven and of the fatness of the earth and plenty of grain and wine. Let peoples serve you, and nations bow down to you. Be lord over your brothers, and may your mother's sons bow down to you. Cursed be everyone who curses you, and blessed be everyone who blesses you!'"***

Summarize the blessing given to Jacob.

The story continues with Esau entering the house soon after Jacob receives the blessing of the firstborn (verses 30-35). Esau summarizes his life in verse 36, ***"Esau said, 'Is he not rightly named Jacob? For he has cheated me these two times. He took away my birthright, and behold, now he has taken away my blessing.' Then he said, 'Have you not reserved a blessing for me?'"***

Isaac summarizes the blessing he gave Jacob (verses 37-38) before he blesses Esau in verses 39-40, ***"Then Isaac his father answered and said to him: 'Behold, away from the fatness of the earth shall your dwelling be, and away from the dew of heaven on high. By your sword you shall live, and you shall serve your brother; but when you grow restless you shall break his yoke from your neck.'"***

Summarize the "blessing" given to Esau.

____

____

____

How would you feel and respond if you were Esau?

____

____

____

The chapter, and story for now, ends with Jacob fleeing for his life because the only thing that brings comfort to Esau is thinking of all the ways he could kill his brother.

Jacob works for his uncle, marries Leah and Rachel, has numerous children, becomes financially successful, and wants to head back home. He left home some 20 years earlier. While traveling, he finds out that Esau is approaching. In fear, he plots an escape route, but

Genesis 33:4 shows a new heart in Esau, ***"But Esau ran to meet him and embraced him and fell on his neck and kissed him, and they wept."***

What emotions do you think Jacob and Esau were experiencing?

____

____

____

Who do you need to forgive or make things right?

____

____

____

"Darkness cannot drive out darkness; only light can do that. Hate cannot drive out hate; only love can do that." Martin Luther King, Jr.

"We must develop and maintain the capacity to forgive. He who is devoid of the power to forgive is devoid of the power to love. There is some good in the worst of us and some evil in the best of us. When we discover this, we are less prone to hate our enemies." Martin Luther King, Jr.

PROPHECY & BIRTH

JACOB & ESAU, DEVOTION 1

Mark O'Connor | *Student Director*

Would it not be great as parents, if God were to let us know well in advance what it was that our children were going to be and what we were supposed to do? I wonder how I would look like a father if that were the case. Would my interactions with my kids be different? Would my personality today be the same?

We sometimes think about how much easier life would be if God would just lay out the path as clear as we could possibly see it. Think about it; if you knew from day one what it was you were going to be doing when you were grown, you would never have to stress about anything. Mark, this is what you were meant for, this is what your wife and kids are meant to do. I mean, how could we make a mess of it?

We see a family in Genesis chapter 25 that had a path laid out for them. From God Himself, Rebekah is told what her boys would be. Both would be leaders of a nation. One would be stronger than the other, but the older would serve the younger. They come into the world as God intended. Esau was full of hair, while Jacob's skin was a smooth as a baby's butt, confirming once again that God knew what He was talking about and is to be trusted. They had an idea of what was going to transpire in the coming years but were unsure of how they were going to get there. This all worked out in the end, but there was a deception involved that we really could not begin to understand. There is a deception on the part of both a wife and son.

It is a very difficult thing to wrestle with, and I would be lying if I said I totally understood it. Here is what I do know. While I am not always going to understand the how and why of the way things happen, I have seen and learned enough to know that it is all part of a much bigger plan than I will ever be able to understand. We can have some peace in that if we begin to look at it through the correct lens. We do not have to know how or why, we just trust that God is in control of taking care of it. It may not be exactly how we want it to go, but it gets us there.

UNIQUENESS & PARENTAL RELATIONSHIP

JACOB & ESAU, DEVOTION 2

Isaiah Combs | *Worship Leader*

I grew up in a large family. There are five of us kids, and my Dad is like having five more people around. I think it is amazing that even though we all grew up together and still spend a lot of time together, we are all very different people. We all have different interests, styles, and personalities. There is a story in Genesis about two brothers named Jacob and Esau. They are the two sons of Isaac, who is Abraham's only son with his wife, Sarah.

The two sons, just like my brothers and I, were opposites. Jacob was more of, for lack of a better term, a Mama's boy, who was more comfortable inside cooking and cleaning. Genesis says he was a quiet man. Jacob's brother, Esau, was the hunter type. Genesis said he was a "Man of the Field." In our society, Esau would probably be called a man's man.

It is easy to figure out who was whose favorite. Jacob, because he spent more time with his mom in the house, was his mom's favorite. We always mocked my mom growing up and even now. We tell her its clear that my little brother Luke is her favorite (It is a joke, and I have an awesome mom). Luke is seven years younger than me, is my mom's baby boy, and is for sure a mama's boy. He and my mom have a special relationship, He was left in the house for seven years with my mom after we older boys had grown up and left the house.

Esau was his dad Isaac's favorite because like all men we think with our stomach (This would get Esau in some trouble later). Esau would feed his dad the meat he would acquire through his hunt and kill. He was also the first born and would receive the birthright and inheritance from his father.

These parent relationships between these four would end up playing a big role in the shaping of God's chosen people.

Genesis 25:27-28 says, ***"When the boys grew up, Esau was a skillful hunter, a man of the field, while Jacob was a quiet man, dwelling in tents. Isaac loved Esau because he ate of his game, but Rebekah loved Jacob."***

It is good to let our children pursue their interests and enjoy them in those moments. Too often parents want to live their life through their child.

ESAU SELLS BIRTHRIGHT

JACOB & ESAU, DEVOTION 3

James Clouse | *Student Pastor*

Do you live for the here and now? Is it important to satisfy the immediate needs in your life? In life, I feel that we often live life for the here and now. We often live life for what can satisfy the immediate need placed before us. When we are hungry, we live in the land of fast food, or the here and now. When we want coffee, there are numerous places whether it be Starbucks or Tim Hortons. When we need stuff, there is usually a mall or shopping center no further than 20 minutes away. While satisfying these needs is not wrong, or a sin, we need to ask ourselves as a church if we live more for the here and now or more for the eternity of our future.

Esau was one who lived for the here and now. Genesis 25:29-34 says, ***"Once when Jacob was cooking stew, Esau came in from the field, and he was exhausted. And Esau said to Jacob, 'Let me eat some of that red stew, for I am exhausted!' (Therefore his name was called Edom.) Jacob said, 'Sell me your birthright now.' Esau said, 'I am about to die; of what use is a birthright to me?' Jacob said, 'Swear to me now.' So he swore to him and sold his birthright to Jacob. Then Jacob gave Esau bread and lentil stew, and he ate and drank and rose and went his way. Thus Esau despised his birthright."***

More people tend to focus on Jacob in this story when realizing that he forced the hand of his brother. But think on Esau for a bit. We first need to understand the importance of the birthright at this time.

God uses the divine birthright to bring the birth of His son Jesus Christ. What an amazing blessing to be used in such a way. So a birthright was not only the inheritance and leadership of his family, but he was in the direct line to Jesus! How can Esau give away such a blessing? Esau gives this all up for a bowl of soup. We do not know if Esau was exaggerating here or if he was truly near death. However, John Calvin writes, "It would have been his true wisdom rather to undergo a thousand deaths than to renounce his birthright; which, so far from being confined within the narrow limits of one age alone, was capable of transmitting the perpetuity of a heavenly life to his posterity also."

Esau missed out on a true blessing to fulfill the here and now. In our own lives, we need to look to the reality of our future instead of the here and now. What is important to me? Is the most important thing about money or success? Is the best choice to climb the corporate ladder? Could it be better to miss a day or two of work to serve the Lord and lead people for eternity to Christ?

I WILL DO IT MYSELF

JACOB & ESAU, DEVOTION 4

Ryan Story | *Location Pastor - Burton*

One of my favorite moments in recent cinema was at the end of *Avengers: Age of Ultron*. During the closing credits the "Mad Titan" Thanos appears and grabs his Infinity Gauntlet and says, "Fine, I will do it myself." Now as the comic book enthusiast that I am, I loved knowing what would be transpiring in the next two Avenger's movies. For years, Thanos was trying to accumulate the infinity stones, and he finally realized that he would have to be the one to do so. Now for those who have not read the comics, this may be a spoiler of Avengers 4, but in the comics, Thanos realizes that his quest for the stones brings nothing but emptiness and Thanos embraces the humble life of a farmer. Thanos realizes that the thing he was working towards ends up being the decision he loathes to the point of wanting to die just so he can see his love, Death.

Comic books and theology are my two strong suits in life. I have always loved reading comics, and I always enjoy reading the Bible. In Genesis chapter 27, the story about Jacob and Rebekah tricking Isaac to get the blessing is one of the most interesting stories in all of Genesis. The part I find so hard to ignore about this story is when Rebekah had trouble conceiving, she and Isaac went to God in prayer. Genesis 25:23 says, ***"And the Lord said to her, 'Two nations are in your womb, and two peoples from within you shall be divided; the one shall be stronger than the other; the older shall serve the younger.'"*** Rebekah knew from the moment Jacob and Esau were born who would be the one in control of the family legacy. Out of God's mouth, He said the older, Esau, would serve the younger, Jacob. If God said it, then it will come true. The question that plagues me is, why did Rebekah not just wait for God's perfect plan to come to fruition?

I have prayed over and pondered this section of Scripture many times. All I can see is Rebekah trying to force God's plan. Rebekah decided that she did not want to wait for God's plan; she wanted to do it her way in her timing. Read Genesis chapter 27 at some point today. Rebekah helps her son con her husband just so Rebekah's favorite would get what she wanted. While this very well could have been God's plan, I do not think God was honoring her sin. Rebekah goes down in history for eternity as a person who lied, cheated, and stole something that God already knew He was going to give.

I feel we all tend to try to force God's plan into existing instead of waiting for His timing. Because of Rebekah's involvement, Esau decides that he is going to kill Jacob, and Rebekah tells Jacob to flee. It is one of the weirdest self-focused "woe is me" moments in the Bible. In Genesis 27:46, Rebekah goes to Isaac and says, ***"Then Rebekah said to Isaac, 'I loathe my life because of the Hittite women. If Jacob marries one of the Hittite women like these, one of the women of the land, what good will my life be to me?'"*** Rebekah is distraught over the fact that her son had to flee when she was the reason he had to flee! In my mind, this is the justice of the Lord on display. She tried to force what God already had planned into a reality.

Do you ever feel like you are chasing after something or feel like you hate your current circumstances? I have seen people want to be married so badly that they hate the fact that they are single. There is no realization that their singleness is a gift that God gave them for this stage of their life. I know this is a hard thing to read, trust me there is apprehension to type this, but sometimes we have to be able to wait on God, even for something that is good. Rebekah could not wait, she took it upon herself and caused a whole lot of family drama just because she could not be patient.

BLESSED & BLESSING

JACOB & ESAU, DEVOTION 5

Dr. Randy T. Johnson | *Growth Pastor*

"Jacob left Beersheba and went toward Haran. And he came to a certain place and stayed there that night, because the sun had set. Taking one of the stones of the place, he put it under his head and lay down in that place to sleep. And he dreamed, and behold, there was a ladder set up on the earth, and the top of it reached to heaven. And behold, the angels of God were ascending and descending on it! And behold, the Lord stood above it and said, 'I am the Lord, the God of Abraham your father and the God of Isaac. The land on which you lie I will give to you and to your offspring. Your offspring shall be like the dust of the earth, and you shall spread abroad to the west and to the east and to the north and to the south, and in you and your offspring shall all the families of the earth be blessed. Behold, I am with you and will keep you wherever you go, and will bring you back to this land. For I will not leave you until I have done what I have promised you.' Then Jacob awoke from his sleep and said, 'Surely the Lord is in this place, and I did not know it.' And he was afraid and said, 'How awesome is this place! This is none other than the house of God, and this is the gate of heaven.'"
Genesis 28:10-17

This might be the first time you have ever read this story. Jacob had a life-altering dream. I have read that everyone dreams, but that not everyone remembers their dreams. Jacob had a dream and it embedded his mind the whole next day and throughout his life. His dream was important to him because he knew God made a promise to him in his dream.

Genesis 28:18-22 tells what Jacob did once he had been blessed by God, ***"So early in the morning Jacob took the stone that he had put under his head and set it up for a pillar and poured oil on the top of it. He called the name of that place Bethel, but the name of the city was Luz at the first. Then Jacob made a vow, saying, 'If God will be with me and will keep me in this way that I go, and will give me bread to eat and clothing to wear, so that I come again to my father's house in peace, then the Lord shall be my God, and this stone, which I have set up for a pillar, shall be God's house. And of all that you give me I will give a full tenth to you.'"***

Jacob was blessed by God, so he wanted to be a blessing to God. He also chose to set up a visual reminder for himself so that when he saw it, the stone would remind him of God's blessing.

What do you do when you have been blessed by God? Do you look for ways to bless Him through others? I encourage you to "count your many blessings." Look for God to bless you and then set up a visual reminder for yourself. Journal of the event. Write the date in your Bible. Post a picture or plant a tree that every time you see it, you remember the blessing from God. Be blessed and be a blessing!

ESAU FORGIVES JACOB

JACOB & ESAU, DEVOTION 6

Michael Fox | *Creative Director*

Have you ever needed to be forgiven for something? I have! I have broken things, mistreated friends and family, and used hurtful words. If you have experienced forgiveness, you know how powerful it can be. Ultimately, God has forgiven us for our sin through the sacrifice of His Son, Jesus. This is a beautiful thing, something we do not deserve. In Genesis chapter 33, we see a picture of forgiveness played out in the story of Jacob and Esau, twin brothers in the Old Testament.

If you are not familiar with the story, take a moment to read Genesis chapter 27. In Genesis 27:14-19, we see the story unfold when Jacob stole the blessing of his father from Esau, who was entitled to it: ***"So he went and took them and brought them to his mother, and his mother prepared delicious food, such as his father loved. Then Rebekah took the best garments of Esau her older son, which were with her in the house, and put them on Jacob her younger son. And the skins of the young goats she put on his hands and on the smooth part of his neck. And she put the delicious food and the bread, which she had prepared, into the hand of her son Jacob. So he went into his father and said, 'My father.' And he said, 'Here I am. Who are you, my son?' Jacob said to his father, 'I am Esau your firstborn. I have done as you told me; now sit up and eat of my game, that your soul may bless me.'"***

Skipping ahead a little, we see Esau's reaction to Jacob taking the blessing that was rightfully his. Genesis 27:41 says, ***"Now Esau hated Jacob because of the blessing with which his father had blessed him, and Esau said to himself, 'The days of mourning for my father are approaching; then I will kill my brother Jacob.'"***

At this point, there was a bit of family drama. One brother stole something that was rightfully his, something rather large. His mother helped him do it. Now, Jacob's mother encourages him to basically run away and hide, as his brother wants to kill him. Work your way through the story, and in Genesis 33:4 when Jacob and Esau finally meet again, we see forgiveness play out, ***"But Esau ran to meet him and embraced him and fell on his neck and kissed him, and they wept."***

Is there someone in your life today that you might need to forgive? Is there someone you offended or wronged, and you need to seek forgiveness? As you reflect and pray on this, here are a few promises from God about forgiveness.

"Bearing with one another and, if one has a complaint against another, forgiving each other; as the Lord has forgiven you, so you also must forgive." Colossians 3:13

"Pay attention to yourselves! If your brother sins, rebuke him, and if he repents, forgive him, and if he sins against you seven times in the day, and turns to you seven times, saying, 'I repent,' you must forgive him." Luke 17:3-4

"If we confess our sins, he is faithful and just to forgive us our sins and to cleanse us from all unrighteousness." 1 John 1:9

14

LEAH & RACHEL

DR. RANDY T. JOHNSON,
GROWTH PASTOR

I have a silly philosophy; I believe any item of food can be improved by adding cheese, chocolate, or bacon to it. I am not saying it is healthy, but people add cheese to hamburger, vegetables, and even apple pie. Have you heard of chocolate covered bacon or bacon flavored ice cream? It is common to put some bacon in the "healthy" green beans. Fruit is regularly dipped in chocolate because many believe, "If it is not chocolate, it is not dessert."

What is your favorite meal, snack, or dessert?

____

____

____

While cheese, chocolate, and bacon can add some flavor to any recipe, too much is still too much. Last Christmas, our family went to a Brazilian Steakhouse. They had sixteen different ways they prepared the meat. There was chicken, steak, pork, and of course bacon. It was too good, but more is not always better. Vanilla is helpful in baking, but too much can wreck the treat. A 4" lift on a truck looks cool (even though I am too short to get in the truck), but enough is enough. In the Book of Genesis, Jacob found out that one wife is good, but two wives can cause some strife.

The saga of Jacob with Leah and Rachel starts off as a beautiful love story. Genesis 29:9-20 records how Jacob met the ladies, ***"While he was still speaking with them, Rachel came with her father's sheep, for she was a shepherdess. Now as soon as Jacob saw Rachel the daughter of Laban his mother's brother, and the sheep of Laban his mother's brother, Jacob came near and rolled the stone from the well's mouth and watered the flock of Laban his mother's brother. Then Jacob kissed Rachel and wept aloud. And Jacob told Rachel that he was her father's kinsman, and that he was Rebekah's son, and she ran and told***

her father. As soon as Laban heard the news about Jacob, his sister's son, he ran to meet him and embraced him and kissed him and brought him to his house. Jacob told Laban all these things, and Laban said to him, 'Surely you are my bone and my flesh!' And he stayed with him a month. Then Laban said to Jacob, 'Because you are my kinsman, should you therefore serve me for nothing? Tell me, what shall your wages be?' Now Laban had two daughters. The name of the older was Leah, and the name of the younger was Rachel. Leah's eyes were weak, but Rachel was beautiful in form and appearance. Jacob loved Rachel. And he said, 'I will serve you seven years for your younger daughter Rachel.' Laban said, 'It is better that I give her to you than that I should give her to any other man; stay with me.' So Jacob served seven years for Rachel, and they seemed to him but a few days because of the love he had for her."

Is love at first sight possible?

____

____

____

What business agreement was made?

____

____

____

What kind of things are worth waiting for today?

____

____

____

The great love story takes a drastic shift as the deceiver is deceived. In Genesis 29:21-30, Laban tricks Jacob, ***"Then Jacob***

said to Laban, 'Give me my wife that I may go in to her, for my time is completed.' So Laban gathered together all the people of the place and made a feast. But in the evening he took his daughter Leah and brought her to Jacob, and he went in to her. (Laban gave his female servant Zilpah to his daughter Leah to be her servant.) And in the morning, behold, it was Leah! And Jacob said to Laban, 'What is this you have done to me? Did I not serve with you for Rachel? Why then have you deceived me?' Laban said, 'It is not so done in our country, to give the younger before the firstborn. Complete the week of this one, and we will give you the other also in return for serving me another seven years.' Jacob did so, and completed her week. Then Laban gave him his daughter Rachel to be his wife. (Laban gave his female servant Bilhah to his daughter Rachel to be her servant.) So Jacob went in to Rachel also, and he loved Rachel more than Leah, and served Laban for another seven years."

Who did Jacob previously deceive?

How is Jacob deceived in this story?

How is deception wrong? How does it hurt the deceiver?

The majority of the story of Leah and Rachel centers around the "Baby Contest." Each woman goes to great lengths to get Jacob's attention and love. It gives them a sense of value. The drama is mainly recorded in these three passages.

"When the Lord saw that Leah was hated, he opened her womb, but Rachel was barren. And Leah conceived and bore a son, and she called his name Reuben, for she said, 'Because the Lord has looked upon my affliction; for now my husband will love me.' She conceived again and bore a son, and said, 'Because the Lord has heard that I am hated, he has given me this son also.' And she called his name Simeon. Again she conceived and bore a son, and said, 'Now this time my husband will be attached to me, because I have borne him three sons.' Therefore his name was called Levi. And she conceived again and bore a son, and said, 'This time I will praise the Lord.' Therefore she called his name Judah. Then she ceased bearing." Genesis 29:31-35

"When Rachel saw that she bore Jacob no children, she envied her sister. She said to Jacob, 'Give me children, or I shall die!' Jacob's anger was kindled against Rachel, and he said, 'Am I in the place of God, who has withheld from you the fruit of the womb?' Then she said, 'Here is my servant Bilhah; go in to her, so that she may give birth on my behalf, that even I may have children through her.' So she gave him her servant Bilhah as a wife, and Jacob went in to her. And Bilhah conceived and bore Jacob a son. Then Rachel said, 'God has judged me, and has also heard my voice and given me a son.' Therefore she called his name Dan. Rachel's servant Bilhah conceived again and bore Jacob a second son. Then Rachel said, 'With mighty wrestlings I have wrestled with my sister and have prevailed.' So she called his name Naphtali. When Leah saw that she had ceased bearing children, she took her servant Zilpah and gave her to Jacob as

a wife. Then Leah's servant Zilpah bore Jacob a son. And Leah said, 'Good fortune has come!' so she called his name Gad. Leah's servant Zilpah bore Jacob a second son. And Leah said, 'Happy am I! For women have called me happy.' So she called his name Asher. In the days of wheat harvest Reuben went and found mandrakes in the field and brought them to his mother Leah. Then Rachel said to Leah, 'Please give me some of your son's mandrakes.' But she said to her, 'Is it a small matter that you have taken away my husband? Would you take away my son's mandrakes also?' Rachel said, 'Then he may lie with you tonight in exchange for your son's mandrakes.' When Jacob came from the field in the evening, Leah went out to meet him and said, 'You must come in to me, for I have hired you with my son's mandrakes.' So he lay with her that night. And God listened to Leah, and she conceived and bore Jacob a fifth son. Leah said, 'God has given me my wages because I gave my servant to my husband.' So she called his name Issachar. And Leah conceived again, and she bore Jacob a sixth son. Then Leah said, 'God has endowed me with a good endowment; now my husband will honor me, because I have borne him six sons.' So she called his name Zebulun. Afterward she bore a daughter and called her name Dinah. Then God remembered Rachel, and God listened to her and opened her womb. She conceived and bore a son and said, 'God has taken away my reproach.' And she called his name Joseph, saying, 'May the Lord add to me another son!'" Genesis 30:1-24

"Then they journeyed from Bethel. When they were still some distance from Ephrath, Rachel went into labor, and she had hard labor. And when her labor was at its hardest, the midwife said to her, 'Do not fear, for you have another son.' And as her soul was departing (for she was dying), she called his name Ben-oni; but his father called him Benjamin. So Rachel died, and she

was buried on the way to Ephrath (that is, Bethlehem)." Genesis 35:16-19

List the name of Jacob's children with the corresponding mother.

Leah	**Zilpah**	**Bilhah**	**Rachel**
1.	1.	1.	1.
2.	2.	2.	
3.			
4.			
5.			
6.			
7.			

What surprised you about the story?

____

____

____

In Genesis chapter 29 we read, ***"Leah's eyes were weak, but Rachel was beautiful in form and appearance."*** Rachel (meaning "ewe") was beautiful, while Leah (meaning "cow") was not pleasant to the eyes. However, Genesis chapter 30 starts off with the phrase, ***"When Rachel saw that she bore Jacob no children, she envied her sister."***

What does envy mean?

____

____

____

How does envy hurt us today?

____

____

____

"Jealousy is both reasonable and belongs to reasonable men, while envy is base and belongs to the base, for the one makes himself get good things by jealousy, while the other does not allow his neighbor to have them through envy." Aristotle

The Bible warns about the dangers of unconfined envy.

James 3:16 says, ***"For where jealousy and selfish ambition exist, there will be disorder and every vile practice."***

Proverbs 14:30 says, ***"A tranquil heart gives life to the flesh, but envy makes the bones rot."***

Galatians 5:19-21 says, ***"Now the works of the flesh are evident: sexual immorality, impurity, sensuality, idolatry, sorcery, enmity, strife, jealousy, fits of anger, rivalries, dissensions, divisions, envy, drunkenness, orgies, and things like these. I warn you, as I warned you before, that those who do such things will not inherit the kingdom of God."***

Envy is dangerous and can consume us, but it does not have to control us.

1 Corinthians 10:13 says, ***"No temptation has overtaken you that is not common to man. God is faithful, and he will not let you be tempted beyond your ability, but with the temptation he will also provide the way of escape, that you may be able to endure it."***

JACOB WRESTLES WITH GOD

LEAH & RACHEL, DEVOTION 1

Isaiah Combs | *Worship Leader*

When I was a kid, my brothers and I would wake up on Saturday mornings and would watch our favorite wrestler, Hulk Hogan. He was the best. After we finished watching, we would then engage in some brotherly wrestling of our own. We would practice our best wrestling moves on each other, and most of the time get in trouble because we would break something in the house. As we grew older, we all became bigger and stronger, and the wrestling became a little more intense. To this day we still will wrestle my Dad to get back at him for all the times he beat us at wrestling as kids.

You can read a lot about a person when you wrestle with them. You find out how strong that person is, how hard they are willing to work to beat you and are they willing to do anything to win? Their true character will come out through adversity and struggle.

In the Bible, God has a one-on-one wrestling match with Jacob. I know what you are thinking, "God could beat Jacob at any time with one finger." I believe God was trying to find some things out about Jacob's character. God found out that Jacob was the perfect man to be the namesake of Israel.

Genesis 32:22-32 records the match, ***"The same night he arose and took his two wives, his two female servants, and his eleven children, and crossed the ford of the Jabbok. He took them and sent them across the stream, and everything else that he had. And Jacob was left alone. And a man wrestled with him until the breaking of the day. When the man saw that he did not prevail against Jacob, he touched his hip socket, and Jacob's hip was*** *put out of joint as he wrestled with him. Then he said, 'Let me go, for the day has broken.' But Jacob said, 'I will not let you go unless you bless me.' And he said to him, 'What is your name?' And he said, 'Jacob.' Then he said, 'Your name shall no longer be called Jacob, but Israel, for you have striven with God and with men, and have prevailed.' Then Jacob asked him, 'Please tell me your name.' But he said, 'Why is it that you ask my name?' And there he blessed him. So Jacob called the name of the place Peniel, saying, 'For I have seen God face to face, and yet my life has been delivered.' The sun rose upon him as he passed Penuel, limping because of his hip. Therefore to this day, the people of Israel do not eat the sinew of the thigh that is on the hip socket, because he touched the socket of Jacob's hip on the sinew of the thigh."*

HIS BEST

LEAH & RACHEL, DEVOTION 2

Holly Boston | *Women's Ministry Director*

I am privileged to be the mother of an amazing young man with Autism. There are three words I would use to describe John "Carter": loving, sensitive, and compliant (to a fault). When Carter was young, I often tried to talk to him about Jesus and the sacrifice He made for him on the cross. I was always met with Carter sobbing and unable to listen. I was so afraid he would never come to know Christ. After all, if he struggled with having relationships with people he could see and hear, how would he ever experience a personal relationship with his Savior? Realizing there was nothing I could do, I prayed and gave my boy to God. Three years later, Carter came to me and said, "I want Jesus in my heart." I then witnessed him pray the most beautiful prayer, tell his entire extended family (unbelievers who assumed he knew Christ because I do), and then practice baptizing himself in a hot tub. All of it was unprompted by Mom. If this is not God's best, I do not know what is.

When I was asked to write about Jacob marrying Leah and Rachel, I considered topics like sowing and reaping, patience, love, and envy. But the comment I kept coming back to was that there was no indication that Jacob prayed before searching for a wife. In Genesis chapter 29, we learn that Jacob apparently fell in love at first sight, ***"Leah's eyes were weak, but Rachel was beautiful in form and appearance"*** (Genesis 29:17). Jacob was clearly following his flesh, not the Spirit. In 1 Samuel 16:7, we are taught that God does not choose people according to their appearance but the heart. We would be wise to do the same.

If you continue to read the story, you will see that Laban (future father-in-law) agreed to give Rachel to Jacob in exchange for seven years of work; the customary price for a bride. After seven years, Jacob asked for Rachel, and through some crazy plot of deceit, Laban gave Jacob Leah instead of Rachel. How a man sleeps with a woman and does not realize it is not his wife is beyond comprehension. But, I digress. The story continues with Jacob continuing to pursue what he wants: Rachel. He agreed to another seven years of work and took a second wife. Please note: Still no praying. A battle ensues between the wives. There is barrenness, hatred, envy, and strife, not at all what God has in mind for us. Jeremiah 29:11 (NIV) says, ***"'For I know the plans I have for you,' declares the LORD, 'plans to prosper you and not to harm you, plans to give you hope and a future.'"***

Was all the pain and strife a result of not praying? Could all the heartache have been avoided? I believe so. If you fast forward a generation, you get a glimpse of God's best for Jacob.

"The book of the genealogy of Jesus Christ... Abraham was the father of Isaac, and Isaac the father of Jacob, and Jacob the father of Judah..." (Matthew 1:1-2).

Jacob's son, Judah, was chosen to be part of the lineage of Jesus Christ. It does not get any better than that! The kicker is Leah was his mother, not Rachel. This leaves many questions: Was he just supposed to marry Leah? Could he have received the fulfillment of God's promises through Leah and avoided all the drama and pain by praying and asking God if Rachel was His choice? I know that if I had gone immediately to God with my concerns about Carter, it would have saved me a lot of sleepless nights. At any time during those three years I could have gone to Carter and told him that he needed to pray to receive Jesus and he would have. He was obedient. But God in His mercy and grace intervened and answered my prayer in a way that I would never again question Carter's salvation. That is His best!

There is a second lesson. If you too have failed to give a decision or situation to God and went off on your path, there is hope. Joseph, son of Jacob, was chosen to save his entire family from a devastating famine (Genesis chapters 45-46). Guess who his mother was? Rachel (Genesis 30:23). That is awesome, but it is not His best. The lesson: God's mercy and grace trump all our mistakes and incredibly, all our sins. Though Jacob and his wives experienced the consequences of pursuing their desires, their way, God worked it all for good. Romans 8:28 (NIV) says, ***"And we know that in all things God works for the good of those who love him, who have been called according to his purpose."***

I do not know about you, but I want God's best! Sometimes God's plan requires us to endure pain to shape us and transform us. I do not see the need for unnecessary stress and chaos. As for me, I will pray then proceed.

NEVER ENOUGH

LEAH & RACHEL, DEVOTION 3

Ryan & Cathy Story | *Location Pastor - Burton*

Have you ever met someone who constantly seems negative? Negative people seem to have a skill at finding the bad in any situation that arises. It can seem that no matter what good may actually come their way, it just never seems to be enough. It does not matter what good seems to be in front of them, there is always something that could be better, cleaner, quieter, less full, more full, or any other issue they might deem as bad. While this mentality can be detrimental in itself, negativity can be abundantly even more destructive within a family. In Genesis chapters 29 and 30 we read about two sisters who are ruled by envy in their relationship with one another.

When we meet these two sisters, Jacob has been sent by his mother, Rebekah, to her brother Laban. Jacob sees Rachel, Laban's daughter, at a well and falls in love with her. Genesis chapter 29:16-17 informs us that, ***"Laban had two daughters the name of the older was Leah and the name of the younger was Rachel. Leah's eyes were weak, but Rachel was beautiful in form and appearance."*** One can imagine the rift these known differences may have caused between these sisters. I am certain that most people would not want to go through life being defined by the way they look. Jacob and Laban struck a deal that Jacob would work for seven years and at the end of that time, he would get to marry Rachel. After those seven years of work had passed and the wedding was to take place, Laban switched the daughters and Jacob ended up with Leah instead of Rachel. Jacob looked at Laban and in verse 25 said, ***"What is this you have done to me? Did I not serve with you for Rachel? Why then have you deceived***

me?" Think for just a moment about how this would have made Leah feel. Jacob and Laban agreed that Jacob would finish the wedding week, and then he would marry Rachel in exchange for another seven years of work. In verse 31 we are told, ***"When the Lord saw the Leah was hated, he opened her womb, but Rachel was barren."*** Leah ended up with four sons, while Rachel had none. Genesis 30 begins, ***"When Rachel saw that she bore Jacob no children, she envied her sister."***

Rachel was most likely not used to being outshined by her sister Leah. The song Never Enough sung by Loren Allred in the movie The Greatest Showman has a catchy chorus:

"These hands could hold the world,
but it will
never be enough,
never be enough for me.
Never, never, for me."

All I can think as I write this devotion is that this would have been Rachel's theme song. She had a husband who was willing to work for fourteen years just to be with her; she has been described as beautiful in form and appearance, but yet she finds herself envious of her sister. This envy led to a back and forth between the sisters of giving their servants to bear children for them and trading and making deals to be with their husband.

I have to believe that this was not the relationship God had intended for these sisters to have. When we approach life with this "never enough" mentality, we only bring harm to ourselves and to the others around us. People who should be our biggest supporters and standing in our corner, end up being our adversaries. Instead of letting our envy, anger, or hurt drive our actions with others we should take a note from 1 Thessalonians 5:11, which states, ***"Therefore encourage one another and build one another up."*** What power and strength can come from us encouraging and supporting one another. There is a common quote that states, "A chain is only as strong as its weakest link." Reacting in a negative fashion weakens our link in the church of Christ. This is not God's will for us. Proverbs 14:30 writes, ***"A tranquil heart gives life to the flesh, but envy makes the bones rot."***

How different could Leah and Rachel's relationship have been if instead of reacting in envy, they reacted in love to one another? How could relationships in your life look different if you chose to respond in more peaceful and uplifting ways? How could your relationship with God be improved if it was not constantly being tested because you feel you should have something better in your life? Trust that God has given you everything you need; His grace is sufficient enough for every situation you are and will encounter.

RACHEL'S SONS

LEAH & RACHEL, DEVOTION 4

Josh Lahring | *Production Director*

The story of Jacob and Rachel is one of love, sin, deceit, and irony. The Bible tells us that Jacob loved Rachel and labored for seven years just to have her hand in marriage. Genesis 29:20 says, ***"So Jacob served seven years to get Rachel, but they seemed like only a few days to him because of his love for her."***

If you have ever loved, you know the love that Jacob had for her. He was willing to do anything to be with her. However, when Jacob went to be with her on their wedding night, Rachel's father and sister plotted to trick him. Instead of Jacob sleeping with Rachel, it was Leah instead. This may remind you of a story two chapters earlier when Jacob and his mother plotted against his brother to receive his father's blessing.

Now Jacob is married to Leah, and he is angry that he was tricked. The father says to finish the bridal week with Leah, and he will give him Rachel as well for another seven years of labor. Now Jacob finally has the wife he loves. As you can imagine Leah is bitter that he loves Rachel more.

However, the Bible says that Rachel could not bear children, but Leah did. Genesis 30:1 (NIV) explains, ***"When Rachel saw that she was not bearing Jacob any children, she became jealous of her sister. So she said to Jacob, 'Give me children, or I'll die!'"*** Now Rachel, who is loved, is bitter at her sister that she gave their husband children.

By now Leah had given Jacob four sons, so Rachel was extremely jealous. However, Rachel was more loved than Leah and Leah was jealous that Rachel was loved. All through chapter 30, it is a war of jealousy between Rachel and Leah to give their husband more children.

Then in verses 22-24 (NIV), the Bible says, ***"Then God remembered Rachel; he listened to her and enabled her to conceive. She became pregnant and gave birth to a son and said, 'God has taken away my disgrace.' She named him Joseph, and said, 'May the Lord add to me another son.'"***

Rachel was bitter and became selfish. Instead of seeking God and waiting patiently upon Him, she did things her own way; she had her servant have children with her husband. It did not work out well for Sarah with Hagar, and it did not work out well here either. In both cases, God decided to bless the women with children.

In all of our mistakes and sinfulness God still hears us and listens to the cry of our hearts. He will not abandon you. Although we have gone our own ways and are selfish and bitter, He still listens and blesses us.

When God blesses us with something, it is easy to take it for granted and not see how blessed we are. Most of the time we get so focused on one thing we want but fail to see all the other blessings God has been giving us. Sometimes we receive our blessing, but we want more rather than being thankful. Right after giving birth to her first child, Rachel so desperately longed for another that she named him Joseph and said, ***"May the Lord add to me another son!"*** God did give her another son. In chapter 35, she had another son but she died after childbirth.

WHAT IS IN A NAME?

LEAH & RACHEL, DEVOTION 5

Richie Henson | *Production Director*

I was given the name Richard after my grandfather on my mother's side. My name means "strong leader or ruler,"and I can tell you, this fact has had zero bearing on my life. I think the same could be said for many people in America. All of us have names that in all likelihood have a "meaning," but that meaning does not impact our daily life. Due to this, I find the stark contrast of names in the Old Testament to be intriguing. It seems that no one in the Old Testament was named arbitrarily. Instead, each name has a very specific meaning that in some way relates to the narrative of said person's life.

With respect to names and meaning, I think we are hard pressed to find a more interesting story than Jacob. Jacob begins his life, for lack of a better term, a hustler. He schemes and connives to get his way. In fact, at one point, Jacob even wrestles who appears to be Jesus. As Jacob wrestles with Jesus, he refuses to relent until he receives a blessing. Part of the blessing given was a name change. However, this name change appears not to stick until much later in the story.
At the outset of Genesis chapter 35, Jacob has once again been forced to flee due to an unresolvable conflict with his neighbors. God instructs Jacob to flee to Bethel and to set up an altar there. As Jacob follows God's instructions, Jacob's enemies become afflicted, and Jacob is saved. It is at this point that God reminds Jacob of the name change given earlier in his life.

Genesis 35:10 says, ***"And God said to him, 'Your name is Jacob; no longer shall your name be called Jacob, but Israel shall be your name.' So he called his name Israel."***

The name Israel means, "God fights." In essence, God is telling Jacob that no matter what comes, Jacob will receive the promise because God fights for him.

Our names do not always mean much to us, but what is undoubtedly meaningful is what God calls us. God names us so specifically. He calls us loved, saved, set apart, and friend. This world and the devil continually work to tear us down. I personally struggle with being reminded that I could never be good enough. No matter how hard I work, it is true that Richard Craig Henson will never be the person he needs to be. However, I know that with God, I am no longer Richard Craig Henson, I am Dikaioumenoi ("justified" Romans 3:24), Kleronomos ("heir" Romans 8:17), and Kainh Ktisiv ("new creation" 2 Corinthians 5:17). My given name has little day-to-day meaning for me, but what God calls me, means everything.

TWELVE TRIBES

LEAH & RACHEL, DEVOTION 6

James Clouse | *Student Pastor*

Have you ever been put in a position where God was able to use your own sinful behavior for His good? God has to remind me all the time that my own sin can cause disastrous consequences, but it is also amazing to see the ways that God has used my past sins and the sins of those around me to help me grow.

Genesis 35:22-26 says, ***"While Israel lived in that land, Reuben went and lay with Bilhah his father's concubine. And Israel heard of it. Now the sons of Jacob were twelve. The sons of Leah: Reuben (Jacob's firstborn), Simeon, Levi, Judah, Issachar, and Zebulun. The sons of Rachel: Joseph and Benjamin. The sons of Bilhah, Rachel's servant: Dan and Naphtali. The sons of Zilpah, Leah's servant: Gad and Asher. These were the sons of Jacob who were born to him in Paddan-aram."***

God did not intend for Jacob to sin against his family and run away. God did not intend for Jacob to work for Laban and have his father-in-law trick him to sleep with the wrong daughter. Jacob's past is full of sin, as is all of ours. But we see an amazing thing happen with all the children that Jacob had with both Leah and Rachel. Yet, we see the birth of the twelve tribes of Israel.

The first three children will not receive their own tribe because of the sin in their lives, but the rest of Jacob's, or Israel's, children will see flourishing tribes come forth. Here we see the amazing power of redemption. God has used the sin of Jacob, the sins of those around him, and the sins of his children to create twelve tribes that will go on to create kingdoms. God has redeemed Jacob and his family to create and to fulfill His promises.

In our own lives, we see this amazing redemption through the power of Jesus Christ. Christ has redeemed us with His blood. So when we come before our Father with our sins, we are sanctified through the amazing power of Christ's redeeming blood. This does not mean that we will not be punished or see the consequences of the sins in our lives, but rather God can use those sins to either help us grow or to help others around us.

The next time that you sin, which will happen, come before the Father and ask for forgiveness. Ask God to have Him use that sin to help you grow in your walk with Him. Ask the Father how you can now move on with your life to help others away from that sin. If you have dealt with alcohol abuse, come before God and ask for forgiveness and let Him use that sin to help others. The same goes for other sins that others around us struggle.

15

JOSEPH & BROTHERS

DR. RANDY T. JOHNSON,
GROWTH PASTOR

When I was in college, I was talking with two close friends, and we decided to triple date. One of the guys suggested going to a musical. Once I realized he was serious, I agreed. We went into Detroit to the Fisher to see *Annie*. It was a great evening that my wife and I still hold fondly. The show was great, but we felt Carol Burnett in the movie version of *Annie* was even better. She was hilarious.

That night opened up a new world to us. We then returned to the Fisher to see *The Phantom of the Opera* (the movie is excellent, too). We loved it. We then proceeded to visit the Pantages Theatre in Toronto (movie) and the Warton Center in Lansing. When I was in Paris, I visited the actual theatre.

Finally, we went to the Fox in Detroit to see *Joseph and the Amazing Technicolor Dreamcoat.* Donny Osmond played the part of Joseph. When my wife first suggested the date, I was shocked and excited that there was a musical based on a Bible story.

Have you seen a musical? If so, which one?

____

____

____

Joseph and the Amazing Technicolor Dreamcoat was impressive, and it is always important to study the Bible and see how accurate the show is to the text. Joseph's childhood can be divided into five different sections. It is covered in Genesis chapter 37.

1. Joseph was daddy's boy.

Genesis chapter 37 tells us a little about Joseph's childhood. Not much detail is given, but some things stand out above the rest.

Joseph was his father's favorite son. That sounds simple, and many people just read on past it. However, think about it. Jacob had his favorite.

It is common for a teacher to be accused of having a teacher's pet. I taught for 29 years, and I had my favorites. Typically, those who took on more responsibility received more privileges. That seems pretty basic.

Did your parents have a "favorite?" (If you are an only child, hopefully it is you)

____

____

____

Genesis 37:1-4 says, ***"Jacob lived in the land of his father's sojournings, in the land of Canaan. These are the generations of Jacob. Joseph, being seventeen years old, was pasturing the flock with his brothers. He was a boy with the sons of Bilhah and Zilpah, his father's wives. And Joseph brought a bad report of them to their father. Now Israel loved Joseph more than any other of his sons, because he was the son of his old age. And he made him a robe of many colors. But when his brothers saw that their father loved him more than all his brothers, they hated him and could not speak peacefully to him."***

Why was Joseph Jacob's favorite son?

____

____

____

How did Jacob show his favoritism of Joseph?

____

____

____

Did Joseph's brothers notice the favoritism? If so, how did they respond?

____

____

____

2. Joseph was a dreamer.

I used to have a poster that said something like, "Some people dream of greatness while others stay awake and do something about it." Dreaming can be good. Martin Luther King Jr. had a dream, and he strived daily to do something about it. His impact is still felt today as a positive leader and role model.

It is clear from Genesis 37:5-11 that Joseph was a dreamer. His situation was unique in that his dream had him instead of him having his dream.

"Now Joseph had a dream, and when he told it to his brothers they hated him even more. He said to them, 'Hear this dream that I have dreamed: Behold, we were binding sheaves in the field, and behold, my sheaf arose and stood upright. And behold, your sheaves gathered around it and bowed down to my sheaf.' His brothers said to him, 'Are you indeed to reign over us? Or are you indeed to rule over us?' So they hated him even more for his dreams and for his words. Then he dreamed another dream and told it to his brothers and said, 'Behold, I have dreamed another dream. Behold, the sun, the moon, and eleven stars were bowing

down to me.' But when he told it to his father and to his brothers, his father rebuked him and said to him, 'What is this dream that you have dreamed? Shall I and your mother and your brothers indeed come to bow ourselves to the ground before you?' And his brothers were jealous of him, but his father kept the saying in mind."

Why was it important for Joseph to share his dream?

____

____

____

Who do you feel believes in you?

____

____

____

"Faith is all that dreamers need to see into the future." Jim Stovall

Side note: Rachel died giving birth to Joseph's younger brother, Benjamin. Some critics use this passage trying to show errors in the Bible. They wonder how his father and mother could bow down to him in the future if she is dead. However, remember Leah would have acted as Joseph's mother. All Jacob's sons would have viewed Leah as their mother. By the way, his dream did come true.

3. Joseph was despised.

Despised is a strong word, but I could not think of a harsher word that began with the letter "D." Joseph's brothers disregarded, disdained, and detested him. They hated him and wanted him out of their lives.

It is heart-wrenching to realize this is how mankind felt about Jesus the Messiah, ***"He was despised and rejected by men, a man of sorrows and acquainted with grief; and as one from whom men hide their faces he was despised, and we esteemed him not"*** (Isaiah 53:3). I believe the word "despised" is used twice for emphasis. How could we not only miss Him but deride Him?

Genesis 37:12-21 tells us of the brothers' feelings toward Joseph, ***"Now his brothers went to pasture their father's flock near Shechem. And Israel said to Joseph, 'Are not your brothers pasturing the flock at Shechem? Come, I will send you to them.' And he said to him, 'Here I am.' So he said to him, 'Go now, see if it is well with your brothers and with the flock, and bring me word.' So he sent him from the Valley of Hebron, and he came to Shechem. And a man found him wandering in the fields. And the man asked him, 'What are you seeking?' 'I am seeking my brothers,' he said. 'Tell me, please, where they are pasturing the flock.' And the man said, 'They have gone away, for I heard them say, 'Let us go to Dothan." So Joseph went after his brothers and found them at Dothan. They saw him from afar, and before he came near to them they conspired against him to kill him. They said to one another, 'Here comes this dreamer. Come now, let us kill him and throw him into one of the pits. Then we will say that a fierce animal has devoured him, and we will see what will become of his dreams.' But when Reuben heard it, he rescued him out of their hands, saying, 'Let us not take his life.'"***

How does this passage describe the brothers' feelings about Joseph?

____

____

____

The brothers viewed Joseph as the enemy; do you think he felt the same about them?

____

____

____

Do you have someone who considers you an enemy? What have you done about it? What should you do about it?

____

____

____

The brothers were supposed to be in Shechem but were thirteen miles away in Dothan.

Why do you think they were not where they were expected to be?

____

____

____

"Christianity preaches the infinite worth of that which is seemingly worthless and the infinite worthlessness of that which is seemingly so valued." Dietrich Bonhoeffer

4. Joseph was defended.

I raised my son to know how to fight, but with the mindset that there would be a better way to solve problems other than his fists. However, I will admit, he did not get in trouble when he fought defending someone else.

Even though Joseph was despised, Reuben was willing to take a stand for him. Genesis 37:22-24 describes the situation, ***"And***

Reuben said to them, 'Shed no blood; throw him into this pit here in the wilderness, but do not lay a hand on him'—that he might rescue him out of their hand to restore him to his father. So when Joseph came to his brothers, they stripped him of his robe, the robe of many colors that he wore. And they took him and threw him into a pit. The pit was empty; there was no water in it."

Why did Reuben want Joseph thrown in the pit?

___

___

___

5. Joseph was disposed of by his brothers.

I wonder what Joseph thought while in the pit. I think he probably heard a lot of their conversation and it would make anyone anxious.

Genesis 37:25-28 continues the story, ***"Then they sat down to eat. And looking up they saw a caravan of Ishmaelites coming from Gilead, with their camels bearing gum, balm, and myrrh, on their way to carry it down to Egypt. Then Judah said to his brothers, 'What profit is it if we kill our brother and conceal his blood? Come, let us sell him to the Ishmaelites, and let not our hand be upon him, for he is our brother, our own flesh.' And his brothers listened to him. Then Midianite traders passed by. And they drew Joseph up and lifted him out of the pit, and sold him to the Ishmaelites for twenty shekels of silver. They took Joseph to Egypt."***

How does the phrase ***"they sat down to eat"*** relate to the tone of the story?

Is there any significance to the sale price?

Genesis 37:29-36 appears to give the end of the story, ***"When Reuben returned to the pit and saw that Joseph was not in the pit, he tore his clothes and returned to his brothers and said, 'The boy is gone, and I, where shall I go?' Then they took Joseph's robe and slaughtered a goat and dipped the robe in the blood. And they sent the robe of many colors and brought it to their father and said, 'This we have found; please identify whether it is your son's robe or not.' And he identified it and said, 'It is my son's robe. A fierce animal has devoured him. Joseph is without doubt torn to pieces.' Then Jacob tore his garments and put sackcloth on his loins and mourned for his son many days. All his sons and all his daughters rose up to comfort him, but he refused to be comforted and said, 'No, I shall go down to Sheol to my son, mourning.' Thus his father wept for him. Meanwhile the Midianites had sold him in Egypt to Potiphar, an officer of Pharaoh, the captain of the guard."***

How many poor choices (sins) are recorded in this story?

How does Joseph's early life relate to "the rest of the story?"

Is there a situation in your life that you need to trust God will use in a special way?

JOSEPH AS DAD'S FAVORITE

JOSEPH & BROTHERS, DEVOTION 1

Wes McCullough | *Production Director*

"Now Israel loved Joseph more than any other of his sons, because he was the son of his old age. And he made him a robe of many colors. But when his brothers saw that their father loved him more than all his brothers, they hated him and could not speak peacefully to him." Genesis 37:3-4

Favoritism seems to be a genetic problem for this family. Isaac favored Esau while Rebekah favored Jacob. Of his wives, Jacob favored Rachel over her sister, Leah. Of his sons, Jacob favored Joseph. The case can be made that Rachel, being the love of Jacob's heart, was his "first" wife while he actually married Leah first. Joseph, as Rachel's firstborn and coming in Jacob's old age, would definitely have a special place in his father's heart.

I can definitely say I am my father's favorite son, primarily because he only had one. However, when my sisters married, I noticed a certain change. My parents welcomed my sisters' husbands into the family with the same love they had for me. I have also seen them love my wife as their own daughter. My parents' attitude and actions make me proud and have been an example to follow in all my family relations.

There are several lessons we can learn from this story. 1 John 2:9 says, ***"Whoever says he is in the light and hates his brother is still in darkness."*** Matthew 5:23-25 provides some directions for such a situation, ***"So if you are offering your gift at the altar and there remember that your brother has something against you, leave your gift there before the altar and go. First be reconciled to***

your brother, and then come and offer your gift. Come to terms quickly with your accuser while you are going with him to court, lest your accuser hand you over to the judge, and the judge to the guard, and you be put in prison."

Furthermore, 1 John 3:15 says, ***"Everyone who hates his brother is a murderer, and you know that no murderer has eternal life abiding in him."*** At the root of it all is hate which Proverbs 10:12 addresses, ***"Hatred stirs up strife, but love covers all offenses."*** Hate will lead to other sins. It will cause you to become someone you are not and do things you are against. Combat hate with forgiveness and love. Jesus taught us to love and forgive, and we would do well to honor those instructions.

I HAVE DREAMED A DREAM

JOSEPH & BROTHERS, DEVOTION 2

Kenny Hovis | *Prison Ministry Director*

Growing up, I spooked easily. I did not like going out in the dark or walking into the house at night with the lights out. I would have wild nightmares, seeing little guys in top hats flying around my room, slamming into my leg, causing it to go numb. Dreams have been used throughout history to tell the future, bring enlightenment to situations, and remember things that happened in our past. Though I have never had God speak to me directly through a dream, I have had a couple instances where in my dreamtime as an adult, I have been challenged spiritually.

Both occurrences involved me in a physical altercation with demons. I had not watched a scary movie, used an Ouija board, or went to a fortune teller. I just went to bed, fell asleep, and the only thing I can remember was literally wrestling with a demon, and on both occasions losing until crying out Jesus' name. The dreams seemed, as all dreams while in them, real. So much so, that the sounds that I was making scared my wife enough that she started to wake me both times, but I woke up on my own just before being shook. I was sweating and breathing heavy as though I had been in an actual physical confrontation. As I said, dreams can seem very real.

In Genesis 37:5-11, we find Joseph having two dreams, both seeming very real, and then him sharing those dreams with his family. In both instances, Joseph's dreams foretell him ruling over his family. Verse 7 says, ***"Behold, we were binding sheaves in the field, and behold, my sheaf arose and stood upright. And behold, your sheaves gathered around it and bowed down to my sheaf."***

Then again in verse 9, ***"Then he dreamed another dream and told it to his brothers and said, 'Behold, I have dreamed another dream. Behold, the sun, the moon, and eleven stars were bowing down to me.'"*** As a result of him telling his siblings and parents his dreams, he is hated and despised by his brothers, and they plot to get rid of him. This sets Joseph on a path that will try his faith in God, people, and government. In the end, God weaves His divine will through Joseph and his family's lives to make his dreams come to pass, which in turn saves his family's lives.

Though I am no Joseph, I too have had a couple dreams of a similar nature. This is what I have gleaned from them. We battle every day with an adversary that wants to get rid of us, destroy us, and see us doubt whether God loves us or even knows that we exist. The Bible says in Job 16:9, ***"He has torn me in his wrath and hated me; he has gnashed his teeth at me; my adversary sharpens his eyes against me."*** Also, 1 Peter 5:8 says, ***"Be sober-minded; be watchful. Your adversary the devil prowls around like a roaring lion, seeking someone to devour."*** Our adversary, the devil, wants to influence us to make choices that will burn our world to the ground, divide our families, and cause confusion. This is where he thrives and dwells. We cannot conquer him on our own, just like in my dreams. Only by invoking the name of Jesus into our lives, in every situation, challenge, tragedy, venture, ministry, or relationship do we have a chance to defeat him.

Just as in the case of Joseph, we cannot trust in our own power to overcome our adversary and the obstacles he places in front of us. We will only gain victory in our lives when we invoke the name of God the Father, Jesus Christ's work at Calvary, and the ongoing work of the Holy Spirit into every aspect of our existence. When this formula is used, God will weave His divine will through our lives so that our dreams may come to pass and that our eternal lives will be saved!

BROTHERLY SHOVE

JOSEPH & BROTHERS, DEVOTION 3

Gareth Volz | *Senior (55+) Director*

Today as we look at the story of Joseph and his brothers in Genesis chapter 37, we see how jealousy can lead to hatred, disobedience, and a breakdown of the relationship in the family. Joseph came from a dysfunctional family. His father, Jacob, had two full-fledged wives – Leah and Rachel, and two concubines – Bilhah and Zilpah. Leah was the mother of Reuben and Judah, while Rachel was the mother of Joseph and Benjamin. The other brothers were the children of the concubines. Additionally, we read in verse 3 that Jacob (Israel) loved Joseph more than any of his other sons because he was the son of his old age. Verse 4 tells us that because of this, Joseph's brothers hated him so much that they could not speak peacefully to him.

Verse 2 tells us that at the age of 17, Joseph was shepherding his father's flocks along with his brothers, and he brought a bad report to Jacob about them. Joseph was not a tattletale, but apparently, the head shepherd, as evidenced by his coat of many colors. You might say Joseph was a white collar (supervisory) worker, while his brothers were blue collar workers – and they did not have a good working relationship. Here was disobedience to the working relationship the father wanted.

Beginning at verse 12, we read that the brothers were tending the flocks near Shechem, and Jacob asked Joseph to go and check on the job they were doing. Joseph willingly accepted the task, and when he got to Shechem, he could not find his brothers nor the flocks. Joseph asked around and found out that his brothers had gone to Dothan, about 20 miles away. This was disobedience to where their father had sent them.

As you read further in the chapter, you will find that the brothers plotted to kill Joseph. Reuben, however, convinced them just to throw Joseph into a pit, sell him to some passing slave traders, and tell their father he was killed by a wild animal. This was disobedience in the form of treachery, lying, and cover-up.

We find that Joseph was a picture of Jesus in the Old Testament. He was sent by his father to his other children. He was not accepted, and he was rejected by his own. The same was true of Jesus (John 1:9-11).

Shechem in the Bible is a picture of the world. Joseph's brothers were shepherding the flock near Shechem (the world) and then moved farther away from the father to Dothan.

The questions we need to ask ourselves as God's children are:

1. Do we truly love our Heavenly Father with all our heart?
2. Do we truly love our brothers and sisters in the Lord?
3. Are we happy with the assignment that our Heavenly Father has given us, or are we jealous of the assignment He has given to others we know?
4. Are we spending our time flirting with the things of the world?

"Blessed is the man who walks not in the counsel of the wicked, nor stands in the way of sinners, nor sits in the seat of scoffers; but his delight is in the law of the LORD, and on His law he meditates day and night." Psalm 1:1-2

HATRED & JEALOUSY

JOSEPH & BROTHERS, DEVOTION 4

Jill Osmon | *Assistant to the Lead Team*

"They saw him from afar, and before he came near to them they conspired against him to kill him. They said to one another, 'Here comes this dreamer. Come now, let us kill him and throw him into one of the pits. Then we will say that a fierce animal has devoured him, and we will see what will become of his dreams.'" Genesis 37:18-20

Bitterness, hatred, and jealousy are not new. Something from deep within us can react to the mere perceived slight from anyone. Joseph's brothers come to this moment with a wealth of history piled up into a heap of anger. Joseph was the favorite, Joseph was clearly anointed by God, Joseph had the coat, and Joseph had the dreams to remind his brothers of these very things.

Does this story instantly bring someone to mind that reminds you of Joseph? Is there someone in your life who seems to have it all, knows they have it all, and reminds you that they have it all? Replace dreams and coat with social media and success, and maybe then you can imagine someone. It makes you discontent, and in that discontentment, it opens a harshness that spreads like cancer to every aspect of your life. You find yourself secretly wishing upon them failures and messes because their life highlights what you do not have.

Hatred and jealousy say more about us than it does about the person we have decided to point out all of our frustrations. We are wounded, hurt, and wondering why God has lavished such favor on someone else. It makes us react out of a place that is unhealthy and harmful. Joseph's brothers were not psychotic, evil people. They were wounded and reacting, and we have all been there. I have been reading a book, "Uninvited," and this statement has stuck with me, "The only thing I've seen work in my life to protect my heart from these deep wounds is the constant pursuit of the sweetest grace."

Take a moment, think through your life, find those places, situations, and people that pull out the bitterness, hatred, and jealousy. Pursue grace with them and for them. God's favor does not exclude anyone from hurt and difficulties. We are all in need of God's grace, to pursue it, give it, and receive it from each other.

REUBEN TAKING A STAND

JOSEPH & BROTHERS, DEVOTION 5

Mary Jane Johns | *Worship Leader*

Firstborns are an interesting group of people. Eldest children set the standard. They are reliable, conscientious, strong-willed, controlling, and overachievers. The greatest quality of firstborns is that of loyalty. I am the youngest of seven kids, so I do not fully understand this whole thing. However, I do know my sister Gail. She is eighteen years older than me. Gail was a senior in high school when my mom carefully broke the news to her. She was ecstatic! Out of all of us seven kids, Gail is the best at caring that we stay connected. She is steady, full of integrity, makes lists, and most of all has character; she is full of truth. Gail has seen adversity through suffering from multiple sclerosis yet, she remains faithful, strong, and really works at communicating with her siblings. My mom would say that she was really tough on her because my parents really did not know what they were doing! Gail tends to be a rule follower, a wonderful leader, a bit bossy, and direct (I love her anyway!). She is just like my mom. Someone has to lead this messy Strader family of seven kids. She calls herself the matriarch.

There is a guy in the Bible whom I feel might display many of the same characteristics as a typical oldest child. Reuben, the son of Jacob and Leah, is the eldest sibling in the band of twelve brothers. However, Jacob (who had many wives) was partial to his wife, Rachel. Apparently, he loved her more. Okay, so this is wrong on so many levels. Anyway, I will continue on with our story. Rachel gave birth to two sons, Joseph and Benjamin. Unlike our family (for real), Jacob showed favoritism to Joseph by giving him a coat with brilliant colors. All of the brothers were extremely jealous of Joseph. Reuben (who was a bit cocky) and his ten brothers decided to attack their brother.

Genesis 37:21-22 records, ***"But when Reuben heard it, he rescued him out of their hands, saying, 'Let us not take his life.' And Reuben said to them, 'Shed no blood; throw him into this pit here in the wilderness, but do not lay a hand on him' –that he might rescue him out of their hand to restore him to his father."***

Joseph's brothers hated him with a jealous passion. It was pretty ugly. They wanted to kill him through starvation and thirst by throwing him in the deep pit in the middle of nowhere. Reuben was not a big fan of Joseph but, he did not want him dead, and felt the weight of displeasing his father. I believe Reuben was still trying to honor his father and follow the rules even with his dysfunctional family. In his mind, killing Joseph was not an option. Completely losing him was definitely not what he had planned.

Genesis 37:29-30 adds, ***"When Reuben returned to the pit and saw that Joseph was not in the pit, he tore his clothes and returned to his brothers and said, 'The boy is gone, and I, where shall I go?'"***

Reuben completely freaked out when Joseph was gone from the pit when he got there to set him free. It was never his intention to have Joseph die. I can only speculate why he went back. That is where he showed family loyalty. Reuben was responsible for his younger brothers, and he had let his father down. He tore his clothes, which is a sign of remorse and grieving. He panicked and lied to cover it all up to his father. Meanwhile, Joseph was picked up out of the pit and sold into slavery in Egypt. However, we will leave the story there.

There is much about this story that is questionable, and I can not be sure of Reuben's ulterior motives. His commitment to his father and younger brothers were completely changed after this account. I would like to think he was a broken man, but seriously, who knows?

Maybe he was a bit less self-righteous and cocky. He was more diligent in his protection of Benjamin after Joseph was sold into slavery.

Loyalty, strength, and concern for parents' approval are huge to firstborn children. My sister Gail would lay down her life for her siblings. In fact, we are all that way. I cannot even fathom being so jealous of my brother that I wanted him to die. It is a foreign concept to me, yet this is the case with Reuben and his ugly and uncompassionate brothers. Jealousy brings about ruin in the lives of families. Do not let it rule yours.

TYPOLOGY

JOSEPH & BROTHERS, DEVOTION 6

Philip Piasecki

My brother is three years younger than me. This age gap allowed us to be pretty close friends through the years. We always had our own group of friends, but we would always enjoy hanging out with each other as well. Whether it was playing one-on-one on the basketball court, or playing PlayStation against each other, we have always been very competitive with one another. The most frustrating thing for me was when he started getting older and actually getting better at me in some things! All of a sudden I did not always beat him in basketball. I had to finally come to terms with the fact that he was better than me. He went on to play some college basketball, all I ever played was intramurals. My team did win the Oakland University Intramural Basketball tournament, so I have that on my resume. There were times when I would be jealous of his talent, but for the most part, I was always very excited for him. That is why reading the story of Joseph is so difficult for me; I cannot ever imagine being so jealous of a sibling that you would be willing to sell them into slavery.

The story of Joseph has so many great moral principles we can take from it, but we must be careful that morality is not always the only thing we take from the Old Testament Scriptures. The whole Old Testament constantly is pointing toward the coming of Jesus; we just have to be looking for the correlations.

Genesis 37:28 says, ***"Then Midianite traders passed by. And they drew Joseph up and lifted him out of the pit, and sold him to the Ishmaelites for twenty shekels of silver. They took Joseph to Egypt."***

We see here that Joseph was bought for the price of a slave, does that ring any bells? Look at the account in Matthew chapter 26 where Judas is seeking to betray Jesus.

Matthew 26:14-16 says, ***"Then one of the twelve, whose name was Judas Iscariot, went to the chief priests and said, 'What will you give me if I deliver him over to you?' And they paid him thirty pieces of silver. And from that moment he sought an opportunity to betray him."***

Here we find the Scripture where Jesus is sold for the price of a slave as well. Joseph was betrayed by those closest to him, in the same way that Jesus was betrayed by Judas. The Old Testament is filled with the foreshadowing of what was going to happen to Jesus. When we read the Old Testament, there will be new life breathed into it if we approach it through the lens of Jesus. There is so much more to the Scriptures than just morality. There is a Savior who loved us and died for us. Our desire should be to honor and glorify Him, and through that, we will live moral lives. Joseph's story is a beautiful picture of Jesus' sacrifice for us, how He loves us even though we constantly sin against Him, and how He will show us mercy when we ask for it. Let the story of Joseph help you better understand that character of our Lord and Savior.

16

JOSEPH & POTIPHAR'S WIFE

DR. RANDY T. JOHNSON,
GROWTH PASTOR

I am intrigued by the competition of setting up Dominoes in such a way that when you push over one, it leads to hundreds and even thousands falling. It appears the world record has been set by a twelve-person German team (ironically they call themselves the "sinners"). They spent more than a week setting up 270,000 Dominoes.

The illustration of Dominoes has often been used to show a slippery slope effect of one poor decision leading to many others. I believe the opposite is true also. One good decision makes the next right decision easier to make.

The story of Joseph and Potiphar's wife shows both sides of the coin. She lived a life of deceit and selfishness, while Joseph built upon his integrity each step of the way.

What other principles can be taught through Dominoes?

____

____

____

Genesis chapter 39 contains the next piece of the puzzle after Joseph's brothers sold him into slavery. The first ten verses set the stage.

"Now Joseph had been brought down to Egypt, and Potiphar, an officer of Pharaoh, the captain of the guard, an Egyptian, had bought him from the Ishmaelites who had brought him down there. The Lord was with Joseph, and he became a successful man, and he was in the house of his Egyptian master. His master saw that the Lord was with him and that the Lord caused all that he did to succeed in his hands. So Joseph found favor in his sight and attended him, and he made him overseer of his house

and put him in charge of all that he had. From the time that he made him overseer in his house and over all that he had, the Lord blessed the Egyptian's house for Joseph's sake; the blessing of the Lord was on all that he had, in house and field. So he left all that he had in Joseph's charge, and because of him, he had no concern about anything but the food he ate.

Now Joseph was handsome in form and appearance. And after a time his master's wife cast her eyes on Joseph and said, 'Lie with me.' But he refused and said to his master's wife, 'Behold, because of me my master has no concern about anything in the house, and he has put everything that he has in my charge. He is not greater in this house than I am, nor has he kept back anything from me except you, because you are his wife. How then can I do this great wickedness and sin against God?' And as she spoke to Joseph day after day, he would not listen to her, to lie beside her or to be with her." Genesis 39:1-10

Why was Joseph successful?

____

____

____

What excuses could Joseph have used to "justify" him choosing to sin?

____

____

____

When we sin, who all is affected?

____

____

____

Potiphar's wife represents the worldview of a lot of people today, "It is all about me." How is this shown in the passage?

____

____

____

Joseph saw a bigger picture and lived to a higher standard. He could have sulked and complained that life was not fair, but he held to his dream. He, like some men in the Book of Daniel, held his standards. Although he was removed from any form of accountability, he kept his compass at True North.

Genesis 39:11-18 continues the story, ***"But one day, when he went into the house to do his work and none of the men of the house was there in the house, she caught him by his garment, saying, 'Lie with me.' But he left his garment in her hand and fled and got out of the house. And as soon as she saw that he had left his garment in her hand and had fled out of the house, she called to the men of her household and said to them, 'See, he has brought among us a Hebrew to laugh at us. He came in to me to lie with me, and I cried out with a loud voice. And as soon as he heard that I lifted up my voice and cried out, he left his garment beside me and fled and got out of the house.' Then she laid up his garment by her until his master came home, and she told him the same story, saying, 'The Hebrew servant, whom you have brought among us, came in to me to laugh at me. But as soon as I lifted up my voice and cried, he left his garment beside me and fled out of the house.'"***

Just a reminder, temptation is not sin. We are not sure if Joseph was tempted, but the assumption is that he was. Sin starts in the mind, moves toward the heart, and is brought to completion through the body. Joseph had a proper mindset that did not allow any Dominoes to fall downward.

Who does Potiphar's wife blame for the situation?

What was Joseph's response to the "invitation?"

How does this story relate to today?

It is good to remember that the rest of the story is not always the rest of the story. Genesis 39:19-23 closes the section, ***"As soon as his master heard the words that his wife spoke to him, 'This is the way your servant treated me,' his anger was kindled. And Joseph's master took him and put him into the prison, the place where the king's prisoners were confined, and he was there in prison. But the Lord was with Joseph and showed him steadfast love and gave him favor in the sight of the keeper of the prison. And the keeper of the prison put Joseph in charge of all the prisoners who were in the prison. Whatever was done there, he was the one who did it. The keeper of the prison paid no attention to anything that was in Joseph's charge, because the Lord was with him. And whatever he did, the Lord made it succeed."***

Do you think Potiphar believed his wife? Why or why not?

What is said of Joseph in prison?

___

___

___

Why do you think the passage omits any record of Joseph defending himself?

___

___

___

Although Joseph did not appear to have a problem with lust, Genesis chapter 39 is the starting point for most biblical discussions on the topic. There are other passages that address the topic of lust.

"The righteousness of the upright delivers them, but the treacherous are taken captive by their lust." Proverbs 11:6

"Flee also youthful lusts: but follow righteousness, faith, charity, peace, with them that call on the Lord out of a pure heart." 2 Timothy 2:22 (KJV)

"I will not set before my eyes anything that is worthless. I hate the work of those who fall away; it shall not cling to me." Psalm 101:3

"'Food is meant for the stomach and the stomach for food'—and God will destroy both one and the other. The body is not meant for sexual immorality, but for the Lord, and the Lord for the body." 1 Corinthians 6:13

"Do not desire her beauty in your heart, and do not let her capture you with her eyelashes." Proverbs 6:25

Which verse stands out the most to you? Why?

____

____

____

"Love is the great conqueror of lust." C.S. Lewis

LONELY CIRCUMSTANCES, NEVER ALONE

JOSEPH & POTIPHAR'S WIFE, DEVOTION 1

Ben Kirkman | *Director of Facilities*

"Now Joseph had been brought down to Egypt, and Potiphar, an officer of Pharaoh, the captain of the guard, an Egyptian, had bought him from the Ishmaelites who had brought him down there. The LORD was with Joseph, and he became a successful man, and he was in the house of his Egyptian master." Genesis 39:1-2

As you consider the story of Joseph, what words would you use to describe his life?

Joseph dealt with some crazy circumstances. You find him doing right and living in obedience to the authority in his life yet "bad" things continue to happen to him. Think about it: as a teenage boy, he obeyed his father by going to check on his brothers, and while he was there they sold him into slavery. What emotions, thoughts, and feelings would you have had if your family sold you into slavery? I imagine you would feel abandoned and betrayed; this would be an extremely scary and lonely place to be. It seems that over and over again we find the circumstances of Joseph's life putting him in a position of potential loneliness.

Have you ever been there? Maybe it was not to the extremes that Joseph had to deal with, but the trials of life can leave you feeling frustrated, disappointed, and all alone. What do you do when you are put in a place where you feel all alone? How do you respond when you are trying to do what is right, you are trying to follow the Lord, and you still find yourself in a painful situation?

You can gain a lot of help and hope if you step back and look at the big picture of Joseph's life. We have the advantage of seeing Joseph's whole story from start to finish. We can see God at work even in the painful days of Joseph's life. We can see God working out His perfect plan. We can see God intricately working to preserve a nation and to fulfil His plan.

God sees the big picture. God knows the whole story from beginning to end. As Joseph was going through those difficult days, he may not have understood why, but he knew he served a God he could trust, and he faithfully faced each trial. No matter how lonely he may have felt, he knew he was never truly alone. Genesis 39:2 says, ***"The LORD was with Joseph."*** Joseph knew that God was with him and that, in every step of his life, God was at work. Joseph testified to this reality. In Genesis 50:20, he said, ***"As for you, you meant evil against me, but God meant it for good, to bring it about that many people should kept alive, as they are today."***

No matter what trial or difficult circumstance that you may face, no matter how lonely you may feel, remember, you are not alone. God is there; He is completely aware of what is going on, and He has a plan for you. Trust in Him, rest in Him, and lean on Him for strength and comfort. We serve an amazing God!

JOSEPH & SUCCESS

JOSEPH & POTIPHAR'S WIFE, DEVOTION 2

Roger Allen | *Recovery Director*

What is success? Is it a big house, bankroll, toys, retirement, or some other vain attempt of a monument to ourselves? Is it a legacy that has temporal value, or is it an eternal substance that is hard to define and categorize? Is it one that is actually bigger than ourselves? In Genesis, we are introduced to Joseph, the eleventh and most favored son of his father. Clothed in a coat of many colors, he lived the life of the most loved. Already jealous, his brothers started planning his end when he told them his dream.

Genesis 37:5-8 says, ***"Now Joseph had a dream, and when he told it to his brothers they hated him even more. He said to them, 'Hear this dream that I have dreamed: Behold, we were binding sheaves in the field, and behold, my sheaf arose and stood upright. And behold, your sheaves gathered around it and bowed down to my sheaf.' His brothers said to him, 'Are you indeed to reign over us? Or are you indeed to rule over us?' So they hated him even more for his dreams and for his words."***

We all have had a "Joseph" in our life. Whether it was a sibling or a co-worker, we all know that one person that stands out above the crowd. It is the one that even at our best seems to bring out the envy in us. Typically, as we get older, we assume that we understand the futility of such emotions but, envy knows no age, only circumstance. I recall the first time that I had such anger and envy. When I was around eight years old, I was spurred on by my older brother to wrestle a neighbor kid. He was smaller than me, so I figured this would be easy. Face down in the dirt, I soon realized what it meant to be envious. I had always looked up to my brother and to be humiliated in front of him was the worst thing in the world to me. I seethed with anger just as Joseph's brothers did.

As the story of Joseph unfolds, we are introduced to the plot to destroy him. Taken captive and sold into slavery by his brothers (Genesis 37:12-35), Joseph becomes part of the household of Potiphar where he quickly found favor. Elevated to the superintendent, Joseph's star began to shine again only to be dimmed by a false accusation by Potiphar's spurned wife (Genesis 29:1-20). Sent to prison, Joseph once again proved he could be trusted. In charge of the prisoners, he showed that integrity and wisdom would bring trust in an otherwise trustless society. Interpreting the dreams of those imprisoned by Pharaoh, he also showed that the hand of the Lord was upon him. Eventually, Joseph was called to interpret a dream for Pharaoh. Advising him of the coming famine, Pharaoh raised him to be second in command in all of Egypt. As the famine continued throughout the land, Joseph's stature grew.

By the second year of the famine, many from the surrounding areas were sent to Egypt to buy food including his family. Now was the time for Joseph's revenge. His brothers were at his mercy. He could get even. Yet, instead of an instant death sentence, he would have some fun. Never letting on to who he was (it had been twenty years), Joseph began the payback. At any time he could end their lives and have his retribution, yet he did not. After playing it out, Joseph ended his ruse and reunited with his family.

Joseph certainly was not perfect. He had a prideful streak that cost him his freedom. Rejected by those closest to him, he paid a high price. Yet, that price paid dividends to him and his family (Romans 8:28-29). Steadfast through his trials he brought salvation to them. The hand of the Lord, his integrity, and wisdom allowed him to succeed where others fail. Psalm 41:11-12 says it best, ***"By this I know that you delight in me: my enemy will not shout in triumph over me. But you have upheld me because of my integrity, and set me in your presence forever."***

OTHERS BLESSED BECAUSE OF JOSEPH

JOSEPH & POTIPHAR'S WIFE, DEVOTION 3

Jen Combs | *Women's Ministry*

"His Master saw that the Lord was with him and that the Lord caused all that he did to succeed in his hands. So Joseph found favor in his sight and attended him, and he made him overseer of his house and put him in charge of all that he had. From the time that he made him overseer in his house and over all that he had, the Lord blessed the Egyptians house for Joseph's sake; the blessing of the Lord was on all that he had, in house and field." Genesis 39:3-5

Do you take notes in your Bible? Or are you one of those that just cannot bring themselves to write in God's Word? I am a major note taker. I write all over the place, up the side of the margin, in the spaces provided, in any blank space that is available. I take notes from sermons I have heard, write definitions of words I have not a clue what they mean, and attach timelines of history. But mainly, I take notes because I have a terrible memory. Right next to this passage I have a note that says, "Do people see Christ in me?" It gets me thinking. In my everyday life, in the mundane, do people see the light of Christ in me? Do they see a difference in me? Am I taking opportunities that the Lord gives to shine His light?

The other day I was at the gym and had missed the previous week because we were out of town. They were talking about raising money for a family, I was trying to put all of the pieces together but could not. So I bugged one of the girls after to update me. She, with tear-filled eyes, told me while standing on the gym mat that her friend's young daughter was going to pass away. I had the opportunity to give the standard answer, "Oh, I am so sorry, let me know if I can do anything." Or I could grab this lady who I did not know, with my sweaty, stinky, hot mess of a self, and pray with her right then and there. I have walked away from those opportunities far too many times in my life to hate the feeling of conviction, knowing I was supposed to do something and did not. So praise God, I prayed with her, and now I have that opened door to talk to her about things of the Lord.

How can you let your light shine today? Are you looking for opportunities? Are you praying for opportunities? Are you willing to feel uncomfortable so people can see the Lord in you? Joseph experienced some pretty tough and traumatic situations in his life. He was abandoned, sold, and imprisoned just to name a few. Even through all of these things, it says that his master saw that the Lord was with him. This challenges me. In the rough seasons of life, do people see me and say, the Lord is with her? Unbelievers especially are watching how we as followers of Christ handle the difficult circumstances we encounter. Joseph's story should encourage us to let our light shine before men, no matter the situation.

AUDIENCE OF ONE

JOSEPH & POTIPHAR'S WIFE, DEVOTION 4

Dr. Randy T. Johnson | *Growth Pastor*

"From the time that he made him overseer in his house and over all that he had, the Lord blessed the Egyptian's house for Joseph's sake; the blessing of the Lord was on all that he had, in house and field. So he left all that he had in Joseph's charge, and because of him he had no concern about anything but the food he ate." Genesis 39:5-6

The main point of this passage seems quite clear. God blessed Joseph. He not only blessed Joseph, but He blessed everyone and anything around Joseph. Potiphar and his estate were flourishing because God blessed him through Joseph.

However, I think there is another aspect that is too often missed: Joseph was faithful to God. Joseph had been belittled by his brothers, thrown in a pit, threatened death, sold into slavery, taken far from home, and humanly speaking had no hope of ever seeing his dad again. All sense of normality was gone. As he served in the house of Potiphar, he was faithful. He was faithful to God; therefore, he was diligent with his work. He was a hard worker. He was a hard worker when Potiphar was watching, but he was a hard worker when Potiphar was not home, too. With Joseph in charge, Potiphar ***"had no concern about anything."***

The key to Joseph's success was that he had an audience of One. There was only One that he wanted to impress. In everything he did, he was working for God. God was the focus of his diligence.

It can be difficult to work for an unbeliever or a godless person. It can be tempting to slack off when no one is watching. It can be hard to press forward when we are not appreciated. It can be challenging to give our best when it is not acknowledged. It is easy to follow the crowd. However, Joseph knew One was always watching. He was the One Joseph strived to please.

Galatians 1:10 challenges us, ***"For am I now seeking the approval of man, or of God? Or am I trying to please man? If I were still trying to please man, I would not be a servant of Christ."***

As servants of Christ, we need to live it. When "no one" is watching, remember One is watching. When many are watching, focus on the One, the true and living God.

NO SIN AGAINST OTHERS

JOSEPH & POTIPHAR'S WIFE, DEVOTION 5

Noble Baird | *Community Center Director*

A few years back, I was out at my buddies farm up in Attica. Connor's parents own a massive horse farm with tons of land. He and his father spent some time building a shooting range in the back of their property in the woods. There are no houses around the range, and they had the perfect set up with a huge dirt hill backing the range. So, as Connor and I usually did on nice summer afternoons, we went out to the range on the farm and practiced shooting. One day we decided to run through some drills with live ammo. Our goal was to practice moving forward down the 200-yard range, alternating our forward position with our rifles, until we were 25 yards out and we pulled out our sidearm, hitting the targets in front of us, and finished the drill in unison. We ran through this drill several times that afternoon; however, there was one main factor that held us together and allowed us to complete the drill successfully and without injury: trust.

As we continue on in the story of Joseph, he has overcome many hardships already; however, he is about to experience one of the morally most difficult situations of his life. In Genesis 39:7-10, we have the account of Joseph's interaction with his master's, Potiphar, wife. Starting in verse 7, ***"And after a time his master's wife cast her eyes on Joseph and said, 'Lie with me.' But he refused and said to his master's wife, 'Behold, because of me my master has no concern about anything in the house, and he has put everything that he has in my charge. He is not greater in this house than I am, nor has he kept back anything from me except you, because you are his wife. How then can I do this great wickedness and sin against God?' And as she spoke to***

Joseph day after day, he would not listen to her, to lie beside her or to be with her."

Joseph's life was full of literal highs and lows. Here, Joseph is at a truly incredible milestone in his life. Yes, he is still in slavery; however, as we read in this passage, he has no limitations. He is head over all of Potiphar's household, and there is nothing that belongs to Potiphar that he does not trust with Joseph. The only thing that is not shared between the two is Potiphar's wife, for obvious reasons.

You see, the reason why Potiphar never questioned or doubted allowing Joseph, one of the slaves he purchased, with his household and all he owned was rooted in the trust he had. Potiphar literally trusted Joseph with his life. Not only was Joseph a true man of God, but he understood the trust he had gained with Potiphar and never wanted to ruin or place himself in situations that could compromise that trust. However, Potiphar's wife had a hidden agenda and was overcome with sin. She had her eyes on Joseph and tried to be with him. Yet, because of the man he was and his identity in the one true God, he was not going to compromise the trust with his master and his character. So, he fled from sin and did not sin against his master.

As you go throughout your week, you will face temptations and trials just as Joseph did. I want to challenge you to stay strong, not to compromise, and flee from that sin as Joseph did. Joseph knew that trust was hard to gain and could be lost in seconds, but he did all he could to not sin against his master. Flee temptation and do not compromise.

NO SIN AGAINST GOD

JOSEPH & POTIPHAR'S WIFE, DEVOTION 6

Noble Baird | *Community Center Director*

Yesterday, we talked about trust. Arguably, it is one of the top three, if not the most, foundational part of any relationship. As I sit in Starbucks, I am reminded of this foundational characteristic. You see, four years ago I came on staff here at The River and had the privilege of doing an eight-month internship. During that time, I was joined by a young man named James Mann who I had never met but heard a lot about. Over the next eight months, James took on a summer internship here, and we were together pretty much every day. Whether we were cleaning toilets, arranging the storage in the warehouse on our maintenance Monday, or hanging out with the students at Fusion and accidentally breaking lights with a soccer ball (which we ended up having to fix), we were constantly serving and doing life together. Out of this, I gained not only a true partner in ministry but a friend who I call my brother.

Joseph makes a very pointed statement in Genesis 39:9. It was one that I read over several times, often thinking that the whole point of this passage was simply to focus on Joseph fleeing from sin and possible adultery. However, in verse 9 it reads, ***"He is not greater in this house than I am, nor has he kept back anything from me except you, because you are his wife. How then can I do this great wickedness and sin against God?"*** From a human standpoint, Joseph is literally facing a rock and a hard place as he seemingly has two options. He can either run from Potiphar's wife and not sin against his master, or he can succumb to sin and not have his position as head of the household at stake. We know the outcome and how he does indeed run; however, him fleeing from temptation was bigger than just not sinning against his master, Potiphar. At the end of the passage, Joseph says, ***"How then can I do this great wickedness and sin against God?"*** Joseph's relationship with his Heavenly Father, was way more important to him than his earthly stature and glory.

While I am writing this, James is sitting across from me getting things in order for our kids camp this summer, and yes he did order a massive milkshake from Starbucks. All kidding aside, we are never alone in this life and in the ministry that God has placed us. Paul had Barnabas, Elijah had Elisha, Peter had Mark, Moses had Aaron, and we could go on for quite a while naming off all the amazing duos in God's Word. One continued common theme amongst them all was that of trust. It was through that foundational characteristic of trust that they pushed each other, encouraged one another, and challenged one another daily. As they did so, they understood this foundational truth of our faith as followers of Christ of not compromising our relationship with the Father and sinning against Him, just as Joseph proclaimed and understood.

So, as you finish up this week or maybe you are just beginning, remember these two truths that we see prevalent in the life of Joseph. He did not want to compromise his trust and relationship with those around him whose trust and respect he had gained. Yet, more importantly, he fled sin so that he would not sin against God. Never take those close friends for granted, keep them close, and never be afraid to challenge and encourage one another in Christ.

17

PRISON TO PALACE

DR. RANDY T. JOHNSON,
GROWTH PASTOR

I am inspired by Rags-to-Riches stories. In 2011, Business Insider listed fifteen people who went from "failure" to the top of the Forbes' list. This is some of the people who were listed.

1. John Paul DeJoria – He lived in his car before his John Paul Mitchell Systems made him into a 900 million dollar company.
2. Ursula Burns – She is the CEO of Xerox, but grew up in a housing project on Manhattan's Lower East Side.
3. Howard Schultz – He also grew up in the projects (Brooklyn) before discovering, and now leading, Starbucks.
4. Leonardo Del Vecchio – He was an orphaned factory worker whose eyeglasses empire today makes Ray-Bans and Oakleys.
5. J.K. Rowling – She lived on welfare before creating the Harry Potter franchise.
6. Sam Walton – He is the well-known founder of Wal-Mart, but he started off by milking cows and selling magazines in Oklahoma.
7. Oprah Winfrey – She has openly shared how she turned a life of hardship into inspiration for a multi-billion-dollar empire.

Do you personally know of a rags-to-riches story?

____

____

____

I want to be careful not to imply that making a lot of money makes one successful or happy. The Bible is clear that money cannot buy anyone a spot in Heaven. However, it is amazing to see God orchestrate Joseph's life from a pit to prison and finally to the palace.

It is ironic that Joseph's dreams put him in the pit, but the interpretation of dreams put him as second in command in the palace.

Genesis 39:20-23 speaks of innocent Joseph being thrown in prison, ***"And Joseph's master took him and put him into the prison, the place where the king's prisoners were confined, and he was there in prison. But the Lord was with Joseph and showed him steadfast love and gave him favor in the sight of the keeper of the prison. And the keeper of the prison put Joseph in charge of all the prisoners who were in the prison. Whatever was done there, he was the one who did it. The keeper of the prison paid no attention to anything that was in Joseph's charge, because the Lord was with him. And whatever he did, the Lord made it succeed."***

What do we know about the Lord from this passage?

____

____

____

What do we know about Joseph from this passage?

____

____

____

1. Joseph interpreted the cupbearer's dream.

Joseph is in jail, and even though the outcome does not look promising, he holds onto his dreams from God and stays positive. He is in jail but acts free. He ends up caring for other inmates. While he is doing time, two noteworthy men join him. After a while, they both have a dream on the same night. Joseph first interprets the dream of the cupbearer. He gets to share the good news.

Genesis 40:1-15 says, ***"Some time after this, the cupbearer of the king of Egypt and his baker committed an offense against*** *their lord the king of Egypt. And Pharaoh was angry with his two officers, the chief cupbearer and the chief baker, and he put them in custody in the house of the captain of the guard, in the prison where Joseph was confined. The captain of the guard appointed Joseph to be with them, and he attended them. They continued for some time in custody. And one night they both dreamed—the cupbearer and the baker of the king of Egypt, who were confined in the prison—each his own dream, and each dream with its own interpretation. When Joseph came to them in the morning, he saw that they were troubled. So he asked Pharaoh's officers who were with him in custody in his master's house, 'Why are your faces downcast today?' They said to him, 'We have had dreams, and there is no one to interpret them.' And Joseph said to them, 'Do not interpretations belong to God? Please tell them to me.' So the chief cupbearer told his dream to Joseph and said to him, 'In my dream there was a vine before me, and on the vine there were three branches. As soon as it budded, its blossoms shot forth, and the clusters ripened into grapes. Pharaoh's cup was in my hand, and I took the grapes and pressed them into Pharaoh's cup and placed the cup in Pharaoh's hand.' Then Joseph said to him, 'This is its interpretation: the three branches are three days. In three days Pharaoh will lift up your head and restore you to your office, and you shall place Pharaoh's cup in his hand as formerly, when you were his cupbearer. Only remember me, when it is well with you, and please do me the kindness to mention me to Pharaoh, and so get me out of this house. For I was indeed stolen out of the land of the Hebrews, and here also I have done nothing that they should put me into the pit.'"*

Joseph saw that the men were troubled. Do you notice when others are hurting?

____

____

____

What did Joseph say about dreams in general?

____

____

____

What request did Joseph have of the cupbearer?

____

____

____

The cupbearer had an esteemed position. He tasted the wine to make sure it was suitable for the king or Pharaoh. They would often have a close relationship as they spent meals together. Joseph knew the cupbearer would have the king's attention.

2. Joseph interpreted the baker's dream.

The baker heard the cupbearer's good news and asked for an interpretation of his dream. His news would not be good; it was bad news.

Genesis 40:16-19 says, ***"When the chief baker saw that the interpretation was favorable, he said to Joseph, 'I also had a dream: there were three cake baskets on my head, and in the uppermost basket there were all sorts of baked food for Pharaoh, but the birds were eating it out of the basket on my head.' And Joseph answered and said, 'This is its interpretation:***

the three baskets are three days. In three days Pharaoh will lift up your head—from you!—and hang you on a tree. And the birds will eat the flesh from you.'"

How do you think the baker responded for the next three days?

____

____

____

Are you willing to challenge others even if the answer might hurt their feelings?

____

____

____

The story continues that in three days it was the Pharaoh's birthday and he was having a party. He decided to call for his cupbearer and baker. What is a birthday party without a cake? However, Joseph's interpretation was correct, and even though the cupbearer was reinstated to his position, the baker was sentenced to death. Unfortunately, the cupbearer forgot to mention anything about Joseph to the Pharaoh.

3. Joseph interpreted the Pharaoh's dream.

The next chapter refers to the Pharaoh having some dreams, ***"After two whole years, Pharaoh dreamed that he was standing by the Nile"*** (Genesis 41:1).

Pharaoh dreams of seven fat cows that come out of the Nile. He then sees seven skinny cows come out of the River and eat the fat cows. He then had a similar dream with ears of grain. Verse 8 gives his response, ***"So in the morning his spirit was troubled, and he***

sent and called for all the magicians of Egypt and all its wise men. Pharaoh told them his dreams, but there was none who could interpret them to Pharaoh."

The chief cupbearer then remembered Joseph and mentioned how he helped him with his dream. The Pharaoh called for Joseph. Verse 15 says, ***"And Pharaoh said to Joseph, 'I have had a dream, and there is no one who can interpret it. I have heard it said of you that when you hear a dream you can interpret it.'"***

Joseph's answer in verse 16 could be a life verse, ***"Joseph answered Pharaoh, 'It is not in me; God will give Pharaoh a favorable answer.'"*** I love how the New International Version translates this passage, ***"'I cannot do it,' Joseph replied to Pharaoh, 'but God will give Pharaoh the answer he desires.'"*** Joseph summarizes our lives, "I cannot, but God!"

What thoughts does this give you of Joseph?

____

____

____

How can this phrase ("I cannot, but God!") relate to us today?

____

____

____

Joseph then interpreted the dreams as seven fruitful years followed by seven years of famine. Joseph then said, ***"Now therefore let Pharaoh select a discerning and wise man, and set him over the land of Egypt. Let Pharaoh proceed to appoint overseers over the land and take one-fifth of the produce of the land of Egypt during the seven plentiful years. And let them gather all the food***

of these good years that are coming and store up grain under the authority of Pharaoh for food in the cities, and let them keep it. That food shall be a reserve for the land against the seven years of famine that are to occur in the land of Egypt, so that the land may not perish through the famine" (Genesis 41:33-36).

What was Joseph's advice?

___

___

___

Verses 37-39 continue the story, ***"This proposal pleased Pharaoh and all his servants. And Pharaoh said to his servants, 'Can we find a man like this, in whom is the Spirit of God?' Then Pharaoh said to Joseph, 'Since God has shown you all this, there is none so discerning and wise as you are.'"***

What does this passage imply about the Pharaoh?

___

___

___

What does this passage say about Joseph?

___

___

___

Joseph kept his cool. He focused on each day to see what God placed before him. He knew God was in control. God gifted him, and he used that gift for God's glory. He gave God all the credit.

It is not as though Joseph had a bad day and then everything was okay. When we take a closer look at these passages, we realize the challenge Joseph faced for a long time.

4. Joseph patiently waited for his time.

Most scholars agree that Joseph was still a teenager when he was thrown into the pit and then sold into slavery by his brothers. Time becomes our enemy when we try to be the one in control. Joseph knew God was in control of every detail in his life.

I have underlined some key phrases in these verses.

***"Some time after this,** the cupbearer of the king of Egypt and his baker committed an offense against their lord the king of Egypt."* Genesis 40:1

"The captain of the guard appointed Joseph to be with them, and he attended them. They continued for some time in custody." Genesis 40:4

***"After two whole years,** Pharaoh dreamed that he was standing by the Nile."* Genesis 41:1

***"Joseph was thirty years old** when he entered the service of Pharaoh king of Egypt. And Joseph went out from the presence of Pharaoh and went through all the land of Egypt."* Genesis 41:46

How long do you think Joseph was in prison?

___

___

___

What are you going through that seems to be endless?

___

___

___

What can you learn through the process of your "prison term?"

___

___

___

Willie Nelson has said, "The early bird gets the worm, but the second mouse gets the cheese." It may sound like a silly quote, but for Joseph, "What if?" What if he never was falsely accused, would his gift never be used and he would be a slave for life? What if the cupbearer had told the Pharaoh about Joseph, would he have gone home to his family and all of Israel struggle due to the famine?

God's timing is not just right; it is best. He is never too early or too late. Rest on His plan and see what He has for you today. Make a difference for Him.

GOD CAUSED SUCCESS

JOSEPH IN PRISON, DEVOTION 1

Ryan Story | *Location Pastor - Burton*

If you have ever read the story of Joseph, which hopefully you have been reading your Bible through this book, you will notice that Joseph always seems to have some horrible circumstance befall him. His brothers hated him and sold him into slavery while his brother Reuben was on his way back to save him from the pit where he had left Joseph. Joseph ended up getting a good working relationship with the captain of Pharaoh's guard, and all things were going well. Eventually, Joseph was wrongly accused of a sexual act despite the fact that he fled; because of this he was put into a political jail that most likely housed the worst of the worst. More up and down moments happen to the son of Jacob, but the one thing that remained true in Joseph's life is that despite all the unfortunate circumstances that befell him, he always had God with him.

Genesis 39:22-23 says, ***"And the keeper of the prison put Joseph in charge of all the prisoners who were in the prison. Whatever was done there, he was the one who did it. The keeper of the prison paid no attention to anything that was in Joseph's charge because the Lord was with him. And whatever he did, the Lord made it succeed."*** Even in the worst circumstances, Joseph always seemed to end up being favored by God. Even when we fast-forward in Joseph's story, God always seems to have a way of making everything fall into place. Joseph was not successful for any other reason than because God was always with him. God worked everything out for Joseph to complete what God wanted him to do. We live in a world where it just seemed that some people have "better luck" than others. We look at other people and might think that their wealth, health, family, spiritual walk, children, spouse, and attitude is just better than ours. Then we start thinking that God has skipped over us and given all of His blessings to another. The truth is we are not in control of how God works out the situation, and we are only in control of our response to the situation.

As I studied my way through Joseph's life while he was in Egypt, it seemed to me that you could divide everything into two parts. In every situation, Joseph did his best to honor God. In every situation, Joseph always seemed to work hard. Now not that we can unlock the secret to making God bless us, but I do think there is some truth to God being with Joseph and God found favor with him. Go back and read every lousy thing that happened to Joseph. You will not be able to find any moment where he complained, gossiped, or slandered anyone. Joseph's attitude was always showing whom he served. Likewise, in every bad situation that befell him, Joseph always displayed a terrific work ethic. If I was sold into slavery, then thrown into jail for a crime I did not commit, I cannot see myself wanting to be the inmate of the year. However, Joseph showed us that in every situation we must work as if it is God who is in control of even the seemingly darkest of times. We cannot make God bless us, but we can find the blessing in every situation. So instead of looking at the bleakness, look for how you can show how amazing the Lord you serve is.

INTERPRETS PRISONER'S DREAMS

JOSEPH IN PRISON, DEVOTION 2

Debbie Gabbara | *Assistant to the Gathering Pastor*

Do you dream at night? I do not dream very often, but my husband has crazy dreams all the time. There are many mornings that he wakes up to tell me of the wild adventure he had during the night. He will often ask me what I think his dream meant. After I tell him that I have no idea, we laugh and decide that maybe he should watch less TV before bed.

Scattered through the Bible, we see God speaking to people through their dreams. In the book of Genesis, we meet Joseph. He had dreams that seemed crazy to his family. His brothers, the sun, moon, and stars were bowing before Joseph. They certainly did not understand what that meant and hated the thought that Joseph might rule over them. But, God would use dreams and interpretation of dreams in incredible ways in Joseph's life.

Because of jealousy and anger towards him, Joseph was sold into slavery by his own brothers. He was later put in prison for a crime he did not commit. I wonder if the dreams God had given him so long ago ever came to mind?

Scripture tells us in Genesis chapter 40 that while in prison, the king's cupbearer and baker were also imprisoned with Joseph. One day he noticed they were sad and asked why. The men were upset because they both had dreamed the night before and were not able to go to the professionals that were used to interpret dreams. Joseph said that true interpretation would come from God, and asked them to tell him their dreams.

The Lord helped Joseph that day to know the meaning of the dreams of the cupbearer and the baker. One man heard that he would return to his previous position with the king. God told Joseph that the other man would be killed within three days. Could it be that his dream was a warning of an immediate decision he needed to make about his faith in God?

Much time would pass before Joseph would see the fruition of the dreams he had as a teenager. He would go through years of trying times before he saw the great plan that God had for his life as ruler over Egypt. Through it all, Joseph honored God and helped others. God blessed Joseph and those around him.

Sometimes God sends dreams in the night, and sometimes He whispers them into our heart. What are you dreaming? Even if the dream is unclear, continue to seek God and follow Him; He is always faithful, and His ways are perfect.

"This God—his way is perfect; the word of the LORD proves true; he is a shield for all those who take refuge in him." Psalm 18:30

"AFTER TWO WHOLE YEARS"

JOSEPH IN PRISON, DEVOTION 3

Joshua Combs | *Lead Pastor*

Something was supposed to happen. Joseph was a man to whom lots of things happened that should not have seemed to. He was born the favorite son of his father and declared to be so with the extravagant gift of a coat (robe) of many colors. But Joseph's life of luxury and privilege would come crashing down. He would be beaten by his brothers, sold into slavery, falsely accused of sexual assault, imprisoned, and forgotten. Every time a glimmer of hope shines on him, there is a sudden and dramatic change of circumstances, and a seemingly more destructive storm rocks his life. Hope is hanging but by a thread.

Genesis chapter 41 finds Joseph forgotten in prison with no end in sight. He had become a trustee in the jail, but that responsibility and privilege paled in comparison to being in his father's house or even a slave at Potiphar's estate. A glimmer of hope came when he translated a dream for a high ranking official who had been sent to Joseph's jail. But once that man had been restored to his position, he conveniently forgot his little stint behind bars and the people he met there, including the dream interpreter, Joseph.

The Bible (Genesis 41:1) simply says, ***"After two whole years..."*** Time had ticked by, and Joseph must have realized that like his brothers and Potiphar's wife, someone else had mistreated him. Years would go by with no word from the palace.

The Scripture uses the word "whole." That is just like God. He does not try us one second longer or shorter than is absolutely necessary. God's refining process is often compared in scripture to refining gold. Job, in his desperate plea to God, states, ***"But [God] knows the way that I take; when He has tried me, I shall come out as gold"*** (Job 23:10). We often long for glory, but the pain and trial must always come first. God was not needlessly trying Joseph. God's plan was working perfectly. God's timing was perfectly on schedule. We, like Joseph, need to trust the Lord even in the difficult years. They may seem long, but "after" is worth the refinement.

PHARAOH'S DREAMS

JOSEPH IN PRISON, DEVOTION 4

Pat Bedell

In Genesis chapter 41, Pharaoh had a few dreams which he could not decipher. He dreamt of seven healthy and bountiful cows and then dreamt of seven thin and ugly cows. The ugly and thin cows then ate the healthy and bountiful cows. Then Pharaoh dreamt of a stalk of grain that had seven healthy and plentiful ears. Then he also dreamt of thin and weary ears that swallowed up the healthy and plentiful ears. Pharaoh was baffled by these dreams and called for all of the magicians and wise men in all of Egypt to meet with him. None of the magicians or wise men could decipher what Pharaoh's dreams were about.

Pharaoh then called for Joseph. Joseph shaved and changed his clothes and came before Pharaoh. He asked Joseph to interpret his dream. Genesis 41:16 says, ***"Joseph answered Pharaoh, 'It is not in me; God will give Pharaoh a favorable answer.'"*** Pharaoh then goes on to repeat his dreams to Joseph. Joseph then gave Pharaoh the interpretation that the seven healthy and plump cows and seven plentiful ears were a metaphor for seven years of "great plenty." The seven thin and ugly cows along with the seven thin and weary ears were a metaphor for seven years of famine. Pharaoh took Joseph's interpretation and used it to prepare. For the seven years of plenty, he used what was needed, but saved up for when the years of famine came. When the seven years of famine came, Pharaoh was prepared, and the land of Egypt survived.

There are several times throughout the year when I am secluded from all of the distractions of life and reflect on my life. It is a time to self-evaluate, make new goals for myself, and measure my progress as a person. There have been times when I can reflect on how awesome God is and how all the blessings in my life are so abundant. Then there are times when I put on a facade. Things in life are so messed up, I just can not seem to get anything right, and that I am a mess.

This devotion is meant to help you and me understand that there are seasons when everything is absolutely amazing. It is when your marriage is strong, your kids are healthy and doing well, and you just got a promotion at work. You are on cloud nine, and there is nothing that can take your smile away. Then there are seasons when you feel like an outcast, an obligation, a hindrance, and a terrible person. You may have dealt with a death close to family, had a relapse into an addiction, or just caved into sin again. We are all guilty of sin, and it can be an emotionally draining feeling. The devil certainly does not help when we are down in our faith.

Like Pharaoh, we need to approach our faith on a large scale. We always see God when all is great in life, but always seem to turn our back and be angry with God when all is not going well. We need to rejoice and give thanks for the blessings we have in our lives, and we need to understand that when our "famine" comes, we are prepared to endure the hardship and ultimately learn God's will. His plans are perfect. I would like to challenge you that the next time you have to endure a "famine," you would give thanks to God and be quick to listen and slow to be angry. Know that He is in control, and He is with you all of the time.

SPIRIT OF GOD IN HIM

JOSEPH IN PRISON, DEVOTION 5

Gareth Volz | *Senior (55+) Director*

In Genesis 41:38-39 we read, ***"And Pharaoh said to his servants, 'Can we find a man like this, in whom is the Spirit of God?' Then Pharaoh said to Joseph, 'Since God has shown you all this, there is none so discerning and wise as you are.'"***

I think that probably the greatest compliment that can be given to a true follower of God is that others can see evidence of God's Holy Spirit in them. Galatians 5:22-23 tells us, ***"The fruit of the Spirit is love, joy, peace, patience, kindness, goodness, faithfulness, gentleness, self-control; against such things there is no law."*** Every believer is indwelt by God's Spirit when they accept Jesus as their Savior. However, the Fruit of the Spirit reveals how filled the believer is with God's Spirit. Being filled with God's Spirit is a voluntary choice to surrender control of your life to the Holy Spirit's control. Examining Joseph's life shows how the Fruit of the Spirit was revealed in him.

A quick review of Joseph's life showed that he was his father's favorite son, which made his brothers jealous. This was made worse when, as a teenager, he had a dream that one day his brothers would all bow down to him. He told them this, and they sold him into slavery, telling their father he was killed by a wild animal. While he was a slave, he resisted the sexual flirtation of his master's wife, and for doing what was right, was falsely accused and thrown into prison. While in prison, he interpreted the dreams of two of Pharaoh's servants who also had been thrown into prison, giving credit for the interpretation to God. When both interpretations proved correct, and one was executed and one restored to his former position, he was forgotten by the latter and languished in prison. Finally, when Pharaoh was troubled by a dream, and none of his wise men could interpret it, Pharaoh's cupbearer remembered Joseph and told Pharaoh he knew someone who could interpret the dream. Joseph did so, giving credit to God, and this is when Pharaoh saw evidence of God's Spirit in him.

What evidence did Pharaoh see in Joseph's life?

1. Faithfulness: Faith gave him the ability to discern right from wrong as Potiphar's slave, confidence to assure Pharaoh's servants (and later Pharaoh himself) that interpretations belong to God, and God's interpretations are true.
2. Patience: Though Joseph was taken from a lavish life and sold into slavery, thrown into prison, and forgotten, he had the patience that God would work in his life for good.
3. Kindness and Goodness: Joseph was kind to Pharaoh's servants in prison, caring enough to share God's truth with them, even while he was suffering.
4. Love: Joseph's unwavering love for God is seen throughout his trials in Egypt.
5. Peace: Joseph was at peace because he knew God was ultimately in control, not Pharaoh.
6. Love and Joy: Joseph's love for God was evident in his declarations that it was God – not himself – who should receive credit for the dream interpretations and results. This led to joy for not only Joseph but Pharaoh and ultimately Joseph's family.

It is my prayer that I will be filled with God's Spirit and it will be evident to all. I pray that is your desire as well.

NAMES

JOSEPH IN PRISON, DEVOTION 6

Carole Combs | *Women's Ministry*

Names - We all have them. Some are given to us by our parents, and some are given to us by our friends. Many parents have toiled over hundreds of names to choose that perfect name for their child. They want the name with the perfect meaning that fits their child. Often times they want to include a family name as well. I was born on Christmas Day. My mother told me that her choice of names for me was Holly, Joy, and Carol. I became my parents Christmas Carole (Mom added an "e" just to be different). The Urban dictionary defines my name as "song of happiness."

Names have been important since the time of the creation of the world. In Genesis 1:20, we see that Adam is naming the animals and birds. God knew it was a good thing not to call everything an "it." Recorded in the book of Genesis there was a son born to a husband and wife named Jacob and Rachel. They named him Joseph (Genesis 30:22-23). The Bible tells us that Joseph was Jacob's favorite son. However, this brought Joseph many problems amongst his older siblings (Take the time to read Genesis chapter 37). Joseph ended up in Egypt. He was away from his family and sold into slavery by his brothers. God blessed Joseph and the Egyptian household that he was overseeing (Genesis chapter 39). The events in Joseph's life turned quickly upside down as if his life had not already been like a roller coaster. Joseph ended up in prison (Genesis chapters 39-40). Two years later, Joseph was still in prison, but God was still protecting and using Joseph no matter what his outward circumstances were. The Pharaoh of Egypt had a disturbing dream that could not be interpreted by his subjects. However, the King's cupbearer remembered a cellmate that he once shared a cell with named Joseph. Joseph had interpreted a dream for him. The Pharaoh was willing to give Joseph a shot at the interpretation of the dream. Joseph emphatically told the Pharaoh that his ability to interpret dreams was not in his own abilities, but it was God who worked through him. Joseph not only interpreted the dream but gave a detailed plan on what to do and how to live with the unfolding plan of the dream that was about to become a reality. The Pharaoh was very pleased with what he heard. He rhetorically asked those around him where he could find such a man to undergo the large task of preparing for the reality of the dream. The Pharaoh looked at Joseph and told him he was the man! Joseph would be over Pharaoh's house and all Pharaoh's people. The will of the people would be at Joseph's command. The coronation began. The Pharaoh took his signet ring from his hand and put it on Joseph's hand. He clothed him in garments of fine linen and put a gold chain around his neck. He rode in the second chariot while servants cried out, "Bow the knee." Joseph became the grand vizier or prime minister to govern all the people of Egypt. He was second only to Pharaoh himself.

A document from the Tomb of Rekhmire in the Late Bronze Age says that the vizier is the "grand steward of all Egypt. All activities of the state are under his control." The Egyptian Empire at one time stretched from modern-day Syria in the north to modern-day Sudan in the south and from the region of Jordan in the east to Libya in the west. Pharaoh wanted to integrate this Hebrew into the Egyptian society. As part of the coronation, Pharaoh would change Joseph's Hebrew name to an Egyptian name. He gave him a wife from the upper echelon of women, too. Title and prestige went along with Joseph's job promotion. Not much has changed in society several centuries later.

Joseph's new name was Zaphenath-paneah (Genesis 41:45). The

meaning of his name has been problematic for translators and biblical historians. Many have attempted to decipher this Egyptian name. A significant Egyptian name with great meaning would be very important to precede the grand vizier. All who would hear it would know its meaning and its importance. The name Zaphenath-paneah is divided into two parts. It would be like our first name and our middle name. Egyptologists generally accept that the second name, paneah, means "life" or to provide life. Jerome, a theologian and historian (420 AD) believed the second name means "preserver of the world." As we look at the entire name, it becomes more exciting. Egypt was about to experience seven years of abundance and seven years of famine. Joseph was to oversee and manage these very important fourteen years of history in Egypt. It was a matter of life and death. The Pharaoh did not worship the God of the Hebrew Joseph, but he surely recognized that there was a divine presence with him (Genesis 41:38). He named him Zaphenath, meaning "The one appointed by the God." People may not know your God, but they should see something different about you, too. Joseph or Zaphenath-paneah, the one appointed by the God to provide life, saved the Egyptians as well as the Hebrew people from death (It is a wonderful story to read in detail in Genesis chapters 37-50).

The book of Genesis was written by Moses over a thousand years before Christ. Moses recorded an amazing prefigure of the life of Jesus in the story of Joseph. Jesus was the one appointed by God to provide life. Joseph foreshadowed the life of Jesus Christ. We all can live life in abundance, but there will come a day that we will come up short. We cannot in our own ability sustain or maintain our own lives.

Mankind was helpless, but God sent His one and only Son, His favorite, to provide you and me life. There must be a time in your life when you accept and trust in God's Son for your life here and for all eternity. It will never be in your own merit or your own abundance. ***"Therefore God has highly exalted him and bestowed on him the name that is above every name, so that at the name of Jesus every knee should bow, in heaven and on earth and under earth, and every tongue confess that Jesus Christ is Lord, to the glory of God the Father"*** (Philippians 2:9-11).

This Christmas Carole trusted in the name of Jesus at twelve years of age. When did you trust in the name of Jesus? If never, why not today?

18

JOSEPH FORGIVES HIS BROTHERS

DR. RANDY T. JOHNSON,
GROWTH PASTOR

In an article written by the Mayo Clinic staff, they wrote a prescription that brought these benefits:

- Healthier relationships
- Improved mental health
- Less anxiety, stress, and hostility
- Lower blood pressure
- Fewer symptoms of depression
- A stronger immune system
- Improved heart health
- Improved self-esteem

The key to this life was letting go of grudges and bitterness. Forgiveness can lead to improved health and peace of mind.

How have you seen the lack of forgiveness consume someone?

____

____

____

The Book of Genesis began with God creating everything, and it was good. However, it did not stay that way. Sin entered the world and affected everyone. As the book ends, we are reminded of sin, but instead of retaliation, we read that Joseph forgave his brothers.

Genesis 50:15-21 says, ***"When Joseph's brothers saw that their father was dead, they said, 'It may be that Joseph will hate us and pay us back for all the evil that we did to him.' So they sent a message to Joseph, saying, 'Your father gave this command before he died: 'Say to Joseph, 'Please forgive the transgression of your brothers and their sin, because they did evil to you." And now, please forgive the transgression of the servants of the God of your father.' Joseph wept when they spoke to him. His***

brothers also came and fell down before him and said, 'Behold, we are your servants.' But Joseph said to them, 'Do not fear, for am I in the place of God? As for you, you meant evil against me, but God meant it for good, to bring it about that many people should be kept alive, as they are today. So do not fear; I will provide for you and your little ones.' Thus he comforted them and spoke kindly to them."

What did the brothers fear? Was it justified?

____

____

____

How does this phrase ***("As for you, you meant evil against me, but God meant it for good")*** relate to your life?

____

____

____

How can acknowledging ***"you meant evil against me"*** be helpful?

____

____

____

T. D. Jakes said, "I think the first step is to understand that forgiveness does not exonerate the perpetrator. Forgiveness liberates the victim. It's a gift you give yourself."

List some of the ways God used evil for eventual good in the life of Joseph.

____

____

____

The concept of forgiveness has two specific aspects that need to be addressed.

1. God is willing to forgive us.

Kirk Cameron realized God's willingness to forgive when he said, "I could see that it was God's forgiveness and His mercy that I needed, and that was provided through Christ on the Cross for those who will receive Him as Lord and Savior. That is how I came to Christ."

Scripture is clear about God's forgiveness.

"If we confess our sins, he is faithful and just to forgive us our sins and to cleanse us from all unrighteousness." 1 John 1:9

"As far as the east is from the west, so far does he remove our transgressions from us." Psalm 103:12

"Who is a God like you, pardoning iniquity and passing over transgression for the remnant of his inheritance? He does not retain his anger forever, because he delights in steadfast love. He will again have compassion on us; he will tread our iniquities underfoot. You will cast all our sins into the depths of the sea." Micah 7:18-19

When we confess our sins, God forgives us. He removes our transgression as far as possible (east to west). He even casts our sin into the depths of the ocean. The key is for us to accept His forgiveness and not to spend time fishing in those seas "bringing up" past sins that are forgiven.

Billy Graham said, "Man has two great spiritual needs. One is for forgiveness. The other is for goodness."

Have you accepted God's forgiveness?

____

____

____

What sin do you need to confess to Him now? How will you avoid repeating the sin?

____

____

____

2. We need to be willing to forgive others.

Matthew 18:21-35 gives a challenging analogy on forgiveness.

"Then Peter came up and said to him, 'Lord, how often will my brother sin against me, and I forgive him? As many as seven times?' Jesus said to him, 'I do not say to you seven times, but seventy-seven times. Therefore the kingdom of heaven may be compared to a king who wished to settle accounts with his servants. When he began to settle, one was brought to him who owed him ten thousand talents. And since he could not pay, his master ordered him to be sold, with his wife and children and all that he had, and payment to be made. So the servant fell on his knees, imploring him, 'Have patience with me, and I will pay you everything.' And out of pity for him, the master of that servant released him and forgave him the debt. But when that same servant went out, he found one of his fellow servants who owed him a hundred denarii, and seizing him, he began to choke him, saying, 'Pay what you owe.' So his fellow servant fell down and pleaded with him, 'Have patience with me, and I will pay you.' He refused and went and put him in prison until he should pay the debt. When his fellow servants saw what had taken place, they

were greatly distressed, and they went and reported to their master all that had taken place. Then his master summoned him and said to him, 'You wicked servant! I forgave you all that debt because you pleaded with me. And should not you have had mercy on your fellow servant, as I had mercy on you?' And in anger his master delivered him to the jailers, until he should pay all his debt. So also my heavenly Father will do to every one of you, if you do not forgive your brother from your heart.'"

How much was the man forgiven?

____

____

____

How much have you been forgiven?

____

____

____

How much was owed to the man?

____

____

____

Who do you need to forgive?

____

____

____

2 Corinthians 5:17 says, ***"Therefore, if anyone is in Christ, he is a new creation. The old has passed away; behold, the new has come."***

How does this verse relate to the topic of forgiveness?

____

____

____

T. D. Jakes said, "We think that forgiveness is weakness, but it's absolutely not; it takes a very strong person to forgive." He added, "Forgiveness is about empowering yourself, rather than empowering your past."

GENESIS 50:15-21

JOSEPH FORGIVES BROTHERS, DEVOTION 1

Wes McCullough | *Production Director*

"When Joseph's brothers saw that their father was dead, they said, 'It may be that Joseph will hate us and pay us back for all the evil that we did to him.' So they sent a message to Joseph, saying, 'Your father gave this command before he died: 'Say to Joseph, 'Please forgive the transgression of your brothers and their sin, because they did evil to you." And now, please forgive the transgression of the servants of the God of your father.' Joseph wept when they spoke to him. His brothers also came and fell down before him and said, 'Behold, we are your servants.' But Joseph said to them, 'Do not fear, for am I in the place of God? As for you, you meant evil against me, but God meant it for good, to bring it about that many people should be kept alive, as they are today. So do not fear; I will provide for you and your little ones.' Thus he comforted them and spoke kindly to them." Genesis 50:15-21

Here we see one of the more incredible stories of forgiveness in the Bible. Because of his brothers, Joseph had been thrown down into a well, nearly killed, sold into slavery, and imprisoned for years. When they reunite, Joseph is second in command of all Egypt and could have had his brother killed for what they did to him. Incredibly, there is no animosity in Joseph's heart toward them, and their submission to him brings him to tears.

Why was Joseph not out for revenge? Verse 20 is the key, ***"You meant evil against me, but God meant it for good."*** Joseph did not blame his brothers for the hard parts of his life. His enslavement was not directly because of his brothers. Joseph chose to see the big picture of God's plan. He resolved that God had allowed events in his life to put him in just the right position to save his family and even their nation. Joseph accepted God's plan, good and bad, and it saved his heart from sinful attitudes.

You will have hard times in life. They may last for days, weeks, months, or years. Remember that this life is temporary and strive to secure your eternal salvation.

"Blessed is the man who remains steadfast under trial, for when he has stood the test he will receive the crown of life, which God has promised to those who love him." James 1:12

1 JOHN 1:9

JOSEPH FORGIVES BROTHERS, DEVOTION 2

Chuck Lindsey | *Reach Pastor*

"If we confess our sins, He is faithful and just to forgive us our sins and to cleanse us from all unrighteousness."
1 John 1:9 (NKJV)

Have you ever been so thirsty, that all you can think about is a drink of water? Have you ever been so tired, that all you can see is your bed? Maybe you have been so hungry, that everywhere you looked you saw cheeseburgers. A few years back, my wife and I tried dieting through Weight Watchers. I remember being so hungry one day that as I drove down the road, I found myself looking at road kill with longing. Yikes!

What a refreshing thing a drink of water is to a person who is dying of thirst. What a satisfying thing it is to sit down when exhausted. Food tastes so good when you feel like you are starving.

This is what forgiveness is like. It is like a cool drink of water when you are dying of thirst. It is like the finest of meals to a man who is starving. Forgiveness is like trying to hold the weight of the world above your head for as long as possible, and finally being allowed to let go.

This is what it must have felt like for Joseph's brothers. For years they carried the weight of what they had done to their brother. For years they tried to carry the weight of their guilt, deception, wrongdoing, and shame. No amount of sleep gave them rest from it. No drink or food helped to alleviate the load. Their sin crushed them. Such is the nature of sin.

How refreshing it must have been to confess their sin, to finally admit their wrongdoing. A few months back, my youngest son (at the time of this writing 5 years old) asked to talk to me "alone." We went into the bedroom, and he broke down sobbing. As I tried to console him, I asked what had happened. It took a few minutes for him to get out the words, "a few weeks ago, I took some candy from the candy drawer, snuck it into my room and ate it all after you put me in bed. I am so sorry daddy!" I told him I forgave him and we both cried. He cried because of the weight of his guilt. I cried because of the beauty of forgiveness.

Put yourself in the brothers' sandals for a moment. What was it like to finally admit what they had done, to finally put that great weight down? They were exhausted. Come what may, they had finally put it down. How it must have felt for them to hear then Joseph speak in kindness to them, forgiving them for all that they had done and offering them all of the blessings that were his to give. They change from being almost completely crushed under the weight of their sin to the elation of true forgiveness and mercy. What a moment that must have been.

1 John 1:9 demonstrates how simple forgiveness really is. Notice the words, ***"If we confess our sins."*** That is our part, and that is a big ***"if"*** is it not? That ***"if"*** implies that we see that we have sin. That ***"if"*** implies that we see our need to not only confess our sin, but it confesses our need for forgiveness. But do not miss the simplicity of it. ***"If we will confess our sin,"*** emphasizes that if we will just admit it. If we will finally just say the same thing about our sins as God says about it (that is what ***"confess"*** means) then, ***"He is faithful and just to forgive us our sins and to cleanse us from all unrighteousness."*** It is so simple. If we will see our need, call sin what it is, and admit to God that we are sinners who need to be forgiven and saved, He will forgive us and cleanse us from all of our

sin! This will be more refreshing than any drink of water or bite of bread. Jesus said it will be like a "fountain of water" springing up within us always satisfying.

John 7:37-38 (NKJV) says, ***"On the last day, that great day of the feast, Jesus stood and cried out, saying, 'If anyone thirsts, let him come to Me and drink. He who believes in Me, as the Scripture has said, out of his heart will flow rivers of living water.'"***

MATTHEW 18:21-35

JOSEPH FORGIVES BROTHERS, DEVOTION 3

Isaiah Combs | *Worship Leader*

The story of Joseph in the Bible is one of the best examples of forgiveness. If you would like to read the story, it is found in Genesis chapters 37-50. However, here is a shortened version.

Joseph seemed to brag a lot about the dreams God gave him and it is obvious that Joseph is his father, Jacob's favorite. The ten older brothers do not like the bragging and favoritism. They become bitter as their hatred grows. So they sell their brother into slavery, and they tell Jacob that Joseph was eaten by a wild animal. Joseph spends the next ten to fifteen years as a slave and then in prison.

The Pharaoh (AKA King of Egypt) has a dream that only Joseph is able to interpret. Pharaoh is pleased with Joseph and made him second in charge over all of Egypt.

The dream Joseph interpreted was that there was going to be a famine for seven years after the present seven years of abundance. So Joseph sets up Egypt to make it through the famine and have so much food that people would travel from all over to get food from Egypt.

Josephs brothers were some of the people that needed food. So when they came to Egypt to get food, Joseph recognized them. Instead of killing or making slaves out of the brothers, he forgives them. Genesis 50:20 is a very powerful verse, ***"As for you, you meant evil against me, but God meant it for good, to bring it about that many people should be kept alive, as they are today."*** Joseph chose forgiveness before he even saw his brothers. He knew that God had forgiven him for the things he had done. He knew God was guiding his path the whole time.

Jesus gives a parable in Mathew 18:21-35 after Peter asks Him a question about forgiveness. The parable speaks of a servant (servant 1) who owed a lot to the king. He had no way that he could pay for it. The king had every right to make servant 1 and his family slaves until the debt was paid. Instead, the rich man showed pity on servant 1 and forgave him his debt.

Servant 1 then went out and to find servant 2 that owned him a little money. Servant 2 asked for mercy, but the other servant refused and ordered him to be thrown into jail until he could pay him back. When the king found out that servant 1 did not forgive servant 2, he had servant 1 thrown in jail until he can pay him back.

This is what Jesus requires us to do. We are servant 1 who has been forgiven for an amount that is unpayable. We have been forgiven for everything we have ever done. So, Jesus requires us to forgive others for the large and small things they do to us. Forgiveness is hard. But since we have been forgiven for so much, we should forgive others, too.

MICAH 7:18-19

JOSEPH FORGIVES BROTHERS, DEVOTION 4

Dr. Randy T. Johnson | *Growth Pastor*

I am not a fisherman. I was not raised in a family that excelled at fishing. The largest fish my dad caught was a Northern Pike. We all celebrated until we found out that 19 inches was too small to keep. I remember sitting in the canoe waiting for the bobber to disappear. Putting worms on a hook was not very exciting, and I soon realized that the main bait on the lake was me; mosquitoes loved me. To make matters worse, my little sister drew back her rod to cast her line but did not look back to see if the "coast" was clear. I got hooked. I am not saying I got "hooked" on fishing; I am saying that she literally hooked my arm. A few stitches later, I retired from the fascinating sport of fishing. As if it could not get worse, my wife's dad loved ice fishing. Adding frostbite to a horrible hobby just brought a new category for a nightmare.

This week we have been focusing on how Joseph forgave his brothers. You might be thinking, "What does fishing have to do with forgiveness?" Micah 7:18-19 says, ***"Who is a God like you, pardoning iniquity and passing over transgression for the remnant of his inheritance? He does not retain his anger forever, because he delights in steadfast love. He will again have compassion on us; he will tread our iniquities underfoot. You will cast all our sins into the depths of the sea."***

God is amazing! When we confess our sins, He does not hold it over us. He does not stay angry. He shows love and compassion. He is even willing to cast ***"all our sins into the depths of the sea."*** I want to remind you to stop fishing. Do not pull those past sins back out of the water. Let them drown.

Satan wants us to feel defeated. Remember: Misery loves company. Too often we revisit past sins and beat up ourselves. God has forgiven us, and we need to walk in confidence. God has cast our sins into the sea, so we need to put out a sign that says, "No Fishing Allowed."

PSALM 103

JOSEPH FORGIVES BROTHERS, DEVOTION 5

Sierra Combs | *Women's Ministry Director*

Dear Mom. I am so sorry...Can you please forgive me? I hope you still love me. Do you still love me? Love, Colbie.

I woke up to this letter on my pillow recently, written by my six-year-old daughter. I left out the details of her trespass, but to honest, it was pretty minor. Unfortunately, as you can see from her sad and questioning note, my reaction was not as kind and understanding as it should have been. When I read her words that morning, my heart sunk. I felt like I had just been stabbed with a dagger to my heart. This is my daughter, whom I love more than words could ever describe. There is nothing I would not do for her. While her disobedience and mistakes can make me angry, frustrated, and sad, there is nothing that she could ever do that would change the way I feel about her. Yet, there she was, praying that I would forgive her and hoping that I still loved her (the daggers are still fresh here and I think they always will be). Within seconds of reading the letter, I ran to her room, scooped her up in my arms, and told her how much I adore her. I told her that she was forgiven and that there is not a mess up too big that would ever cause me to stop loving her.

Perhaps you find yourself feeling like my Colbie did that morning. Maybe you messed up. Maybe you messed up so bad, and you find yourself saying, "God I am so sorry! Can you please forgive me? I hope you still love me. Do you still love me?" Maybe you do not even want to wait around for the answer because you are sure it is going to be, "No." Is this you? Friend, let me just tell you a little bit about the Father. He is wild about you! He loves you so much that He sent His Son, Jesus, to die on a cross for every poor choice. If you confess your sin and call on Him to be your Savior, He is faithful to forgive. He is right there waiting to scoop you up in His arms and tell you how much He loves you. Are you still doubting it? Flip to Psalm 103:8-12. Highlight and memorize it. It says:

"The Lord is merciful and gracious,
slow to anger and abounding in steadfast love.
He will not always chide,
nor will he keep his anger forever.
He does not deal with us according to our sins,
nor repay us according to our iniquities.
For as high as the heavens are above the earth,
so great is his steadfast love toward those who fear him;
as far as the east is from the west,
so far does he remove our transgressions from us."

Do you know how high the heavens are above the Earth? The galaxies are infinite! That is how much He loves you. Do you know how far the east is from the west? Think about it. If you travelled north, eventually you would hit the north pole and then start heading south, until you hit the south pole and started heading north again. But if you turn to the east, you will keep going east. And if you turn to the west, you will keep going west. Both roads just keep going on forever in their specific directions. That immeasurable distance is how far He removes our transgressions from us. All we need to do is ask. With His blood that was shed on the cross, He wipes the slate clean. Thank you, Jesus!

2 CORINTHIANS 5:17

JOSEPH FORGIVES BROTHERS, DEVOTION 5

Debbie Kerr | *Office Administrator*

"Therefore, if anyone is in Christ, he is a new creation. The old has passed away; behold, the new has come."
2 Corinthians 5:17

The first Bible verse I learned as a child is, ***"Be kind to one another, tenderhearted, forgiving one another, as God in Christ forgave you"*** (Ephesians 4:32). Born again believers in Jesus Christ, who have been forgiven of all their sins, should always have a forgiving spirit, right? If only it was that easy. If you have a pulse and are not living on a deserted island, I am pretty sure you deal with the issue of forgiveness. While it is possible and necessary, it requires a transformation from the inside out. That is what the Apostle Paul is talking about in 2 Corinthians 5:17. If we are now in Christ, we are a completely new creation; the old man has died, and the new man is in control. As believers, we are to take on the image and characteristics of Christ. Jesus died on the cross for the forgiveness of sins. Is it just me, or does anyone else find it hypocritical that we have taken His gift of forgiveness and yet we often feel justified to withhold it from others?

The story of Joseph in Genesis is a great picture of true forgiveness. In fact, Joseph is known as a type of Christ. His story foretells what we will come to know as the grace Jesus has given to all who believe and receive His free gift of salvation. Joseph was severely mistreated by his jealous brothers, thrown into a well, sold into slavery, nearly killed and yet he never retaliated. His response to his brothers came as quite a surprise to them because they knew what they deserved, but instead of yielding his power and authority over them, he said to them, ***"As for you, you meant evil against me, but God meant it for good"*** (Genesis 20:50a). He was able to see the bigger picture and put his own hurt and betrayal aside for the greater good, which was to obey and honor God. We never look more like Christ than when we forgive.

A few reasons why forgiveness is difficult is when the offense is repeated, or there is no apology offered. Deep wounds begin to form, and our hearts begin to harden. The natural tendency is to protect ourselves. This will result in a breakdown in the relationship. We begin to avoid, ignore, and slander. This progression leads to bitterness, resentment, anger, mistrust, and a whole list of toxic emotions and actions.

Jesus is the ultimate example of forgiveness. He was rejected, beaten, mocked, falsely accused, and killed. Yet, as He hung on a criminal's cross, He prayed, ***"Father, forgive them, for they know not what they do"*** (Luke 23:34). The goal of forgiveness, I believe, first and foremost is reconciliation. I encourage you to take a few minutes right now and read Romans 12:14-21. Ask God to reveal any sign of an unforgiving spirit. If our inability to forgive goes unattended and we let bitterness take root, we will soon go from the offended to the offender. It is true that hurting people, hurt people.

2 Corinthians 5:18 says, ***"All this is from God, who through Christ reconciled us to himself and gave us the ministry of reconciliation."***